THE CAMBRIDGE COMPANION TO AUGUST WILSON

One of America's most powerful and original dramatists, August Wilson offered an alternative history of the twentieth century, as seen from the perspective of black Americans. He celebrated the lives of those seemingly pushed to the margins of national life, but who were simultaneously protagonists of their own drama and evidence of a vital and compelling community. Decade by decade, he told the story of a people with a distinctive history who forged their own future, aware of their roots in another time and place, but doing something more than just survive. Wilson deliberately addressed black America, but in doing so he discovered an international audience. Alongside chapters addressing Wilson's life and career, and the wider context of his plays, this *Companion* dedicates individual chapters to each play in his ten-play cycle, ordered chronologically and thereby demonstrating Wilson's notion of an unfolding history of the twentieth century.

CHRISTOPHER BIGSBY is Professor of American Studies at the University of East Anglia and has published more than thirty books covering American theatre, popular culture and British drama, including *Modern American Drama* (Cambridge, 1992), *Contemporary American Playwrights* (Cambridge, 2000), *Arthur Miller: A Critical Study* (Cambridge, 2005) and *Remembering and Imagining the Holocaust: The Chain of Memory* (Cambridge, 2006). He is co-editor, with Don Wilmeth, of *The Cambridge History of American Theatre*, which received the Barnard Hewitt Award for Outstanding Research from the American Society for Theatre Research. He is also an award-winning novelist, has written plays for radio and television, and is a regular radio and television broadcaster.

A complete list of books in the series is at the back of this book

THE CAMBRIDGE
COMPANION TO
AUGUST WILSON

EDITED BY
CHRISTOPHER BIGSBY

CAMBRIDGE
UNIVERSITY PRESS

CAMBRIDGE UNIVERSITY PRESS
Cambridge, New York, Melbourne, Madrid, Cape Town, Singapore, São Paulo

Cambridge University Press
The Edinburgh Building, Cambridge CB2 8RU, UK

Published in the United States of America by Cambridge University Press, New York

www.cambridge.org
Information on this title: www.cambridge.org/9780521685061

© Cambridge University Press 2007

First published 2007

Printed in the United Kingdom at the University Press, Cambridge

A catalogue record for this publication is available from the British Library

Library of Congress Cataloguing in Publication data
The Cambridge companion to August Wilson / edited by Christopher Bigsby.
p. cm.
Includes bibliographical references and index.
ISBN 978-0-521-86606-4 (hardback) – ISBN 978-0-521-68506-1 (pbk.)
1. Wilson, August–Criticism and interpretation.   2. Historical drama, American–History
and criticism.   3. African Americans in literature.   I. Bigsby, C. W. E.   II. Title.
PS3573.I45677Z6   2007
812'.54 – dc22
2007032993

ISBN   978-0-521-86606-4 hardback
ISBN   978-0-521-68506-1 paperback

CONTENTS

CONTENTS

LIST OF CONTRIBUTORS

MARGARET BOOKER *Independent scholar*

STEPHEN BOTTOMS *Leeds University*

MARY L. BOGUMIL *Southern Illinois University*

HARRY J. ELAM, JR. *Stanford University*

SAMUEL A. HAY *Lafayette College*

JOAN HERRINGTON *Western Michigan University*

DAVID KRASNER *Yale University*

JOHN LAHR *Writer and journalist*

FELICIA HARDISON LONDRÉ *University of Missouri, Kansas City*

BRENDA MURPHY *University of Connecticut*

ALAN NADEL *Rensselaer Institute*

KIM PEREIRA *Illinois State University*

MATTHEW ROUDANÉ *Georgia State University*

DAVID K. SAUER AND JANICE A. SAUER *University of Southern Alabama*

NOTE ON THE TEXT

Before his death in 2005, August Wilson completed his cycle of ten plays, each set in a different decade of the twentieth century. They were not written in sequential order beginning with the 1900s, but for the purposes of this book they are presented chronologically so that it is possible to follow the unfolding story of that century as seen from the perspective of a man now recognized as America's most powerful and successful African American playwright.

Chapter 2 was originally published in the *New Yorker* on 16 April 2001 (pp. 50–65), and is reprinted here with the kind permission of the author, John Lahr. American spellings and punctuation have been retained.

The interview with August Wilson originally appeared in the first volume of *Writers in Conversation with Christopher Bigsby*, which I edited for the Arthur Miller Centre for American Studies at the University of East Anglia in 2000.

Christopher Bigsby

LIST OF PLAYS

The following list of the ten plays that make up August Wilson's 'Pitts-burgh Cycle' indicates the decades in which they are set and the year of first production.

Gem of the Ocean 1900s (2003)
Joe Turner's Come and Gone 1910s (1986)
Ma Rainey's Black Bottom 1920s (1984)
The Piano Lesson 1930s (1987)
Seven Guitars 1940s (1995)
Fences 1950s (1985)
Two Trains Running 1960s (1990)
Jitney 1970s (1982)
King Hedley II 1980s (1999)
Radio Golf 1990s (2005)

I

CHRISTOPHER BIGSBY

August Wilson: the ground on which he stood

I am one of those warrior spirits. The battle since the first African set foot on the continent of North America has been a battle for the affirmation of the value and worth of one's being in the face of this society that says you're worthless.

... As Africans prior to coming over here, they existed, and they were the center. Everything revolved around them in their world view. Over here, all of that has been taken and stripped away. So I say, 'Let's look at it. The world is right here in this back yard.' There is no idea that cannot be contained by black life. We have the entire world here ... it all depends on where you're standing ... I'm standing over here.

August Wilson[1]

On 2 October 2005 August Wilson died at the Swedish Medical Centre in Seattle. It was just eight months after the death of another American playwright, Arthur Miller. They came out of different worlds. Miller was descended from immigrants on both sides of the family, Jews who went to America to escape persecution and seek their fortune. And if they subsequently lost the fortune they made, they nonetheless never lost belief in the system that had redeemed them from a far worse fate. To be sure, they encountered prejudice, but even so they slid with some ease into an America which swiftly bore the impress of European Jews as they emerged as entrepreneurs, artists, scientists and intellectuals surprisingly ready to interpret America to itself.

For some, particularly those in middle age at the moment of immigration, the maintenance of the old ways was a priority. For others, the trading of a previous identity was a small price to be paid for the acquisition of a new one. If Jewishness was perceived as a problem, it could be wished away, literally or symbolically. Names could be changed. Miller abandoned his grandparents' god, and though he continued to write works in which Jewish characters were confronted with the implications of their identities, this was not his subject. If his career was that of a man who engaged in a lifelong argument with America, and if he frequently found himself excluded by virtue of his critique, he was in essence a believer in the very values he so often challenged.

In particular, he rejected the notion that assimilation was a form of betrayal. He laid claim to Jewish culture, drained of its religious content, but otherwise took American claims sufficiently seriously to test them in plays in which true believers discovered the flaws of a system which nonetheless offered new possibilities. Wilson's case was fundamentally different, though the two writers met in a shared theatrical tradition, no matter how determined they were to modify and challenge it.

On one side Wilson was a descendant of slaves (while his white father was an immigrant from Europe, this was not an identity that interested him), a people who neither fled persecution nor sought a fortune, though their labour guaranteed it to those who systematically persecuted them. And when freedom from slavery came, such rights as they were granted were swiftly stripped away. Thereafter, a primary function became survival. Yet through all this suffering something new was born, a way of being in the world, strategies of resistance that were simultaneously strategies of self-invention, and by degrees, they, too, began to transform the society they were never quite permitted to join. It was their labour that built the infrastructure, that enabled industry to flourish. Their blood was spilt on foreign battlefields with little offered in return beyond a sustained hostility. Assimilation was not as easily available as it had been even for the Jew who suffered from anti-Semitism. Indeed, for much of the twentieth century assimilation was virtually unattainable. Nor, from Wilson's point of view, was it desirable. 'To make inroads into society,' he observed, 'you have to give up your African-ness . . . if you want to go to Harvard, you have to give up the natural way to do things as blacks . . . I think the process of assimilation to white society was a big mistake. We don't want to be like you.'[2] Of *Two Trains Running* (1990) he said, 'There were two ideas in the play, or at least two ideas that had confronted black America since the Emancipation, the ideas of cultural assimilation and cultural separation. These were, in my mind, the two trains.'[3]

The European immigrant drew a line across history. The past existed only to be transcended. Seemingly, much the same could be said of African Americans. A distant African past had been erased by those who enslaved them, while slavery was not an experience to be claimed, any more than what followed, as new rights were swiftly stripped from the supposedly redeemed. History was what white historians declared it to be, not because they sought to distort but because they were standing on their own ground and not that of others. For Wilson, though, Africa had never been dissected out of the African American, while slavery, as fact and image, was the ineluctable starting point of the American experience. Above all, a disregarded history had to be reclaimed, a history this time written by those whose experience of America had been radically different from that of the European immigrant.

In terms of his own profession, he was too conscious of the black artist's role as entertainer of his oppressor to be happy to celebrate those individuals who took advantage of the escape route seemingly offered by show business in its various forms, any more than he was prepared to welcome the ending of the black baseball league when at last sport began to be desegregated. Something, it seemed to him, was lost in the process. That something, in both cases, was black people's roots in the black community, their role in a complex black culture which could only be damaged by the condescending offer of access to a dominant society. To Wilson, the trade was an unequal one. In fact, he went so far as to regret the Great Migration that had seen millions of black Americans trek north in search of freedom and success as if they were, indeed, true equivalents of Polish Jews or Italian workers ready to be embraced and absorbed as they passed through the Golden Door.

It was not simply that awaiting them, besides genuine emancipation, the vibrant life of the ghetto, emergent political and literary activity, and music which he called the carrier of a culture, were those determined to deny them access to work, housing, rights of all kinds. It was not only that further into the century urban decay, drugs and violence would work to undermine a real sense of community. It was that connections had been broken, people dispersed, personal and public stories interrupted. When eventually integration had become more of a reality, the middle classes, in distancing themselves from the ghetto, distanced themselves, too, from those others who they feared defined them in ways they no longer chose to embrace. For Wilson, the need was for communal strength, an acknowledgement of a shared past and hence a sense of shared identity in the present.

Slavery, in particular, was the source of shame, seemingly best not mentioned. Toni Morrison has spoken of the difficulty she found in approaching it but Wilson remarked that as the Jews at Passover begin by recalling their time as slaves in the land of Egypt, so, too, should black Americans celebrate the moment of their emancipation. Indeed, he called for an annual celebration of the Emancipation Proclamation, and it was notable that while the European Holocaust was marked by a museum in Washington, the nation's capital, the genocide of Africans in the slave trade had no national marker.[4] But it was not only slavery that was suppressed. He noted that his parents, in common he believed with those of his friends, revealed little about their own pasts, not least because they could take no pride in what, he presumed, had been demeaning. But, for Wilson, history was a key. As he observed, quoting his character Aunt Ester, 'If you drop the ball, you got to go back and pick it up' (*Conversations* 157). That is what his plays, in effect, do. They are based on the assumption that it is necessary to retrieve the past before it is possible to go forward. They are about the necessity to pick the ball up.

Miller, too, had been a believer in history. For him, it was a key to the moral self. The linking of action to consequence was an acknowledgement of responsibility, for the individual and society alike. His characters spend much of their lives desperately calling out their names, quite as if, in league with their society, they had conspired against themselves. What undoes them is denial, a refusal to confront their own past actions. Hence the very structuring of his plays was a statement. The birds, he was fond of admonishing, always come home to roost, the more especially, perhaps, in a society so determined to deny the reality of its past, so committed to turning away from history in order to stare into the bright light of a future which alone, Americans had been told, holds true authority.

Wilson, however, is drawn to the past for other reasons. Miller could assume a history that he was able to evoke because its contours were seemingly known. Wilson was about the business of identifying and, in truth, constituting a history. It was not a history contained in the history books. Miller returns to the Depression, to the Second World War, to the Holocaust, to the House Un-American Activities Committee, to filmmaking in the 1960s. This is not the business of Wilson's plays. He was committed to celebrating the lives of those who lived in the interstices of such history. To be sure, they suffered the Depression, were pulled away to war, but it is the daily traffic of individuals who share a mythology, ways of behaving, assumptions about human necessities, who share, in short, a culture, that interested him. Thus, as he explained, his 1930s play *The Piano Lesson*, (1987)

> doesn't deal with the Depression, because I am not interested. I have a 1960s play [*Two Trains Running*], but I don't believe the words Black Power are ever mentioned [in fact, he was worng – they are], and it doesn't deal with Martin Luther King. So what? It deals with the people, people who live their lives in a certain social condition that could not have existed other than in those particular decades . . . I am not particularly interested in history as such. You can get that from the history books.[5]
>
> [His interest was rather in those who] still had to go to work every day . . . still had to pay [the] rent . . . still had to put food on the table. And those events [the assassinations of Martin Luther King and Bobby Kennedy, the antiwar marches] while they may have in some way affected the character of society as a whole, didn't reach the average person who was concerned with just simply living.[6]

In setting himself to chart that other history and that culture over the course of a century, Wilson was not, then, concerned to tell a public history, still less to present the pathology of black life in a racist society. His interest lay elsewhere. The story he set himself to stage was that of the lives of those who while peripheral to a society on the make, to the American century, materialistic, confident in its power, were scarcely peripheral to themselves. They did not cut themselves adrift from the American Dream, even as the door was slammed securely in their faces. The pursuit of happiness, the persistence of hope, defined them no less than those who so casually dismissed them as irrelevant to an unfolding national narrative of triumph. But, to Wilson, they were defined by something more than a desire to merge themselves into the generality.

This was not history in the sense of an accurate retrieval of detailed facts. He changed the date of a Joe Louis boxing match because it suited his dramatic purposes. In writing *Joe Turner's Come and Gone* (1986), he made no effort to research 1911, when it is set. Admittedly, in the background, and shaping the emotional environment of characters who live out the moment-by-moment truths of personal and social existence, are the shifting realities of an unfolding public life. But historical accuracy came second place to a different kind of integrity. Rather than turn to reference books which, he explained, constituted a kind of straitjacket, he listened to the music of each decade, finding there a correlative to the concerns of a community for which music was the carrier of the history of a people whose resilience and cultural resources had been disregarded at times even by themselves.

Wilson was happy to acknowledge that Miller was a part of the dramatic tradition on which he could be said to have drawn, though when he began writing he had read and seen almost no plays (feeling that his wide reading in poetry had inhibited the development of his own voice, he determined not to make the same mistake in the case of drama). He was not happy, however, at suggestions that colourblind casting might be one route for the black actor anxious to assume his or her rightful place in the theatre. Thus he recoiled from the notion of black actors performing *Death of a Salesman* (1949) as an insult, an assault on the black presence, on the grounds that 'Blacks speak differently, think differently; they respond to stimuli differently, (*Conversations* 183). Black families, he insisted, 'would not have those problems and in any case do not resolve problems in that way',[7] in truth an odd comment since the relationship between fathers and sons would, as he himself confessed, prove no less central to Wilson's work than Miller's, while both writers staged the lives of characters desperate to affirm their identities and too easily seduced by myths and values tangential to their needs. The point is, though, that Wilson was concerned precisely to delineate a distinct territory, to refute suggestions that African Americans were no more than a variation on the American theme. Their history, after all, was distinctive and their methods of surviving that history no less so.

For black actors to lend their talents to the classic and modern repertoire of Western drama seemed to him close to a betrayal: 'Our manners, our style, our approach to language, our gestures, and our bodies are not for rent. The history of our bodies – the maimings, the lashings, the lynchings, the body that is capable of inspiring profound rage and pungent cruelty – is not for rent. Nor is the meaning of our history or our bodies for rent.'[8] How, then, could he embrace, as he did, an Afrikaans writer such as Athol Fugard? Presumably, what he responded to was Fugard's placing of the black experience in South Africa at the centre of *Sizwe Banzi Is Dead* (in 1976, the first professional play seen by Wilson, and the play whose impact on him was so great that he felt challenged to equal it), even though Fugard wrote out of a white liberal sensibility forged in part out of a reaction to his own early racism (as a child he had spit in the face of a black servant). Speaking in 1997, however, while acknowledging the importance of Fugard, he suggested that ideally he should have concentrated on the white experience in South Africa, a strange remark given that this was in large part what he did and does, though his attempt to inhabit the sensibility of his black characters was surely at the heart of his resistance to the apartheid regime which he so assiduously challenged.

By the same token, Wilson was unwilling to celebrate the production of black plays by regional theatres, seeing this not merely as tokenism, a kind of theatrical quota system, but as a refusal to acknowledge the primacy of black theatres, denied the kind of funding regularly made available to what he characterized as white theatres, white-managed, white-directed and with, essentially, white subscription audiences, the subscription ethos being one, he thought, which favoured mediocrity.

To be a black American writer was to embrace a complex fate but also to lay claim to more than one tradition. What primarily mattered was a sense of continuity between his life as a writer and his life as a black man in America. Miller had spoken of that same sense of continuity between a personal and aesthetic life but in Wilson's case there was clearly a sense of moral, social, historic obligation. There was, though, a disjunction between the polemical nature of some of his public statements and his plays. His cycle of plays was a statement rather than containing one. They did, in fact, constitute the ground on which he stood in that they recapitulated the history that had gone to consolidate his own identity and that of those whose lives he celebrated in their variety no less than their commonalities. Those plays, from *Gem of the Ocean* (2003) to *Radio Golf* (2005), were not an argument for the significance of black lives – they were a demonstration of it.

Born on 27 April 1945, Wilson grew up in his mother's house at 1727 Bedford Avenue in the Hill District of Pittsburgh (a district in which he would later set his plays, while insisting that they could equally have been set in Detroit or Cleveland). He was the fourth of six children. His father, Frederick (Fritz) Kittel, like Tom's in *The Glass Menagerie* (1945), seems to have fallen in love with long distance. Certainly at the time of Wilson's birth he was hardly a presence and it is, perhaps, no surprise that Wilson would later choose to take his mother's surname, not least because his memories of his father were of a destructively violent man. After his parents divorced, Wilson's mother, Daisy, turned to a black man called David Bedford, a high school football star who had spent twenty-three years of his life in prison for having killed a man during a robbery but who now worked for the city, cleaning sewers. He became Wilson's stepfather and it was he, not Wilson's birth father, who seems to have been a model, though he died when Wilson was twenty-four. No wonder there was never any ambiguity in Wilson's mind about his racial identity. His father's European ancestry, his whiteness, meant nothing to a young boy who lived, literally and symbolically, in his mother's house and whose everyday associations were with a predominantly black world.

Daisy Wilson cleaned houses and the family of seven lived in two rooms. Life was a struggle, but it was not struggle that Wilson later recalled. Deprivation might have characterized their material circumstances; it did not define their lives. The poor surrounded by the poor seldom feel poor. His mother had inherited beliefs, values, practical ways of surviving that she passed to her son who inherited, too, the richness of a wider world, a culture improvised in the face of disregard and prejudice. He afterwords remembered the small daily indignities of growing up black. In Woolworths no paper bags were offered to them. While he would attend St Bridget's church, he and his fellow blacks were considered members of a small church called St Benedict the Moor's, albeit a church that could not hold confession. His mother paid $300 a month for her row-house while a white woman two doors away paid $40.

Nonetheless, Wilson grew up feeling that to become overconcerned with the white world which sought to limit and define black possibility was to succumb to a temptation best resisted. To allow oneself to be defined by those who exclude you, to accept their standards of behaviour and concede their authority, is to limit one's possibilities and be distracted from the business of identifying and celebrating cultural strengths that may have been engendered by oppression but which now stood as a key to identity.

Wilson began to write seriously at the age of twenty, reading his poetry at art shows (since he knew a group of artists) and once at a fashion show, earning himself $50, which in 1966 was serious money. He and others published a small magazine called *Signal* which metamorphosed into *Connection*, which in turn gave way to the Centre Avenue Poets' Theatre Workshop. This was a home for poetry readings and jazz but, in part because of the word 'theatre' in their title, its members began to consider presenting plays. They were now reborn as Black Horizons, putting on a play by Rob Penny (known as Black Rob) with Wilson directing, following a crash course in the local library. It was Penny who introduced Wilson to recordings of Malcolm X's speeches, tapes which he found moving.

Wilson was twenty-three, in 1968, when he co-founded this black arts theatre in Pittsburgh. Knowing little of theatre, he turned to Amiri Baraka's *Four Black Revolutionary Plays* (1969) and to a special issue of the *Tulane Drama Review* (edited by Ed Bullins) whose opening essay by Larry Neal was entitled 'The Black Arts Movement'. In this Neal had laid claim to a 'black aesthetic', quoting 'Brother Knight' as insisting that the 'Black artist must create new forms and new values, sing new songs . . . he must create a new history, new symbols, new myths and legends.'[9] Here, had Wilson but known it, was a template for his later life as a playwright (though when he tried to imitate Baraka's plays he found them alien to his own style). Black Horizons performed their plays in (mostly black) schools, charging fifty cents admission, rising to a dollar, in colleges around Pittsburgh and in Ohio, and even in Jackson, Mississippi. Wilson was both director and actor, learning his skills from a book.

For the black writer, the theatre had a central force. It was a social form which drew on and appealed to the community. It lent itself to polemics, didactics. It was concerned with transformation. What was at stake, though, was not integration, not the appearance of black actors in white musicals (characterized by Neal as 'hipper versions of the minstrel show'), still less 'Negroes acting out the hang-ups of middle-class America' (*TDR* 33). This was to be a theatre that would stage the lives of '*blues people*', and in the person of Baraka find a writer with a 'spiritual outlook', and of 'deep lyricism' since he was 'fundamentally more a poet than a playwright' (*TDR* 36).

That phrase must have had a special resonance for Wilson, for whom the new black theatre came as something of a revelation. Although regarding himself as a poet, and never previously having seen a play, he was attracted by the directness of theatre and set himself to stage all the scripts contained in the *Tulane Drama Review*, which included works by Baraka (still identifying himself as Jones), Bullins, Ben Caldwell, John O'Neal, Sonia Sanchez and half a dozen others. It was an urgent theatre, unapologetic. Neal's article quoted from the black poet Don. L. Lee: 'We must destroy Faulkner, dick, jane, and other perpetuators of evil. It's time for DuBois, Nat Turner, and Kwame Nkrumah. As Frantz Fanon points out: destroy the culture and you destroy the people. This must not happen. Black artists are culture stabilizers, bringing back old values, and introducing new ones. Black Art will talk to the people' (*TDR* 29–30).

This was not to be protest literature in that protest was, by definition, aimed at white audiences in expectation of acceptance. Black art began where protest ended. It was primarily a question of audience. 'The Black Arts Movement', Neal insisted, 'is radically opposed to any concept of the artist that alienates him from his community' (*TDR* 29). That would remain a central tenet of Wilson's own work, work which still lay five years in the future.

Wilson's was never protest literature. Rather, it was an attempt to sustain a culture and to bring the writer into closer alignment with his own community. Like Neal, he was also concerned to propose 'a separate symbolism, mythology, critique, and iconology'. Black power, Neal explained, 'is the necessity for Black people to define the world in their own terms . . . The two movements [Black Arts and Black Power] postulate that there are in fact and in spirit two Americas – one black, one white. The Black artist takes this to mean that his primary duty is speak to the spiritual and cultural needs of Black people' (*TDR* 29). Interestingly, the Kerner Commission Report on Civil Disturbances, also published in 1968, in response to the widespread 'riots' of the previous year, had come to a similar conclusion – that there were two Americas – and the special issue of the *Tulane Drama Review* was published shortly after the assassination of Martin Luther King, after which once again cities across America burned. Bullins and Baraka were at a production of Wole Soyinka's *Kongi's Harvest*, at the Lafayette Theatre, when news of King's death reached them.

Wilson shared all the convictions and objectives identified by Neal but felt inhibited from writing plays. He was still more at home with poetry, drawn to the work of John Berryman and Derek Walcott. Dialogue, in particular, posed problems. But the theatre seemed central to his beliefs and belief was what he had been seeking. As he later explained, in 1968 he had been 'a young man coming into manhood searching for something to dedicate my life to' (*Ground* 11–12).

After a while, though, he was tempted to add playwriting to his newly acquired skills as a director, at first trying, then rejecting, Baraka's poeticized agitprop. Inspired by seeing *Sizwe Banzi Is Dead*, he wrote *Recycle* in 1973 (prompted by the break-up of his first marriage), which was produced by a Pittsburgh community theatre, and *The Coldest Day of the Year* (1976) in which an old man and woman engage in conversation on a park bench (a response, he explained, to the collapse of his relationship with his girlfriend of the time). A poetic work, the latter remained a favourite of his long after he had launched himself into his ten-play cycle, though its language was at odds with that in his later plays. In that same year he wrote *The Homecoming*, a brief play set in a railroad station in which three black men wait for the dead body of Blind Willie Johnson, a blues singer. They encounter two recruiting scouts from record companies, exploiters of black talent, whom they beat. The play was staged by an amateur company. Together with *Ma Rainey's Black Bottom* (1984) and a planned play about Otis Redding, this was to have formed part of a projected trilogy to be called *Dangerous Music*.

The key moment, however, came when, in 1978, Wilson's friend Claude Purdy persuaded him to rewrite a series of poems as a play, *Black Bart and the Sacred Hills* (a musical satire on American society with twenty-seven characters), in 1978 inviting him to St Paul to finish it (a city, incidentally, that Wilson could not at the time locate on a map).

The play ran to 167 single-spaced sheets. After a staged reading by the Inner City Repertory Theatre of Los Angeles, Wilson moved to St Paul (though *Black Bart* would not be performed there until 1981) and worked for the Science Museum of Minnesota, writing a series of brief plays about scientists (Margaret Mead, William Harvey, Charles Darwin) and anthropological subjects, adapting stories from the Northwest Native Americans ('I never could understand why they were willing to pay me so much money to do that', *Conversations* 121) before taking a part-time job as a cook for the Little Brothers of the Poor.

It was in St Paul that Wilson began work on what would become *Ma Rainey's Black Bottom*. He also worked on early versions of *Fullerton Street* (1981), set in the 1940s and concerned with those who had moved north only to end up on welfare, and *Jitney* (1982). Although the Eugene O'Neill Theatre Centre's National Playwrights Conference rejected the latter two (the first receiving a staged reading at the Minneapolis Playwright's Centre and the second a production at the Penumbra Theatre in St Paul), it accepted *Ma Rainey* and Wilson began a personal and professional relationship with the director Lloyd Richards, whose parents had made their way to Detroit in the 1920s by way of Canada and who would subsequently direct the majority of his play cycle.

Richards had started work as an actor, appearing in New York in a play by Molly Kazan, directed by Hume Cronyn and starring Karl Malden, but his reputation was made when he directed Lorraine Hansberry's 1959 Broadway success, *A Raisin in the Sun*. As artistic director of Yale Rep and dean of the Yale School of Drama, appointed in 1978 and 1979 respectively, he was in an ideal position to assist Wilson as his plays moved from their Eugene O'Neill Theatre Centre workshops to initial production at Yale on their way through regional theatres to Broadway. This peripatetic production history became a distinguishing feature of Wilson's plays. *King Hedley II* (1999), for example, was workshopped in Seattle, premiered at the Pittsburgh Public Theatre and, over the course of two months, was then developed in five further cities before opening on Broadway, where it ran for a mere seventy-two performances. Usually the plays would lose an hour or more as they were slimmed down into a final form (*Ma Rainey* beginning life at four and a half hours).

In part, Wilson had to create the audience for his own work. American theatre, he admitted, was largely white. Black Americans, he explained, 'don't go to the theatre primarily because the theatre is not responsive to them'. The very existence of his plays, therefore, seemed to him to begin a crucial change. Often his were the first black plays staged by regional companies, so 'if I have a production there, they will go' (*Conversations* 414). However, he was clear that these were not his primary audience. Whatever his social objectives, he wrote for an audience of one. The process of writing was one of 'walking down this landscape of the self' (*Conversations* 78). The play served its own necessities.

At the same time, despite his emphasis, in *The Homecoming* and *Ma Rainey's Black Bottom*, on the appropriation of black art by white society, and despite his success on Broadway and the prizes which came his way, Wilson was unafraid of this process affecting his own work. It seemed to him that just as black Americans could claim the blues, so they could see his work as part of their tradition, whatever whites might make of it, though he would speak bitterly of the failure of black critics to engage with his work, as he would reproach black colleges for lacking Black Studies programmes.

His reference to the blues is scarcely fortuitous. They lie at the centre of his work, as metaphor and paradigm, the flagbearer, he explained, of self-definition. They constitute what he called a 'sacred book' (*Conversations* 58) offering, as they do, an emotional correlative to the African Americans' response to experience. To Wilson, their significance lay in their power to transmute suffering into affirmation, seemingly random events into form. They were the carrier of a culture (though he explained that he himself could not carry a tune in a bucket), registering the shifting tensions, the resistances, the values of a people for whom music had always been central, a trace element of that African heritage he was anxious to stress, of the slavery that was acknowledged less as historical fact than as a coded memory. Compacted within the blues was black history, a history of defeat and triumph, and his plays embodied precisely that rhythm. The musicians in *Ma Rainey's Black Bottom* come together in their music, even as they are divided in other ways. He speaks of characters looking for their song, that song effectively being their identities as individuals but also part of a culture whose history reaches back beyond their own time. His plays are, in essence, about this need to reestablish a connection.

In *Joe Turner's Come and Gone*, the self-imposed function of one character is to bring people back together, to reunite those who have been broken apart. Although each individual has to heal himself or herself, that process involves a recognition of a community in the present and over time. In particular, they had to recognize that they were African people, despite the passage of time. That African connection becomes stronger the further Wilson moves back in time. In *Joe Turner's Come and Gone*, set in 1911, it is clear but its survival remained an article of faith to Wilson, a survival fostered to the extent that the black community remained discrete, less inclined to fade into the anonymity of American society, were that permitted. That conviction led him in what seemed to some a strange direction, as he regretted the abandonment of the South which he characterized as the ancestral land. It was there, he insisted, that the slaves and their immediate descendants forged the culture to be inherited by their descendants. The move north he thought a mistake.

On 26 June 1996 Wilson addressed the eleventh biennial Theatre Communications Group National Conference at Princeton University. In a speech entitled 'The Ground on Which I Stand' he outlined his personal and dramatic philosophy and in so doing ignited a dispute with Harvard University's Robert Brustein which extended beyond the question of the plight of black theatre in America and issues such as colourblind casting, subscription theatre and the funding of regional theatres. It was a combative speech, challenging the assumptions, rhetoric and policies of those who presumed to speak for and about an American theatre which, Wilson insisted, was more socially, culturally and theatrically various than they presumed. But for Wilson, black theatre was something more than evidence of a culturally diverse society, to be celebrated in theatrical seasons in which artistic directors tipped their hats in the direction of minority authors as though graciously offering access to the great house of a national drama with shared assumptions about the past, myths and values. Black theatre, he insisted, expressed a parallel but neglected history; it reflected a psychology shaped by something other than American pieties; it played a potentially central role in the reconstruction of an identity that had been placed under extreme pressure but was constituted precisely from a series of resistances taking cultural form. The assumptions of white dramatists, he claimed, were not those of black playwrights whose roots lay in radically different experiences and who laid claim to quite other influences.

At the heart of *The Ground on Which I Stand* is an appeal for more black theatres and for the funds that would sustain them. Despite his role in co-founding the Black Horizons Theatre in the 1960s, Wilson had established himself through white institutions – the Eugene O'Neill Theatre Centre, Yale Rep, the Huntington Theatre Company. His plays wended their way to Broadway by way of regional repertory companies, the very League of Resident Theatres against which he fulminated. His point, though, was that he had few alternatives and that this process was not one that could be expected to foster black playwrights, technicians, designers, or, indeed, audiences. The irony, however, was that in his own case he began to write plays precisely when he had left the kind of community that could be expected to host black theatres (today Pittsburgh has a black population of 27 per cent), moving first to St Paul (black population 11.7 per cent) and then, after a divorce, Seattle (8.4 per cent and falling since 1990). As Wilson himself observed, 'I went from a neighbourhood of 55,000 blacks to a state [Minnesota] in which there were only 35,000. This was a tremendous change.' Tremendous and, it turned out, crucial. As he explained later, 'In Pittsburgh it was a question of not being able to see the forest for the trees. The reason I couldn't write dialogue was because I didn't respect the way blacks talked. I didn't see a value in it. I was always trying to alter the language into something else.' When he moved to St Paul, for the first time 'I was removed from the black community and, perhaps as a result, for the first time I began to hear the voices that I had grown up with all my life. And I began to discover, to recognize, the value of those voices and the fact that I did not have to change the way they talked in order to create art. That was one of the really important moments of my life'.[10]

The reason for his emphasis on black theatre was clear enough. His plays themselves may not have been political, in the sense of being shaped to a political objective beyond that implied in the presentation of black life as a central fact and black culture as a rich and living truth. Nonetheless, he insisted that 'All my plays are political.' (*Own Words* 304) Their very existence, and the existence of a vibrant black theatre, was a political fact and as such they could play a vital role. In a language reminiscent of the 1960s, he announced that the black artist could be 'the spearhead of a movement to reignite our people's positive energy for a political and social change that is reflective of our spiritual truths rather than economic fallacies' (*Ground* 40). Plays about history in turn become historical facts with the power to alter consciousness, and if consciousness then actions, assumptions, ambitions, values.

Wilson's was not a theatre which rejected the history of Western theatre. Indeed, he was happy to declare his embrace of it. What he wanted to do was amend it, to infiltrate an African consciousness which drew on influences unique to itself, from black music and ritual through to a spirituality which went beyond that explored and expressed by white writers. He did not reject his American identity; he simply wished to lay claim to it on his own terms. His was not to be a mendicant theatre.

At the same time, he was not afraid to invoke the idea of universality, in the 1930s code for communist, in the 1960s code for a neutered specificity. He was not interested in a separatist theatre, if what was meant by that was that it assumed passions, convictions, aspirations unique to one group. Betrayal, he noted, 'is betrayal whether you are a South Sea Islander, a Mississippi farmer or an English baron. All of human life is universal, and it is theatre that illuminates and confers upon the universal the ability to speak for all men' (*Ground* 45). Indeed, Wilson's 1996 speech, which was to prove so controversial, ended with an encomium to the American spirit and to the power of the American theatre 'to inform about the human spirit'. It ended with the assertion of art's role in reaching 'across that divide that makes order out of chaos' (*Grounds* 44) and with a rededication to the pursuit of happiness, the ground, he concluded, 'on which we all stand' (*Ground* 46).

His own values and assumptions were forged in the 1960s, but his were not the countercultural assertions of those for whom liberation was a matter of personal exploration, nor yet the radicalism of those for whom capitalism was to be challenged in the name of a new romanticism. Even the civil rights movement, so desperate to claim access to American values by way of shared lunch counters, transport, housing, seemed to him beside the point. The key moment came with the emergence of Black Power and its cultural wing, forcefully led as it was by a man who had abandoned his 'slave name', LeRoi Jones, for a new one, Amiri Baraka. Here was a man determined to found exclusively black theatres, to raise the consciousness of a black community alternately relegated to the margins of history and now invited in on condition that it relinquished precisely what was most distinctive. The civil rights movement, as it seemed to him, stood ready to trade memory, a history of suffering, a cultural distinctiveness, for a suspension of discrimination. Baraka, by contrast, reached back to Africa as a central point of reference and proposed a model of resistance rather than subservience traded in for acquiescence.

Baraka's father had been drawn to Marcus Garvey in the early part of the century and although Garvey's ventures frequently foundered, what he had recognized, which others had not, was a communal strength based on a communal distinctiveness. To be sure, the Africa that Garvey invoked was not one he knew, and he was not without a certain imperial presumption, but Baraka, and subsequently Wilson, was concerned to lay claim to a heritage not defined by pathology and suffering. His youth, Wilson explained in 1991, was fired in the kiln of the black cultural nationalism exemplified by Baraka. It was a favourite trope. In 1996 he would insist that Black Power was 'the kiln in which I was fired', (*Ground* 12–13) as elsewhere he spoke of black culture being 'fired in the kiln of slavery' (*Conversations* 105). It was, he insisted, 'a duty and an honor to participate in that historic moment' (*Ground* 12). Nor was it limited to the 1960s. When his daughter went to university in the 1980s, she found herself discussing the great African civilizations, just as many of those drawn to Black Power had done. However, by then this seemed to Wilson beside the point. He had no fascination with Africa itself. In the 1960s he never wore a dashiki and neither then nor in the 1990s did he have any desire to go to Africa. To him, "When the first African died on the continent of North America, that was the beginning of my history" (*Conversations* 210).

It is tempting to think that in 1996 Wilson was retrieving something of his experience of nearly thirty years earlier. The 'self-determination, self-respect and self-defence that governed my life in the '60s,' he explained, 'I find just as valid and self-urging in 1996'. Indeed, he insisted that the 'need to alter our relationships to the society and to alter the shared expectations of ourselves as a racial group I find of greater urgency now than it was then' (*Ground* 13). In his 1968 article Neal had remarked that black people constituted a nation in the belly of white America, an idea he traced to Garvey and the Honourable Elijah Muhammad as Wilson now declared that his roots lay in 'Marcus Garvey and the Honorable Elijah Muhammad'. He was, he declared, what Garvey had called 'a race man'.

More disturbing, however, was what some took to be an anti-Semitic remark. Thus where in 1968 Neal had quoted Baraka's call for poems that will be daggers 'in the slimy bellies/of the owner-jews' (*TDR* 31), in 1996 Wilson spoke of 'financiers', influencing the future of the theatre, and the pernicious effects of 'counting houses'. It was an absurd piece of overinterpretation since Wilson was specifically speaking of the failure to fund black theatres as opposed to regional theatres. But in other respects the Wilson of 1996 was close in spirit to the Wilson of 1968, even though, speaking in 1993, he had confessed that in trying to speak for the people in 1968 he had lost touch with them. His, he admitted, had been the romanticized view of a young man of twenty-three. Not all of that romanticism, however, had drained away with the years.

In an article published in the year of his death, Wilson suggested that if the NAACP, one of whose founders had been W. E. B. DuBois, were to rename itself the National Association of Black People, it would be less concerned with essentially middle-class values and more committed to the needs of the wider community. In his 1996 speech he had rejected DuBois's idea of the Talented Tenth, insisting that it was 'a fallacy and a dangerous idea' which created 'an artificial superiority . . . that only serves to divide us further'. He was not, he asserted, willing 'to throw away as untalented ninety percent of my blood (*Ground* 39). All God's children, he stated, 'got talent'. As if to contradict himself, in 2005 he asserted that the middle class, 'which had adopted the values of the dominant society' and 'given up some of their cultural values', 'have a duty and a responsibility',[11] not quite the talented tenth, perhaps, but plainly a group whom he saw as having succeeded in the terms defined by American society and who were now to be reminded of an obligation of the kind identified by DuBois. Rich or poor, their roots were the same, their history was the same. They came, he suggested, from the same gene pool.

Wilson's lament, though, is not simply that the problems of the deprived are ignored by the well-to-do. It is the immigrant's regret at the price paid for assimilation, a constant refrain of his speeches, articles and interviews. It was a parallel he acknowledged: 'Some people make the choice, it's certainly not only black people – a lot of ethnic Europeans have made that choice completely. They have been so anxious to become Americans that they've changed their names, forgotten the old ways and don't want to be reminded of them.' It was possible, he insisted, to maintain a double identity but materialism was in danger of fostering a new identity, albeit one which, somewhat strangely, he associated with the British class system: 'I think we're all trying to imitate the British to become lords and aristocrats, have a bunch of servants and a gardener, all that kind of stuff' (*American Theatre* 22, 24).

His own identity, he remarked, derived precisely from the black experience in America. 'Before I am anything, a man or a playwright,' he asserted, 'I am an African American. The tributary streams of culture, history and experience have provided me with the materials out of which I make my art.' That culture was

> forged in the cotton fields of the South and tested by the hard pavements of the industrial North . . . The field of manners and rituals of social intercourse – the music, speech, rhythms, eating habits, religious beliefs, gestures, notions of common sense, attitudes toward sex, concepts of beauty and justice, and the responses of pleasure and pain – have enabled us to survive the loss of our political will and the disruption of our history. (*American Theatre* 27)

This was to be the basis of his drama. As he explained:

> I wanted to present the unique particulars of black American culture as the transformation of impulse and sensibility into codes of conduct and response, into cultural rituals that defined and celebrated ourselves as men and women of high purpose. I wanted to place this culture on stage in all its richness and fullness and to demonstrate its ability to sustain us in all areas of life and endeavor and through profound moments of our history in which the larger society has thought less of us than we have thought of ourselves. (*American Theatre* 28)

The black world that formed the focus of Wilson's activities was not peripheral; it did not exist at a tangent, was not a footnote, an appendix, the subtext to a master story. It defined its own parameters. It was not subjunctive, doubtful of its own assertions. Its history might be occluded, subtly coercive by virtue of its suppressions, but that history contained something more than suffering and tainted nostalgia. What he would stage, in the course of the ten-play cycle he presented between 1984 and 2005, was a culture with its roots in a distinctive past.

To Wilson, a significant aspect of black theatre had originally lain in its origins in the slave plantations where performance was a response to white needs and desires but, more importantly, in those performances designed to serve the necessities of those whose imaginations transcended the slave quarters. This was a world of song and dance, of rituals partly reaching back beyond the Middle Passage and partly generated to give shape and form to an experience which had to be given a meaning at odds with that assumed by those who commanded their bodies but not their souls. It is in that sense that Wilson asserts, 'I stand myself and my art squarely on the self-defining ground of the slave quarters, and find the ground to be hallowed and made fertile by the blood and bones of the men and women who can be described as warriors on the cultural battlefield that affirmed their self-worth' (*Ground* 20).

LeRoi Jones's *The Slave* (1964) begins with what appears to be a slave, suddenly transformed into a warrior. It was an emblem of the black theatre of the 1960s. In a similar way, Jones's *Slaveship* (1967) was offered precisely as a reminder of the origin of black suffering and thus the need for a theatre of resistance. Jones's protagonist in *The Slave* has been shaped by white culture and, indeed, is an admirer of it. His transformation thus carries a cost. Much the same could be said of Jones himself, who was in the process of deciding that his life must take a different course. His reinvention as Amiri Baraka was a public declaration that his tussle with ambiguity was at an end. If Wilson had started his career as a playwright, perhaps he might have been drawn to create agit-prop works of the kind Baraka wrote – he did, in fact, briefly try his hand at this. But resistance takes many forms and even at that time Bullins was creating a cycle of plays which explored the nature of black life in America, presenting it not as a series of reactive gestures but as a story of intimate negotiations within the family and the community, plays which Wilson would come to admire. When he finally turned to the theatre, and despite his affirmation of Baraka's centrality, it was that path that Wilson chose to tread. For Bullins was no less concerned with self-determination and in his 1996 lecture Wilson offered a roll-call of those black writers whom he believed had played a significant role: Ron Milner, Ed Bullins, Philip Hayes Dean, Richard Wesley, Lonne Elder III, Sonia Sanchez, Barbara Ann Teer and Baraka.

Four of these had appeared in the 1968 special issue of the *Tulane Drama Review*. It was this explosion of black talent, he declared, that 'remains for me the hallmark and the signpost that points the way to our contemporary work on the same ground', the ground on which, in the title of his lecture, he proclaims himself to stand. Here, after all, were artists prepared to challenge white hegemony over the theatre while black Americans were, in his tart phrase, pointing 'blacks toward the ball fields and the bandstands' (*Ground* 21), which perhaps goes some way to explaining why his first fully produced play was *Ma Rainey's Black Bottom*, which detailed the fate of those who accepted this direction only to see their talents appropriated, and why *Fences* (1985) explores the life of a man for whom the ball field was the source of frustration and despair, if also of triumph.

If Baraka was one source of inspiration, another, Wilson explained, was the artist Romare Bearden, who had spent time in Pittsburgh and whose work celebrated black society. When a study of Bearden's work appeared in 1990, Wilson wrote an introduction. In this he revealed that two crucial discoveries had shaped his own sensibility, Bessie Smith and the blues in 1965 and, in 1977, Bearden's collages which appeared under the collective title *The Prevalence of Ritual*. Here he found 'black life presented on its own terms . . . with all its richness and fullness, in a language that was vibrant and which, made attendant to everyday life, ennobled it, affirmed its value, and exalted its presence'.[12] Thereafter, he explained, he had sought to make his plays 'the equal of his canvases' (*Bearden* 9). Two of his plays would take direct inspiration from individual paintings. *Joe Turner's Come and Gone* was prompted by *Mill Hand's Lunch Bucket* (and two of *Joe Turner's* characters – Seth and Bertha – draw their names from another Bearden painting) and *The Piano Lesson* by Bearden's work of the same name.

The very nature of Bearden's technique – his collages were constructed from discarded scraps, from African and American cut-out figures, bold colours, juxtaposed images unapologetically presented – would prove a clue to Wilson's work, as would Bearden's views on black art. Writing in 1942, Bearden had endorsed the notion that 'The Negro painter should direct his efforts largely from the standpoint of the heritage left him from his African ancestors' (*Bearden* 120). Part of that heritage, he granted in discussing the work of the Nigerian writer Amos Tutuola, was the reality of ghosts, ghosts of the kind that would be invoked by Wilson. Although Bearden had left the South of his birth, he was still drawn to it, while he saw his work as rooted in the world he had known when he was growing up. 'Many artists', he believed, 'take some place, and like a flower, they sink roots, looking for universal implications, like James Joyce did in Dublin and the photographer Mathew Brady did for the Civil War . . . I paint what people did when I was a little boy, like the way they got up in the morning' (*Bearden* 256). Wilson, who set his plays in the place where he grew up, did no less.

Wilson's 1996 speech was polemical in tone. It spoke of the need to resist 'cultural imperialists' who regarded 'blacks as woefully deficient not only in arts and letters but in the abundant gifts of humanity' (*Ground* 22). Such imperialists, he contended, 'view their American culture, rooted in the icons of European culture, as beyond reproach in its perfection' (*Ground* 29). An article in the *New York Times* about the pop singer Michael Bolton had particularly angered him. It cited four white singers as Bolton's influences, along with 'the great black rhythm and blues singers', a phrase which, Wilson suggested, reduced those singers 'to an afterthought on the verge of oblivion'. Thus the history of music becomes 'a fabrication, a blatant forgery' (*Ground* 35). He stressed, as had many before him in the 1960s, the contrasting lexical meanings of the words 'black' and 'white' which constituted the 'linguistic environment that informs the distance that separates blacks and whites in America', invoking Webster's Dictionary as authority.

He challenged Brustein's implication that the cultural products of black dramatists were inferior – embraced, if at all, less for aesthetic than for social reasons. Where Brustein called for writers to meet on the common ground of a single value system, Wilson asked, rhetorically, 'Where is the common ground in the horrifics of lynching? Where is the common ground in the maim of the policeman's bullet? Where is the common ground in the hull of a slave ship or the deck of a slave ship with its refreshments of air and expanse?' (*Ground* 26). It was, in short, history that divided, not the whim of playwrights.

It was history that had to be confronted and acknowledged before a common ground could be opened up, a triumphant history, not merely one of survival but of achievement. It was for black Americans to become custodians of their culture and their lives. For the moment, the only shared space was that provided by theatre, which had its own commonly embraced history; though even here, and somewhat oddly, Wilson mocks those who believe that life cannot be lived and enriched without knowing Shakespeare (the first Shakespeare play he saw was *Othello*, and that not until 1986), oddly because in the same speech he quotes from that same Shakespeare.

What were his own plays designed to do? On that he was clear, if hardly modest. They were to 'contain the sum total of black culture in America, and its difference from white culture' (*Own Words* 294). It was a tall order. Beyond that, the personal histories he staged 'would not only represent the culture but illuminate the historical context both of the period in which the play is set and the continuum of black life in America that stretches back to the 17th century'.[13] He was also prone to make a distinction that was not always clear to others. What he wanted people to derive from his work, he explained, was that his characters were Africans, 'as opposed to black folks in America'. When he talked to an audience at Yale Rep, after a performance of *Joe Turner's Come and Gone*, he asked how many had recognized the characters as African. The response angered him to the point of his losing his temper. As he recalled later in an interview, 'I said, "How many recognize these people as Africans?" There were two hundred people sitting there and about eight raised their hands. I'm very curious as to why they refuse – I have to say it's a refusal because it's so obvious. So many people blocked that, wanting to recognize them as black Americans. I was really surprised to find that' (*Own Words* 302). What is surprising about his surprise is that the phrase 'black Americans' is one he had himself used on many occasions. What, after all, is the distinction he is trying to make?

Despite his invocation of Garvey, Wilson was not interested in going back to Africa but in asserting that Africa was already inside him. Despite growing up at a time of African liberation which some in the 1960s took as a model for political action within America, he did not share Stokely Carmichael's sense of it as a base for exporting revolution. He was closer to Baraka, who, despite the fact that in an early poem he had confessed 'Africa/is a foreign place. You are/as any other sad man here/American',[14] was later drawn to Ron Karenga who had called for a cultural revolution and placed Africa at the centre of that enterprise. Baraka, though, resisted the kind of cultural nationalism which 'uses an ahistorical unchanging never-never-land Africa to root its hypothesis' and was aware that his attachment to things African could be said to be the 'working out of the guilt of the over integrated'.[15] Nonetheless, he adopted the name of Ameer Barakat (the Blessed Prince), later Swahilizing it (and setting himself to learn Swahili). He was thus, he insisted, 'being changed into a blacker individual'. His children were given

African names (Obalaji Malik Ali and Ras Jua Al Aziz), as were Wilson's (Sakina Ansari and Azula Carmen), whose first marriage was to a member of the Nation of Islam. However, that religion came between them and the marriage foundered, though not until Wilson had become a black Muslim, adopting the name Mbulu and selling copies of *Muhammad Speaks*, subsequently remaining respectful of Elijah Muhammad and his teachings, including the bizarre myth of origins which saw whites as the by-product of a failed experiment by black scientists.

Since he had confessed to being the heir to two traditions, the distinction Wilson is reaching for – in opposing black American to African – surely involves one of emphasis. The American is the given, the known. It is territory mapped many times before. As he explained, 'We got the American part together the first hundred years that we were here. We would not be here had we not learned to adapt to American culture' (*Conversations* 70). The African is the suppressed, the unacknowledged, the insufficiently explored. None of his characters denies their American context. It is simply the given that has no need of articulation. What he stages is that dimension largely ignored by the white world and never fully honoured by the black, a distinctiveness which turns not on hybridity but on modes of being forged out of a history that reaches back through the move of a people from the rural south to the urban north, from slavery to redemption, from Africa to America. What he presents is a culture not improvised out of nothing but constructed over time out of experience now encoded in myths, rituals, stories, music, social and personal behaviours. The African owes nothing to America beyond suffering transmuted into form, disregard transcended by shared faiths, marginality nullified by a startling originality of expression. As he remarked in a 1987 interview, 'I think that if we move toward claiming the strongest part of ourselves, which is the African parts, so that we can participate in the society as Africans, we would be all the stronger for it' (*Conversations* 57).

The African American is a forging together of two traditions. Despite the bad faith of one of those traditions, rooted as it is in an arrogant presumptiveness towards others, Wilson respects them both. But, as his anger at the response of the Yale audience suggests, his territory was staked out for him long before when he realized that his own commitment was to what distinguished him from the larger society which accepted him, if at all, only on sufferance, and to that community whose roots lay elsewhere than in a displaced Europe and whose commitments were to something other than an homogenized identity forged out of a desire to reject the past.

What he was trying to do as a playwright was to place black values on stage in what he called '"loud action," simply to demonstrate that they exist and that they are capable of sustenance, and to point out some avenues of sustenance.' That, he explained, was 'what fuels my work – more so than any bitterness or angriness. I don't', he added, 'write from a wellspring of bitterness. I write from a very positive viewpoint of black life and black experience' (*Conversations* 55). He was, he explained, 'working out of a four-hundred-year autobiography, which is the black experience' (*Conversations* 60). He did not write to precipitate social change but to offer a new perspective on lives whose modes of articulation, vision, traditions, assumptions might be distinct and distinguishing but whose human necessities are immediately recognizable. Meanwhile, the elevation of those lives into art itself stood as a statement. To his own mind, he wrote tragedies and at the centre of those tragedies was what Miller, in discussing his own tragic intent, chose to call 'the common people'. Wilson was an Aristotelian in the same way as Miller. His tragic protagonists are flawed. Their struggle with the consequences of such flaws is what compels attention. But these characters were black, in terms of their racial identity, their history, their values.

It was these convictions that led Brustein to believe that Wilson's support of black theatres was a separatist gesture rather than an appeal for the funding of those who had no more stake in theatrical America than he believed them to have in the economic, social and political system which continued to exclude them. But Brustein's argument with Wilson went beyond this. His objection, he explained, was that Wilson seemed old-fashioned. Suzan-Lori Parks might be carrying the torch for the avant-garde but Wilson, he suggested in an article in the *New York Times*

> who always claimed to be establishing black traditions completely independent of any white influence never struck me as being more or less than part of the fine but well-established tradition of social protest domestic drama. The more poetic tradition which he is certainly capable of joining because he is a great creator of language, is more extended, symbolic, subterranean

– this of a man who created a character several hundred years old, and works which featured a conjure man and in which ghosts haunt the present and figures sing their lives, literally and symbolically. Beyond that, however, Brustein suggested that, in choosing to chronicle the oppression of black people through the decades, Wilson had fallen into a monotonous tone of victimization. His plays, he observed, were 'weakly structured, badly edited, prosaic and overwritten'.[16] Wilson responded by describing Brustein as 'a sniper, a naysayer, and a cultural imperialist'.[17] Brustein's suggestion, elsewhere, that funding agencies were supporting inferior work by minority writers rather than challenging work by, implicitly, white writers (though the phrase was not used), merely served to further accommodate Wilson's work, by implication, to a sociological model.

Wilson plainly knew little of the consistency with which Brustein had attacked American playwrights who seemed to him to lack the necessary credentials as avant-garde writers. He had famously written an article entitled 'Why American Drama is Not Literature' and dismissed with equanimity and a certain equality of contempt the work of Miller, O'Neill (despite his own shrewd analysis of his work in *The Theatre of Revolt* (1964)) and Tennessee Williams. His observations about Wilson's plays are almost endearingly wide of the mark. Social protest drama is what Wilson specifically eschews. He claimed only once to have succumbed to pressure to write a more commercial play, one which focused on the plight of an individual – *Fences*, a successful play but one which he thought tangential to the kind of work he was anxious to do. Otherwise, he thought of himself as devising forms appropriate to his subject.

Both men were swinging somewhat widely and wildly. The rhetoric of Wilson's 1996 speech had laid him open to attack and attacks came from more than Brustein. The echoes of Black Power rhetoric prompted responses from Henry Louis Gates, Jr. and Stanley Crouch. For both men, Wilson seemed to be advocating a separatist approach, one, moreover, reinforced, for some, by his refusal to allow the filming of *Fences* without a black director, claiming that specific 'ideas and attitudes that are not shared on the common cultural ground . . . remain the property and possession of the people who develop them'.[18] 'Let's make a rule,' he proposed:

> Blacks don't direct Italian films. Italians don't direct Jewish films. Jews don't direct black American films . . . I want somebody talented who understands the play and sees the possibilities of the film, who would approach my work with the same amount of passion and measure of respect with which I approach it, and who shares the same cultural sensibilities of the characters. The last time I looked, all those directors were black.[19]

In like manner he resisted the idea of the Seattle Rep's Dan Sullivan directing his work on the grounds that he would prefer someone who shared his sensibility and culture and, hence, race.

In one sense his critics were right. Wilson was being overly restrictive. His demands, at times, seemed to challenge the very idea of art as a means of bridging divides. But then, his focus was plainly on black experience. He spoke up for black theatre, which he believed more likely to foster black talent in all dimensions of theatre. When he spoke regretfully of the Great Migration he did seem to be celebrating a supposedly more homogeneous culture, relatively uninflected by the wider culture not least because separatism was the ruling orthodoxy of whites. At the same time, he tended to ignore the coercive realities which defined that culture and which existed, as he well knew, at the whim of white society even as it developed its own coded values.

All this, though, is to ignore the plain thrust of his remarks, not merely in his 1996 speech to the Theatre Communications Group National Conference but in the dozens of interviews to which he had submitted over many years. His subject was black people and their struggle to understand their past and present in the context of an American society that was seemingly content to see them relegated to the margins of history, as of civil society. By almost any indicator, while he was writing they remained the most likely not to be beneficiaries of the free market. They faced unemployment on a scale not experienced by others, lived in parts of cities into which few whites would choose to venture, colluded in their own exclusion from the educational system, drifted, seemingly inevitably, towards prison, and were ravaged by drugs in a parody of paradigms of production and consumption. In one nation, indivisible, they were divided not by a playwright but by economic, social and political forces. Yet this was not Wilson's subject.

He did not advocate separatism. He explored the lives of those who lived in communities with their own traditions, myths, values. Eddie Carbone, in Miller's A View from the Bridge (1955), inhabits such a community, in which the other America exists just beyond the boundaries of conventions forged in another time and place – Sicily. It was not, though, Miller's community. He had his own, equally hermetic when it wished to be, and he staged it in Broken Glass (1994). Wilson chose another community defined partly by exclusion and partly by cohesion.

Wilson did not protest (though in various plays he traces in the boundaries drawn by others): he celebrated. He presented an America that others had not. Which white playwright, after all, even including O'Neill, had even attempted to explore the dynamics of black life, to understand the nature of its strengths, the unspoken, though not unsung, assumptions on which it is based? His references to Africa might seem quaint to those who believe themselves to have encountered it before, but what he means by that is surely clear. And if it is not, then he tries to stage it as remnants of folk myths, shards of stories, half-forgotten rhythms are retrieved from an uninspected past only to merge with those of the country his characters inhabit, a country which has its own myths reaching back to another continent and respected as entirely legitimate traces of a history which, if equally romanticized, has the sanction of authority.

Whenever he finished a play, Wilson would immediately begin working on the next. His last, however, was followed not by another but by the announcement of his liver cancer. He was dead barely five weeks later, at the age of sixty. It would be a sentimentality to say that he had finished his life's work, simply because he had completed the ten-play cycle. There would undoubtedly have been others. Nonetheless, there is a consolation in the completion of his project to remap the century from a black point of view. He had achieved not only what no black playwright had accomplished before him. He had achieved what few white writers had. He had a string of awards which outstripped those of others. He had established himself as a successful Broadway author who nonetheless attracted audiences of a kind unusual for Broadway plays. If America remains, as he insisted, radically divided by race, even in the twenty-first century, he contrived to address both black and white audiences and to discover in the particularities of black life not only those qualities that had sustained and energized that life but also those elements of a common humanity which gave his tragedies their force and more general relevance.

His arguments about strengthening black theatre, which some took to be a defence of separatism, his fanciful notions of a mass return to the South, were never designed as a rejection of an American identity. They were aspects of his desire to embrace that identity from a position of strength, of the need to acknowledge, indeed, that that American identity already bore the impress of those who had always been the protagonists not only of their own drama but of the drama of a society whose amnesia was a threat to its own future.

August Wilson was one of the finest American playwrights of the twentieth century, even as he resisted a view of America as a culture built on homogeneity, requiring the surrender of other identities in order to embrace a singular vision. America, he pointed out, was always in the making. That was its strength. One key aspect of its distinctiveness, however, had been, if not ignored, then relegated to a subtext. That distinctiveness came from a people torn from another continent, destroyed in their passage to a new land not of their choosing, enslaved, evicted from history, demeaned, excluded, but who had survived, recreating themselves, and who, from their struggle in an alien world, had forged a resilient culture which slowly infiltrated the sensibility of those who for centuries had dismissed them as an irrelevance to the national project. These were the people Wilson celebrated, this the culture he staged.

But he was conscious that when he sat down to write, he sat in the same chair as Henrik Ibsen, Miller and Williams, faced with the same problems of crafting a play. He recognised a kindred spirit in Anton Chekhov, though he saw only one of his plays, and that when he was himself well launched as a writer. Conflict was no less central to his work than to that of any other writer. He had no interest in being filed away, labelled for his presumed politics, aesthetics, racial commitments. His primary commitment was to words. That he became the first African American to have his name on a Broadway theatre, the former Virginia Theatre on 52nd Street in New York, was a sign of his achievement in his chosen profession. 'When I do interviews,' he explained, 'I am expected to become some sociologist. I have to speak to the condition of black America. My preference would be: "Let's talk about theatre. Let's talk about art. The fact that I am black is self-evident."'[20] And again, 'I'm a black American playwright . . . I couldn't deny it . . . I make my art out of black American culture . . . That's who I am, that's who I write about . . . in the same manner that Chekhov wrote about the Russians . . . so there's no reason why you can't say "August Wilson, playwright".'[21]

NOTES

1. Jackson R. Bryer and Mary C. Hartig, eds., *Conversations with August Wilson* (Jackson: University of Mississippi Press, 2006), p. 197. Further quotations will be cited parenthetically in the text.
2. David Savran, ed., *In Their Own Words: Contemporary American Playwrights* (New York: Theatre Communications Group, 1988), p. 299. Further quotations will be cited parenthetically in the text.
3. Richard Pettengill, 'The Historical Perspective: An Interview with August Wilson,' in Marilyn Elkins, ed., *August Wilson: A Casebook* (New York: Garland, 1994), p. 208.
4. In February 2006 George W. Bush signed a proclamation establishing a slave burial ground in Lower Manhattan, New York, as a national monument.
5. See chapter 16, 'An interview with August Wilson', p. 207.
6. Pentengill, 'The Historical Perspective', p. 207.
7. Stephen Kinzer, 'A Playwright Casts Himself to Tell His Angry Story,' *New York Times*, 26 May 2003, p. B5.
8. August Wilson, *The Ground on Which I Stand* (New York: Theatre Communications Group, 2001), p. 30. Further quotations will be cited parenthetically in the text.
9. Larry Neal, 'The Black Arts Movement', *Tulane Drama Review*, 12:4 (Summer 1968), p. 30. Further quotations will be cited parenthetically in the text.
10. Bigsby, *Writers in Conversation*, pp. 412–13.
11. Suzan-Lori Parks, 'The Light in August', *American Theatre* (November 2005), p. 22. Further quotations will be cited parenthetically in the text.
12. August Wilson, 'Foreword', in Myron Schwartzman, *Romare Bearden: His Life and Art* (New York: Harry N. Abrams, 1990), p. 8. Further quotations will be cited parenthetically in the text.
13. August Wilson, 'Characters Behind History Teach Wilson About Plays', *New York Times*, 12 April 1992.
14. LeRoi Jones, *Preface to a Twenty Volume Suicide Note* (New York: Corinth Books, 1961), p. 47.

15. Amiri Baraka, *The Autobiography of LeRoi Jones Amiri Baraka* (New York: Freundlich Books, 1984), pp. 253, 255.
16. Kinzer, 1 'A Playwright', p. B5.
17. Simon Saltzman and Nicole Plett, 'August Wilson versus Robert Brustein', in US, Princeton, New Jersey, 22 January 1997, at www.princetoninfo.com/Wilson.html.
18. August Wilson, 'I Want a Black Director', in Alan Nadel, ed., *Essays on the Drama of August Wilson* (Iowa City: University of Iowa Press, 1994), p. 201.
19. *Ibid.*, p. 204.
20. 'A Dialogue Between August Wilson and Javon Johnson', at www.pbs.org/newshour/bb/remember/july_dec05/wilson_10_3.html.
21. Gwen Ifill, 'American Shakespeare (An Interview with August Wilson', at www.webinstituteforteachers.org/phooper/wit2002/awinterview.html.

2

JOHN LAHR

Been here and gone

If anybody asks you who sang this song
Tell 'em
It was little Jimmy Rushing,
He's been here and gone.

The playwright August Wilson lives in a leafy, genteel part of Seattle intended by the city's founding fathers to be the site of the state capitol, and so named Capitol Hill. He moved here in 1994, with Constanza Romero, a Colombian-born costume designer who is now his third wife, and they share a rambling turn-of-the-century house with Azula, their three-year-old daughter. Azula has her father's ear and number, as well as total control of the living room, which, apart from a jukebox and a piano – props from Wilson's productions – hasn't a stick of adult furniture. Wilson, who doesn't drive, is more interested in the inner terrain than the external one; writing, he says, 'is for me like walking down the landscape of the self. . . . You find false trails, roads closed for repairs, impregnable fortresses, scouts, armies of memory, and impossible cartography.'

Wilson does most of his pathfinding below the living room, in a low-ceilinged basement, lit by neon bars, where he goes to sneak cigarettes, listen to records, and wait for his characters to arrive. He writes standing up, at a high, cluttered pine accounting desk, where he can prop his legal pad and transfer his jottings to a laptop computer. Pinned on a bulletin board, just beside where he stands to write, are two quotations, as bold as street signs: 'TAKE IT TO THE MOON' (Frank Gehry) and 'DON'T BE AFRAID. JUST PLAY THE MUSIC' (Charlie Parker). When Wilson looks up from his desk, at the dingy wall with its labyrinth of water pipes, he sees honorary degrees from the University of Pittsburgh, his home town, and from Yale, where his career as a playwright began in 1982 – just two of twenty-three he has accumulated so far, which is not bad for a fifty-five-year-old writer who quit school when he was fifteen.

For years, about two steps behind Wilson's writing table, an Everlast punching bag was suspended from the ceiling. When Wilson was in full flow and the dialogue was popping, he'd stop, pivot, throw a barrage of punches at the bag, then turn back to the work. Recently, however, during a particularly vigorous rewrite of his new play, *King Hedley II*, which opens on Broadway this month, Wilson knocked the bag and its ceiling hook down, and it now rests mournfully in the corner. Wilson has a retired boxer's heft – thick neck, square shoulders, wide chest – and a stomach whose amplitude is emphasized by suspenders that bracket his belly like parentheses. Wilson is the product of a mixed marriage, but, he says, 'the culture I learned in my mother's household was black.' He has a handsome face that is dominated by a wide forehead and a concentrated gaze. He exudes a very specific sense of gravity. He gives away nothing at first, or even second, glance. But when his guard is down, and especially when he's telling a story, you feel what his wife calls 'the sizzle.'

Wilson, who was originally named Frederick August Kittel, after his German father, says that his model for manhood – 'the first male image that I carry' – is not his father but an old family friend, 'the brilliant Hall of Fame prizefighter' Charley Burley. Archie Moore called Burley the best fighter he'd ever faced, and Sugar Ray Robinson refused to box him, but after his glory days as a pugilist were over Burley became a garbageman in Pittsburgh and lived across the street from the impressionable young Wilson. In Burley's Friday-night regalia – hundred-dollar Stetson, cashmere coat, yam-colored Florsheim shoes – Wilson saw something iconic. Burley was one of those black men, Wilson writes, who 'elevated their presence into an art. They were bad. If only in an abstract of style.'

Burley was known as 'the uncrowned champion'; Wilson is known as 'the heavyweight champion' – a nickname given to him by the director Marion McClinton, who is staging *King Hedley II*. McClinton explains, 'It's August's language – the rhythm of hurt, the rhythm of pain, the rhythm of ecstasy, the rhythm of family – which sets him apart and is why we call him the heavyweight champion.' Between 1959, when Lorraine Hansberry had a hit with *A Raisin in the Sun*, and 1984, when Wilson made his sensational breakthrough with *Ma Rainey's Black Bottom*, a play about black musicians' struggle with their white bosses in the twenties, the number of African American plays to succeed on Broadway was zero. (There were, of course, many other black playwrights during this time – Amiri Baraka, Ron Milner, Phillip Hayes Dean, Richard Wesley, and Ed Bullins among them – who won critical praise and a coterie following.) *Ma Rainey* ran for ten months. Almost immediately, Hollywood came calling, mostly with offers for bio-pics of Louis Armstrong, Muhammad Ali, and the like; Wilson wasn't tempted. He asked the Hollywood nabobs why so many black playwrights had written only one play. 'I go, "Where is Lonne Elder? Where is Joseph Walker?" They go, "They're in Hollywood." And I go, "Oh, I see,"' he says. 'I wanted to have a career in the theatre.'

Wilson's success also triggered what McClinton calls 'one of the more major American theatrical revolutions.' His audience appeal almost single-handedly broke down the wall for other black artists, many of whom would not otherwise be working in the mainstream. His plays were showcases for an array of first-rate performers, such as Charles S. Dutton, Samuel L. Jackson, Courtney Vance, Angela Bassett, Ruben Santiago-Hudson, and Laurence Fishburne. And the opportunities for African American playwrights also increased. 'What's happened since 1984 has been incredible,' McClinton says. 'A lot of black writers had doors opened to them basically because August knocked them open. So then you start seeing Kia Corthron, Suzan-Lori Parks, Keith Glover, Robert Alexander, Lynn Nottage, Sam Kelley, Carlisle Brown, Charles Smith, Michael Henry Brown – I could keep going. American theatre now looks toward African-Americans as viable members.'

Wilson followed *Ma Rainey* with six critically acclaimed plays in a row – *Fences* (Pulitzer Prize, Tony Award), *Joe Turner's Come and Gone*, *The Piano Lesson* (Pulitzer Prize), *Two Trains Running*, *Seven Guitars*, and *Jitney*. He actually had drafts of *Fences* and *Joe Turner's Come and Gone* in his trunk before *Ma Rainey* made it to Broadway, and sometime after the success of that play, he has said, it dawned on him that each play he'd written so far was 'trying to focus on what I felt were the most important issues confronting black Americans for that decade.' Wilson gave himself a mission: to continue to chronicle, decade by decade, the 'dazed and dazzling' rapport of African Americans with the twentieth century. *King Hedley II* is set in the 1980s, which leaves only the first and last decades of the century to be written. The plays form a kind of fever chart of the trauma of slavery. Their historical trajectory takes African Americans through their transition from property to personhood (*Joe Turner's Come and Gone*); their struggle for power in urban life (*Ma Rainey*); their dilemma over whether to embrace or deny their slave past (*The Piano Lesson*); the broken promise of first-class citizenship after the Second World War (*Seven Guitars*); their fraught adaptation to bourgeois values (*Fences*); stagnancy in the midst of Black Power militancy (*Two Trains Running*); and their historical and financial disenfranchisement during the economic boom (*Jitney* and *King Hedley II*).

'The average struggling non-morbid Negro is the best-kept secret in America,' Zora Neale Hurston wrote in 1950. Wilson has put that man – his songs, his idiom, his superstitions, his folly, and his courage – on the stage. His plays are not talking textbooks; they paint the big picture indirectly, from the little incidents of daily life. 'People can be slave-ships in shoes,' Hurston said. Wilson's characters are shackled together by something greater than poverty; their bondage is to the caprices of history. 'We's the leftovers,' Toledo, the piano player and only literate member of Ma Rainey's band, tells the other musicians. 'The white man knows you just a leftover. 'Cause he the one who done the eating and he know what he done ate. But we don't know that we been took and made history out of.'

Wilson's work is a conscious answer to James Baldwin's call for 'a profound articulation of the Black Tradition.' He says he wanted to demonstrate that black American culture 'was capable of sustaining you, so that when you left your father's or your mother's house you didn't go into the world naked. You were fully clothed in manners and a way of life.' In the past, playwrights such as Dubose Heyward, Paul Green, and Eugene O'Neill made blacks and black culture the subject of drama; Wilson has made them the object. 'When you go to the dictionary and you look up "black," it gives you these definitions that say, "Affected by an undesirable condition,"' Wilson says. 'You start thinking something's wrong with black. When white people say, "I don't see color," what they're saying is "You're affected by this undesirable condition, but I'll pretend I don't see that." And I go, "No, see my color. Look at me. I'm not ashamed of who I am and what I am."'

Wilson's characters often scrabble desperately, sometimes foolishly, for an opportunity that rarely comes. But when opportunity knocked for Wilson he seized it with a vengeance. He has tried to live his writing life by the Buddhist motto "You're entitled to the work but not the reward"; nevertheless, he has become a very rich man – in 1990, he was the most produced American playwright – and he is only getting richer. After *Seven Guitars*, he and his co-producer, Ben Mordecai, formed a joint venture called Sageworks, which allows Wilson to exercise unusual control over the destiny of his plays – and also to take both a writer's and a producer's share of their profits. A Wilson play has a gestation period like no other in the history of American theatre, and no other major playwright – not Arthur Miller, Tennessee Williams, Eugene O'Neill, or David Mamet – has negotiated the latitude to work so freely. Before a play arrives on Broadway, Wilson refines his story through a series of separate productions. In his rehearsal mufti – black turtleneck and cloth cap – he sits beside the director for almost every hour of every production, and, since *Seven Guitars*, he's taken to 'writing in the heat of the moment.' By the time *King Hedley II* reaches New York, the play, which shows the fragmented life of a Pittsburgh ghetto during the Reagan years, will have been seen, digested, reconceived, and rewritten after productions in Seattle, Boston, Pittsburgh, Chicago, Los Angeles, and Washington. This long reworking, like a brass rubbing, brings the play's parameters and its filigree of detail into bold relief until the drama emerges, as Wilson puts it, 'fat with substance.'

'When I was writing *Joe Turner*,' Wilson says, 'I realized that someone was gonna stand up onstage and say the words, whatever the hell they were.

That's when I realized I had a responsibility to the words. I couldn't have the character say any old thing. There couldn't be any mistakes'. To achieve this sort of focus requires the kind of appetite for victory that is epitomized, for Wilson, by a breed of championship racehorses, which in order to win 'bite their own necks to get more oxygen'. He began his own extraordinary endeavor late, at about forty, and his time is valuable. He does not spend it on the telephone, or watching television, or going to movies (between 1980 and 1991, he saw only two, both directed by Martin Scorsese – *Raging Bull* and *Cape Fear*). His work requires a lot of 'doing nothing' to generate 'brain space.' So Wilson, whom Azula calls 'the slippery guy,' is usually to be found puttering in the crepuscular gloom of his basement, where he communes with himself and, if he's lucky, taps into what he calls 'the blood's memory,' that 'deepest part of yourself where the ancestors are talking.' To do so requires a kind of ritual preparation. 'Before I write something, I wash my hands,' he says. 'I always want to say I approached it with clean hands – you know, a symbolic cleansing.'

Wilson's plays, filled as they often are with visions and visionaries, have a kind of hoodoo of their own, which can seem strange to white viewers, who are often critical of his use of the supernatural. He is a collagist, making Afro-Christian parables, and his plays are best when the real and the spiritual are wedded (*Joe Turner, Seven Guitars, The Piano Lesson*), in order, as he says, 'to come up with a third thing, which is neither realism nor allegory.' Then, his intensity and his natural eloquence – what Henry Louis Gates, Jr., calls 'an unruly luxuriance of language, an ability to ease between trash talk and near-choral transport' – most effectively highlight another comparatively unsung quality of his writing: the ability to unfetter the heart. Under his focussed gaze, characters take on uncanny, sometimes awesome, life, and, unlike most contemporary male playwrights, he can write memorable roles for women as well as men. Wilson's work is not much influenced by the canon of modern Western plays, almost none of which he has read or seen. 'I consider it a blessing that when I started writing plays in earnest, in 1979, I had not read Chekhov. I hadn't read Ibsen. I hadn't read Tennessee Williams, Arthur Miller, or O'Neill,' he says. By then, he had been writing poetry for fifteen years and had read all the major American poets. 'It took me eight years to find my own voice as a poet. I didn't want to take eight years to find my voice as a playwright. To this day, as incredible as it seems, with the exception of his own productions and a few of his friends', Wilson has seen only about a dozen plays.

In the age of the sound bite, Wilson is that most endangered of rare birds – a storyteller. A Wilson tale takes about as long as a baseball game, which is to say a good deal longer than the average commercial play. Although audiences will happily watch sports contests into double overtime, the play of ideas and characters is another matter. In this arena, they are accustomed to what Shakespeare called the 'two hours' traffic,' and Wilson has taken a lot of flak for his capaciousness. According to *The Oxford Companion to American Theatre*, his plays 'lack a sense of tone and a legitimate, sustained dramatic thrust.' This criticism is, to my mind, unjust, but it reflects a distinctive cultural and artistic difference. Virtually all the seminal white postwar plays – *The Glass Menagerie*, *Long Day's Journey Into Night*, *Death of a Salesman* – revolve around the drama of American individualism; they mark a retreat from exterior into interior life. Wilson, however, dramatizes community. 'Community is the most valuable thing that you have in African American culture,' he explains. 'The individual good is always subverted to the good of the community.' Wilson's plays are distinctive – and longer – because society, not just a psyche, is being mediated. They demonstrate the individual's interaction with the community, not his separation from it.

In Wilson's plays, the white world is a major character that remains almost entirely offstage; nonetheless, its presence is palpable – its rules, its standards, its ownership are always pressing in on the black world and changing the flow of things. 'I look around and say, "Where the barbed wire?"' Hedley says, observing that as a slave he would have been worth twelve hundred dollars, and now he's worth three-fifty an hour. 'They got everything else. They got me blocked in every other way. "Where the barbed wire?"' To which his sidekick replies, 'If you had barbed wire you could cut through. You can't cut through having no job.' 'Blacks know the spiritual truth of white America,' Wilson says. 'We are living examples of America's hypocrisy. We know white America better than white America knows us.' Wilson's plays go some distance toward making up this deficiency. For white members of the audience, the experience of watching a Wilson work is often educational and humanizing. It's the eternal things in Wilson's dramas – the arguments between fathers and sons, the longing for redemption, the dreams of winning, and the fear of losing – that reach across the footlights and link the black world to the white one, from which it is so profoundly separated and by which it is so profoundly defined. To the black world, Wilson's plays are witness; to the white world, they are news. This creates a fascinating racial conundrum, one first raised by Baldwin: 'If I am not what I've been told I am, then it means that you're not what you thought you were either!'

August Wilson was born in 1945 in Pittsburgh's Hill District. Although it was just four minutes by car from downtown, the Hill – known then as Little Harlem – was a lively, flourishing, self-contained universe, with its own baseball teams, night clubs, businesses, and newspaper, and its own people, some of them legends who had left its one square mile to sing their distinctive songs to the world: Lena Horne, Erroll Garner, Ahmad Jamal, Earl (Fatha) Hines, Billy Eckstine, George Benson. When Wilson was a child, the Hill had a population of fifty-five thousand; since then, as a consequence of the 1968 riots, urban renewal, and competition from white neighborhoods, to which African-Americans now have putative access, the Hill's boundaries and its buoyancy have shrunk. Today, its rows of small, decrepit houses sit on the sloping land like a set of bad teeth – irregular, decaying, with large gaps between them. Beside one such desolate, littered vacant lot, at the rear of 1727 Bedford Avenue, Wilson grew up. You have to bushwhack your way through a tangle of branches that covers the ten steep steps to the boarded front door of the forty-dollar-a-month apartment where Wilson, the fourth of six children, lived with his mother, Daisy Wilson, and his siblings, Freda, Linda Jean, Donna, Richard, and Edwin.

Daisy ran a structured household that was centered on family activities. 'Monday at seven, the Rosary came on the radio, so we said the Rosary,' Wilson recalls. 'Art Linkletter's "People Are Funny" was Tuesday. We played board games. Then there was the Top Forty. Everyone got to pick a song. If your song got to No. 1, you got a nickel.' The back yard, where Daisy planted flowers and played dodgeball and baseball with her children and, on summer evenings, sat around a card table for games of Tonk, is blocked off now and difficult to see, but in the set for *Seven Guitars* Wilson preserved the ramshackle solace of the place so exactly that when his sister Linda Jean first saw the show she burst into tears. At the core of Wilson's personality is a kind of truculent resolve, which comes, he says, from his mother's example. (Daisy, who planned her own funeral, down to the gown she'd wear, died of lung cancer in 1983; for the past eighteen years, Wilson has returned to Pittsburgh on her birthday to gather with his family and visit her grave.) She was a tall, strong, handsome homebody, who had left school after the seventh grade and lived by the gospel of clear-eyed common sense and competitiveness. For Wilson, the best example of Daisy's brand of bumptious integrity is an incident that took place around 1955. She was listening to a quiz program that was offering a new washing machine to anyone who could answer a question correctly. Daisy knew the answer, and knew that, with six children, a washing machine would be a blessing. But when she won the contest and the promoters found out that she was black, they offered her instead a certificate to the Salvation Army to get a used washing machine. 'Mother said she wanted the new machine or she didn't want any,' Wilson says. 'I remember Julie Burley' – Charley Burley's wife – 'saying to her, "Oh, Daisy, you got all them kids, what difference does it make? Take the washing machine." And my mother said, "Something is not always better than nothing."'

Wilson's sense of his own uniqueness came, at least in part, from his mother's adoring gaze, what Baldwin called 'the crucial, the definitive, the all-but-everlasting judgment.' Wilson was Daisy's much longed-for first son. 'My mother said she would have had eleven girls – she didn't care – she would have kept trying till she had a son,' says Wilson's sister Donna, who remembers being told of her father's disappointment at her own birth. '"Another split-ass," he said.' Freda says, 'Mother seemed to have a need for a male in the house to show leadership. She clearly felt that August was the best and smartest of us, so he should be given the duty of going downtown at the age of ten or eleven to pay the bills. It wasn't just about paying the bills. Her underlying reason was to prepare him for the world.' 'She made me believe that I could do anything,' Wilson says. He adds, 'I wanted to be the best at whatever I did. I was the best dishwasher in Pittsburgh. I really was. I got a raise the first day I was there. When I sit down and write, I want to write the best play that's ever been written. Sometimes that's a fearsome place to stand, but that's when you call on your courage.'

Wilson had a high I.Q.; he also had a gift for language. In kindergarten, he was already entertaining the class with his stories. By the sixth grade, he was turning out love poems for the girls he fancied: 'I would I could mend my festering heart / Harpooned by Cupid's flaming dart / But too far the shaft did penetrate / Alas, it is too late.' At his Catholic grade school, Wilson's intellectual overreaching drove the nuns crazy. 'When they said no one could figure out the Holy Trinity, I was like, "Why not?" I instantly wanted to prove it could be done,' he says. As Wilson grew into adolescence, even his friends acknowledged a certain grandiosity in him; his nickname was Napoleon.

Wilson's hankering to be spectacular was fed not only by his mother's expectations but by his father's abdications. Fritz Kittel considered himself German, although when he had emigrated to America, with his three brothers, in 1915, he was an Austro-Hungarian citizen. The first time he met Daisy, at a neighborhood grocery store, she was shy. At the urging of her grandmother, the next time she saw him she was more flirtatious. They married, but by the time Wilson was born, Linda Jean says, Fritz was staying at the house only on weekends and living in a hotel during the week. Wilson remembers him as 'mostly not there,' adding, 'You stayed out of his way if he was there.' Fritz was, Wilson says, 'an extremely talented baker,' who worked for a while at New York's Waldorf-Astoria. He was also a wine drinker – 'Muscatel by the gallon' – and couldn't keep a job.

The only father-son experience Wilson remembers was being taken down-town by Fritz in a blizzard to get a pair of Gene Autry cowboy boots. 'He gave me a bunch of change, about seventy-five cents, and told me, "Jingle it." To let them know I had money.' Otherwise, his memories focus on his father's hectoring abuse. Wilson refers to ferocious arguments, which some-times ended with Fritz outside heaving bricks at their windows. 'We knew to hide,' Freda says. 'We ran together, we'd fall behind the bed together, then, obviously, someone would sneak up to the window and look down.' If Wilson closes his eyes to conjure up his father, he sees a tall man singing a German song to himself as he comes home from work with three-foot-high brown bags full of baked goods. 'When he got angry, the next thing you know, Dad was just throwing the bags on the floor and stomping and crushing all the doughnuts and things in the bag,' Linda Jean recalls. 'And we needed those morsels.' One Thanksgiving, in a tantrum, Fritz pulled the door off the oven and Daisy had to prop it back up with a stick so the turkey could finish roasting. Fritz's tranquil moments could be as tyrannical as his outbursts. 'He believed in reading the papers,' Freda says. 'We had to sit down. We were not allowed to talk. We were not allowed to play. It was complete silence.' Freda saw him as a displaced person, 'an off-the-boat-type person.' She says, 'I don't think he ever fit here in America. I don't think he ever accepted black people. Or the culture. I think for my whole family there's a deep sense of abandonment.' By 1957, when Wilson was twelve, Daisy had divorced Kittel and taken up with David Bedford, a black man whom she later married. 'I loved the man,' Wilson says of Bedford, an avid reader who was a community leader, and who, Wilson learned, after his death in 1969, had spent twenty-three years in prison.

Wilson inherited his father's volatile temperament. 'He was a kid with a temper,' Freda says. 'And a sorry loser, because, in his mind, if he played to win he should win because he should have figured out whatever strategy was needed to win. And not figuring out that strategy was just highly unac-ceptable to him.' In this regard, Wilson hasn't changed much over the years. 'My goodness, when he got emotional he was mad scary,' says the professor and playwright Rob Penny, who was one of Wilson's closest friends on the Hill. 'You'd think he was gonna snap out, attack you, or beat you up or something. He was very intense.' When he was about twenty, Wilson cuffed his sister Donna and broke her jaw. I asked Constanza Romero what she had found most surprising about Wilson after she married him, and she said, 'His temper – his temper scared me.' She referred to an explosion over a misplaced telephone number. 'He went crazy, absolutely bonkers,' she said. 'He starts speaking very strongly, cussing himself out. He really doesn't allow himself any mistakes, any leeway.'

'I just always felt that the society was lined up against you,' Wilson says. 'That in order to do anything in the world you were going to have to battle this thing that was out there. It wasn't gonna give you any quarter.' For Wilson, the battle began in earnest when he was a freshman at Central Catholic High School, where he was the only black student in his grade and was placed in the advanced class. 'There was a note on my desk every single day. It said, "Go home, nigger,"' Wilson says. The indignities – the shoving, the name-calling, the tripping – were constant; so was Wilson's brawling. The Christian Brothers frequently sent him home by taxi. 'They would have to walk me through a gantlet of, like, forty kids. I would always want to say to them, "But you're not saying anything to these forty guys. You're just escorting me through them as though they have a right to stand here."' Then, one day when Wilson was in his early teens, a student standing in front of him during the Pledge of Allegiance made mention of the 'nigger' behind him. 'I said, "O.K., buddy,"' and, at 'liberty and justice for all,' Wilson punched him. 'We go down to Brother Martin's, and he's ready to send me home. I said, "Hey, why don't we just do this permanently? I do not want to go to school here anymore."' Wilson went next to a vocational school, where the academic content was 'I swear, like fifth-grade work.' When his [auto-mechanic] shop teacher, angry that Wilson had knocked in a thumbtack with a T-square, punched Wilson so hard that he knocked him off his chair, Wilson lunged at the teacher and 'bounced him off the blackboard. "Give me a pink slip," he said. "I'm leaving this school."'

At fifteen, Wilson ended up at Gladstone High School, taking tenth-grade classes but still officially in the ninth grade. He sulked in class, sat in the back, and refused to participate. Then, in an effort to redeem himself in the eyes of a black teacher, who ran an after-school college club Wilson wanted to join, he decided to take one assignment seriously. It was an essay on a historical figure, and Wilson chose Napoleon. 'The fact that he was a self-made man, that he was a lieutenant in the army and became the emperor, I liked that,' Wilson says. He researched it; he wrote it; he rented a typewriter with money he'd earned mowing lawns and washing cars; he paid his sister Linda Jean twenty-five cents a page to type it; and then he handed it in.

'The next day, the teacher asked me to stay after class,' Wilson says. On the paper the teacher had written two marks – A-plus and E, a failing grade. 'I'm gonna give you one of these two grades,' he told Wilson. Suspecting that one of Wilson's older sisters had written the paper, he asked, 'Can you prove to me that you wrote this?' Wilson remembers saying, '"Hey, unless you call everybody in here and have all the people prove they wrote them, even the ones that went and copied out of the encyclopedia word for word, I don't feel I should have to prove anything."' The teacher circled the E and handed the paper back. 'I tore it up, threw it in the wastebasket, and walked out of school,' Wilson says.

Every morning for the rest of the school year, rather than tell his mother he'd dropped out, Wilson walked three blocks to the local library. Over the next four years, by his own estimation, he read three hundred books, spending as many as five hours a day in the library. He read everything – sociology, anthropology, theology, fiction. 'The world opened up,' he says. 'I could wander through the stacks. I didn't need anyone to teach me. All you had to do was have an interest and a willingness to extract the information from the book.' It was about this time that Wilson began to see himself as a kind of warrior, surviving unapologetically on his own terms. The first person with whom he had to do battle was Daisy, whose dashed dreams for her son made her a furious opponent. 'She told him he was no good, that he would amount to nothing,' Linda Jean says. 'It was relentless. It was an agony for him. He suffered many indignities. He was often denied food. She would take the food out of the refrigerator, put it in her bedroom, lock the door, and then go out. He was made to live in the basement for a while. She said he was dirty. She didn't want him in the house upstairs.'

By the time Wilson was banished to the basement, he had decided to become a writer. 'I was like, "O.K., I'm gonna sit here, I'm gonna write some stories. I'll show you,"' Wilson says. 'I was gonna demonstrate my worth to her. I negotiated cooking privileges. I'd get fifteen cents and go buy me three pounds of potatoes. I was gonna demonstrate that I could feed and take care of myself.' He lasted a week. 'My mother was very disappointed,' Wilson says. 'She saw a lot of potential that I'd squandered, as far as she was concerned.' To get out of the house, Wilson joined the Army. He took the Officer Candidate School test and came in second in his battalion, just two points behind the leader. Then, as often happens in Wilson's plays and in his life, he came up against the rules: to be an officer, you had to be nineteen; he was seventeen. And, if he couldn't be an officer, he wasn't interested.

Wilson headed across the country to California, where he worked in a pharmacy, until his father's terminal illness brought him back to Pittsburgh. Wilson and Linda Jean visited their father, who told them stories about being in the Army and the battle of the Argonne Forest. 'Then he suddenly looked up and said, "Who are you?"' Wilson says. 'He basically chased us out of there, but for a couple of hours we had a great time.' On his deathbed, Wilson's father called for his son 'Fritz.' Afterward, Wilson wrote a muted memorial, 'Poem for the Old Man,' which begins by evoking his father in his prime ('Old Fritz, when young / could lay a harem') and ends with Wilson himself ('his boxing boy / Is hitting all the new places / Too soon to make a mark').

Wilson took refuge in the African-American community, and it, in turn, nurtured him and contained him and his rage at his father's abandonment. 'He's so faithful to the blackness. He's faithful like a father – that represents fidelity to him,' says James Earl Jones, who starred in *Fences*. Wilson found another father figure in Chawley Williams, a black drug dealer turned poet, who became his protector on the street. 'August wasn't really black. He was half-and-half,' Williams says. 'He was too dark to be white, and he was too white to be dark. He was in no man's land. I knew he was lost. I was lost. Kindred brothers know one another. We were trying to become men. We didn't even know what it meant.' In time, Wilson would write himself into the center of modern black American history. But when he hit the streets he had no money, no marketable skills, no proven talent. He was, he says, 'searching for something you can claim as yours.'

On April 1, 1964, Wilson walked into downtown Pittsburgh to McFerron's typewriter store and put twenty dollars on the counter for a heavy black Royal Standard in the window. He'd earned the money by writing a term paper – 'Two Violent Poets: Robert Frost and Carl Sandburg' – for Freda, who was then at Fordham University. He lugged the typewriter up the Hill to the basement apartment he'd rented in a boarding house, placed the machine on the kitchen table, put a piece of loose-leaf paper in it, and typed his name. Actually, he typed every possible combination of his name – Fred A. Kittel, Frederick A. Kittel, Frederick A. Wilson, A. Wilson, August Wilson – and settled finally on the last because it looked best on paper. He then laboriously typed a batch of poems. He'd heard that *Harper's* paid a dollar a line, so he sent the poems there. 'They came back three days later,' Wilson says. 'I said, "Oh, I see. This is serious. I'm gonna have to learn how to write a poem." I wasn't deterred by that. I was emboldened.' But because he 'didn't like the feeling of rejection,' Wilson didn't send out another poem for five years. (His first published work was 'Muhammad Ali,' which appeared in *Black World* in 1969.) 'It was sufficient for me to know that I wrote poetry and I was growing as an artist,' he says.

Most sightings of Wilson on the Hill were in restaurants – the White Tower, Eddie's Restaurant, the B & W, Moose's – bent over, scribbling on his tablet or on napkins. Decades later, Wilson would walk through the neighborhood and people would stop him and ask, '"You still drawin'?" I found out later people thought I was a bum,' Wilson says. 'The thing that sustained me was that my idea of myself was different from the idea that society, my mother, and even some of my friends had of me. I saw myself as a grand person.' He adds, 'I saw the pictures of Richard Wright, Langston Hughes – all of them always had a suit on. I thought, Yeah, that's me. I want to be like that.' At a local thrift shop, he bought white shirts for a dime, the broad ties he favored for a nickel, and sports coats for thirty-five cents. In the poetic sphere, he'd come under the influence of Dylan Thomas, and he went through the Black Power movement with a coat and tie and a pipe, intoning poetry in an English accent. 'People thought he was crazy in the neighborhood,' Chawley Williams says. He adds, 'When I met August, I was in the drug world. Here come August. He's sensitive, he's articulate, he has talent, he's trying to write. And the hustlers of the streets is at him. They could get him to do things, 'cause he wanted to belong. He would allow them to come to wherever he stayed at to eat, to get high and shoot their dope, to lie up with different women. They were trying to get him to get high. I put a halt to that.'

Fish love water, it is said, and are cooked in it. But although Wilson swam in this predatory world he never felt threatened. If you ask him now to imagine the street back then, a smile crosses his face; he holds out his big right hand and trembles it. 'A shimmy,' he says. 'The avenue shimmered. Hundreds of people on the sidewalks. Life going on.' The vibrancy ravished him. Once, riding up Centre Avenue in a friend's convertible, Wilson heard gunshots. 'I hopped out of the car and ran down to where the gunshots were,' he says. 'There's this woman chasing the man around the car, and – boom! – she shot him. He was bleeding, and he asked this guy, "Man, drive me to the hospital." The guy said, "You ain't gon' get all that blood in my car!"' Wilson adds, 'I remember one time I didn't go to bed for damn near three days because every time I'd go to bed I felt like I was missing something.'

Although Little Richard, Frankie Lymon and the Teenagers, Chuck Berry, and other rock and rollers had spilled over the back-yard fences of Wilson's childhood, it wasn't until this time that he first heard the blues. For a nickel at a St Vincent de Paul charity shop, he bought a bootleg 78-r.p.m. record on whose tattered yellow label he could make out the words 'Bessie Smith: "Nobody in Town Can Bake a Sweet Jelly Roll Like Mine."' Smith's impudent, unabashed sound stunned him. 'The universe stuttered and everything fell to a new place,' he wrote later. Like James Baldwin, who wrote that hearing Bessie Smith for the first time 'helped to reconcile me to being a "nigger,"' Wilson saw the moment as an epiphany: 'a birth, a baptism, and a redemption all rolled up into one.' Wilson played the new record twenty-two times straight. 'Then I started laughing, you know, 'cause it suddenly dawned on me that there was another record on the other side.' He adds, 'It made me look at the world differently. It gave the people in the rooming house where I lived, and also my mother, a history I didn't know they had. It was the beginning of my consciousness that I was the carrier of some very valuable antecedents.'

Wilson considers the blues 'the best literature we have.' As a way of preparing the emotional landscape for each play of his cycle, he submerges himself in the blues of the period. For *Hedley*, for instance, he's asking himself, 'How'd we get from Percy Sledge's "Warm and Tender Love" to "You My Bitch"?' Even the structure of his sentences – the frequent reiteration of themes and words – owes much to the music's repetitions, its raucous pitch and improvised irony. From *Two Trains Running*: A nigger with a gun is bad news. You can't even use the word "nigger" and "gun" in the same sentence. You say the word "gun" in the same sentence with the word "nigger" and you in trouble. The white man panic. Unless you say, "The policeman shot the nigger with his gun."'

He particularly likes it when singers speak their names in song. 'There's something wonderful about that,' he says. 'They're making a stand. They're saying, "This is me. This is what I have to say."' In the context of what Zora Neale Hurston called 'the muteness of slavery,' the notion of singing solo and making a personal statement is, for African Americans, a comparatively new and extraordinarily potent thing, which Wilson dramatizes in his plays. In his theatrical vocabulary, 'finding a song' is both the expression of spirit and the accomplishment of identity. Some of his characters have a song that they can't broadcast; others have given up singing; some have been brutalized into near-muteness; and others have turned the absence of a destiny into tall talk – the rhetoric of deferred dreams. But Wilson's most brilliant demonstration of 'carrying other people's songs and not having one of my own' – as one character puts it – is in *Joe Turner's Come and Gone*, where a conjure man called Bynum, who has a song, discourses with Loomis, who has been separated from his. Bynum says:

> Now, I can look at you, Mr. Loomis, and see you a man who done forgot his song. Forgot how to sing it. A fellow forget that and he forget who he is. Forget how he's supposed to mark down life . . . See, Mr. Loomis, when a man forgets his song he goes off in search of it . . . till he find out he's got it with him all the time.

Music, in Wilson's plays, is more than slick Broadway entertainment. A juba dance banged out on a table, a work song beaten out with chairs and glasses, a gutbucket blues demonstrate the African American genius for making something out of nothing. They take an empty world, as Ma Rainey says, and 'fill it up with something.'

Blues people, Ralph Ellison once wrote, are 'those who accepted and lived close to their folk experience.' On the Hill, the blues cemented in Wilson's mind the notion that he was somehow 'the conduit of ancestors.' West's

Funeral Home – which figures in *Two Trains Running* – was just around the corner from Eddie's Restaurant, and Wilson, for some deep personal reason and not for art's sake, felt compelled routinely to pay his respects to whoever had died. 'I didn't have to know them. I felt that this is a life that has gone before me,' he explains. From Claude McKay's 'Home to Harlem,' he learned of a hangout in his own neighborhood called Pat's Place – a cigar store with a pool hall in the back – where a lot of the community elders congregated. Pat's Place became Wilson's Oxford, and its garrulous denizens – 'walking history books,' Wilson calls them – his tutors. They called him Youngblood. 'I was just like, "Hey, man, how did you get to be so old, 'cause it's hard out here." I really wanted to know how they survived. How do you get to be seventy years old in America?' Wilson recalls meeting one old man at Pat's Place who said to him, '"I been watchin' you. You carryin' around a ten-gallon bucket. You carry that ten-gallon bucket through life, and you gon' always be disappointed. Get you a little cup. And, that way, if somebody put a little bit in it, why, you got sumpin."' Wilson adds, 'I managed to cut it down to a gallon bucket, but I never did get that little cup.'

'What I discovered is that writing was the only thing society would allow me to do,' he said in 1991. 'I couldn't have a job or be a lawyer because I didn't do all the things necessary. What I was allowed to do was write. If they saw me over in the corner scribbling on a piece of paper they would say, "That is just a nigger over in the corner scribbling on a piece of paper." Nobody said, "Hey, you can't do that." So I felt free.' On the street, as a defensive maneuver, Wilson says he 'learned to keep my mouth shut,' but, according to Chawley Williams, 'when August stood onstage and read his poetry, there was a difference in him that didn't exist at no other time. He stood tall and proud. He stood with that definiteness.' He was supported in this pursuit by his friends in the neighborhood – Williams, Rob Penny, and Nicholas Flournoy, who were all aspiring poets. The group founded the Centre Avenue Poets Theatre Workshop, out of which came the journal *Connection* (Wilson was its poetry editor), then the Halfway Art Gallery, and, from 1968 to 1972, the Black Horizons Theatre, which Wilson co-founded with Penny, who served as house playwright.

During this time, Wilson had a daughter, Sakina Ansari (to whom *Joe Turner's Come and Gone* is dedicated), in a marriage to Brenda Burton, which ended in 1973. 'She moved out with the baby,' Linda Jean says. 'August came home to an empty house. The shock and pain were unbearable to him. In a nutshell, she thought his writing was a waste of time, he wouldn't amount to anything.' Although Wilson himself always felt successful, he says, he still hadn't achieved what he calls, quoting the poet Robert Duncan, 'surety – the line burned in the hand.' He says, 'I had been trying to get to that point. I didn't approach it lightly. I worked concertedly toward growth.' Finally, in 1973, in a poem called 'Morning Statement,' Wilson found his poetic voice:

> It is the middle of winter
> November 21 to be exact
> I got up, buckled my shoes,
> I caught a bus and went riding into town.
> I just thought I'd tell you.

'The poem didn't pretend to be anything else,' Wilson says. 'It wasn't struggling to say eternal things. It was just claiming the ground as its own thing. For me, it was so liberating.' But his liberation as a playwright didn't begin until March 5, 1978, when he moved away from the Hill, to St Paul, Minnesota, where he married Judy Oliver, a white social worker. In doing so, he went from a neighborhood that had fifty-five thousand blacks to a state that had the same number. 'There weren't many black folks around,' he says. 'In that silence, I could hear the language for the first time.' Until then, Wilson says, he hadn't 'valued or respected the way that black folks talked. I'd always thought that in order to create art out of it you had to change that.' Now he missed the street talk and wanted to preserve it. 'I got lonely and missed those guys and sort of created them,' he says. 'I could hear the music'

By the time Wilson reached St. Paul, he'd directed a handful of amateur productions, and his friend the director Claude Purdy had staged a musical satire based on a series of Wilson's poems. But despite a paying gig at the Science Museum of Minnesota, where Wilson wrote children's plays on science-related subjects, he was, by anyone's standard, a theatrical tyro. As early as 1976, he'd begun work on a piece about Ma Rainey, but then, he says, 'it never occurred to me to make the musicians characters in the play. I couldn't have written the characters.' His dialogue had a kind of florid artiness. In one of his early dramatic experiments, which involved a conversation between an old man and a woman on a park bench, the woman said, 'Terror hangs over the night like a hawk.' Wilson had at least one play, *The Coldest Day of the Year*, produced in this stilted style. 'It wasn't black American language,' he says. It wasn't theatre, either.

In the fall of 1977, Wilson came across the work of the painter Romare Bearden. As he thumbed through Bearden's series of collages 'The Prevalence of Ritual,' he discovered his 'artistic mentor.' Bearden's paintings made simple what Wilson's writing had so far only groped to formulate: 'Black life presented on its own terms, on a grand and epic scale, with all its richness and fullness, in a language that was vibrant and which, made attendant to everyday life, ennobled it, affirmed its value, and exalted its presence.' He adds, 'My response was visceral. I was looking at myself in ways I hadn't thought of before and have never ceased to think of since.' In later years, Wilson would stand outside Bearden's house on Canal Street, in New York, 'in silent homage, daring myself to knock.' He didn't knock, but, he has written, if Bearden 'had answered . . . and if I were wearing a hat, I would have taken it off in tribute.' (In the end, Wilson's true homage was his plays, two of which – 'Mill Hand's Lunch Bucket,' which became *Joe Turner*, and *The Piano Lesson* – took their titles from Bearden paintings.)

Years before, Wilson, who then 'couldn't write dialogue,' had asked Rob Penny, 'How do you make characters talk?' Penny answered, 'You don't. You listen to them.' Now, in 1979, when Wilson sat down to write *Jitney*, a play set at the taxi stand that had been one of Wilson's hangouts on the Hill, the penny, as it were, dropped. For the first time, he was able to listen to his characters and let them speak. 'I found that exhilarating,' he says. 'It felt like this was what I'd been looking for, something that was mine, that would enable me to say anything.' For Wilson, the revelation was that 'language describes the idea of the one who speaks; so if I'm speaking the oppressor's language I'm in essence speaking his ideas, too. This is why I think blacks speak their own language, because they have to find another way.' While writing *Jitney*, he proved to himself that he didn't have to reconstitute black life; he just had to capture it.

Wilson sat at Arthur Treacher's Fish & Chips, a restaurant up the street from his apartment in St. Paul, for ten days in a row until the play was finished. At Penny's suggestion, he submitted it to the O'Neill Playwrights Conference, a sprawling estate in Waterford, Connecticut, where each summer about a dozen playwrights are provided with a dramaturg, a director, and a cast to let them explore their flawed but promising plays. The O'Neill rejected *Jitney*; its incredulous author, assuming that no one had read it, submitted the play again. The O'Neill rejected it again. Wilson took serious stock of his newfound calling; his inner dialogue, he says, was '"Maybe it's not as good as you think. You have to write a better play." "I've already written the best play I can write." "Why don't you write above your talent?" "Oh, man, how can you do that?" "Well, you can write beneath it, can't you?" "Oh, yeah."' Wilson turned back to the play on Ma Rainey and began to imagine it differently. 'I opened up the door to the band room,' he says. 'Slow Drag and Cutler was talking about how Slow Drag got his name. Then this guy walked in – he had glasses, carrying the books – he became Toledo. I had discovered them and got them talking.'

On August 1, 1982, the producer Ben Mordecai, who had recently become the managing director of the Yale Repertory Theatre, drove up to Waterford to see his boss, Lloyd Richards. Richards, who is of Jamaican descent, was the head of the Yale Drama School and, for more than thirty years, worked during the summer as the artistic director of the O'Neill. He is a man of few words, most of them carefully chosen. 'Is there anyone here I should meet?' Mordecai asked Richards. 'Meet him,' Richards said, nodding toward the porch of the main building, where Wilson was sitting. When *Ma Rainey's Black Bottom* was accepted at the O'Neill, Wilson stumbled onto the right person at the right place at the right time. Other African Americans, such as Ed Bullins, whose 'Twentieth-Century Cycle' did for South Philadelphia in the 1960s and 1970s what Wilson would do for Pittsburgh, were not as lucky. With access to theatres and to grant-giving agencies, Richards, who had directed *A Raisin in the Sun* on Broadway, was well positioned to usher Wilson's talent directly into the mainstream. Richards became, Wilson wrote, 'my guide, my mentor, and my provocateur,' and all of Wilson's subsequent plays until *Seven Guitars* would follow the same golden path – from the O'Neill to Yale to Broadway.

When *Ma Rainey* went to Yale, in 1984, Richards took over. 'We go into the room with the actors, we read the play,' Wilson says, describing the first day of rehearsal. 'An actor had a question about a character. I started to speak, and Lloyd answered the question. There was another question, and Lloyd answered it again. I remember there was a moment when I thought, The old fox knows what's going on. This is gonna be O.K.' 'We had a pattern of work,' Richards says of their partnership, which in time would become as influential as that of Tennessee Williams and Elia Kazan. 'I would work on it, check it with him, so I included him, but I was the director.' He adds, 'August was very receptive in the early days. He had a lot to learn and knew it. He was a big sponge, absorbing everything.' Richards sent him to the sound booth, to the paint shop, to the lighting designer. 'As he learned structure – playwriting, really – he was also learning everything else,' Richards says.

Richards is not a gregarious man, and his natural reticence complements his collaborative, indirect way of working: 'I try to provoke the artist to find the answer I want him to find.' When Wilson sent Richards a version of *The Piano Lesson*, he says, 'Lloyd calls me up and says, "I think you have one too many scenes there." "O.K., Lloyd, I'll look at that." End of conversation. I go to the play. I see this scene that looks like it's expendable. I pull it out. Talking to Lloyd about something else a couple of days later, I say, "Oh, Lloyd, by the way, I took the scene out." Lloyd says, "Good." To this day, I don't know if we were talking about the same scene.' Richards says, 'He cut the scene that needed to be cut.' He adds, 'August writes wonderful scenes. He must think they're wonderful, 'cause they go on and on and on. To the point where they advance the play much further than it needs to be advanced at that moment.' Wilson's *Fences*, which was the second-most-produced play on American professional stages in 1989, was transformed by Richards, over several productions, from a four-and-a-half-hour first appearance at the O'Neill to its commercial length of less than three hours not just by cutting but by reorganizing. This began Wilson's practice of refining his plays in the regionals. *The Piano Lesson* – which involves a contest for ownership of a prized family piano between a sister, who wants to keep it as a symbol of her African American heritage, and her brother, who wants to sell it to buy land on the plantation where their ancestors were slaves – had still not found a satisfactory ending after a year of touring. It finally got one when Richards suggested to Wilson that the battle between the brother and sister was missing a third party: the spirit of the white family who also had claims on the piano. 'August wrote a wonderful speech describing how the piano came into the family and how they had stolen it from this white family,' Richards says. 'That brought the piece together.'

When *The Piano Lesson* was made into a TV movie, in 1995, Wilson served as a producer, a shift in power that also augured a change in his relationship with Richards. At one meeting, a production designer, Patricia Van Ryker, who hadn't read the original play – which states that the piano's legs are 'carved in the manner of African sculpture,' to represent the characters' African heritage – laid out her plans to decorate the piano with images of plantation life that fit within the time frame of the play. Wilson exploded. 'He was screaming,' Van Ryker recalls. '"How dare you do this! You're insulting my relatives! My race!" It was like I'd thrown kerosene on him.' Richards recalls the moment as 'terrible,' and says, 'I don't function dictatorially. I don't give directives. I saw August in a position of power. I knew I couldn't work for him.'

As Wilson grew in confidence, craft, and stature, it became increasingly difficult for him to play the protégé in the partnership. 'The two of them artistically began drifting apart, which was, I think, a natural thing,' Mordecai says. 'The collaboration wasn't happening at the level it had in earlier years.' As Wilson saw it, 'Lloyd slowed down,' but it's just as true to say that Wilson grew up. When a rewritten version of *Jitney* was up for production at the Pittsburgh Public Theatre, in 1996, Wilson chose as his director Marion McClinton, who had done inventive second productions of many of his earlier plays. Wilson may have lost a kind of father in the split with Richards, but in McClinton he gained a brother. Where Richards's productions were stately, McClinton's are fluid; where Richards's process was formal, McClinton's is relaxed. 'The first conversation we had, August said to me, "My style is I don't talk to the actors,"' McClinton recalls. 'I said, "I don't care if you talk to the actors. Whatever gets the information to them the clearest and cleanest, that's what I'm for."'

'August is a soldier,' McClinton says, and he's referring to more than Wilson's theatrical battles. Wilson, who cites the Black Power movement as 'the kiln in which I was fired,' describes himself as a 'race man.' And his very specific anthropological understanding of American history has led him to some hard, politically incorrect opinions. For instance, he believes that it was a mistake for African Americans to leave the South. 'The blood and bones of two hundred and fifty years of our ancestors are buried in the South, and we came North,' he says. 'I think if we'd stayed South and continued to empower ourselves, in terms of acquiring land – we already had acres of farmland that we owned – we'd have had ten black senators in the United States. We'd be represented. We'd be a more culturally secure and culturally self-sufficient people.'

Wilson's insistence on preserving and sustaining an African-American identity led to a well-publicized argument with Robert Brustein, the artistic director of Boston's American Repertory Theatre, that culminated in a formal debate at New York's Town Hall, in 1997. Among many contrarian points, Wilson argued against the current fashion for 'color-blind casting' – a bias shared by McClinton, who refers to the practice as 'Cyclops casting.' 'It's color-blind in one eye,' he says. 'You're quite aware of the fact that we're black – that's why we're not asked to present that in our performance, where the white actors can bring whatever history and interior self-knowledge they have into a rehearsal process and into the making of character.' In Wilson's view, to mount an all-black production of, say, *Death of a Salesman* is to deny us 'the need to make our own investigations from the cultural ground on which we stand as black Americans.' In his exchange with Brustein, Wilson pointed out the transparent inequity of having sixty-six regional theatres and only one that can be considered black. (He subsequently conceived and supported the African Grove Institute for the Arts, an organization that promotes African-American theatre.) In America, 'the subscription audience holds the seats of our theatres hostage to the mediocrity of its tastes, and serves to impede the further development of an audience for the work that we do,' he said. 'Intentional or not, it serves to keep blacks out of the theatre, where they suffer no illusion of welcome anyway.' This call for an African American theatre was immediately seized upon by the press as separatist, despite the fact that Wilson himself disputed the label. 'We are not separatists, as Mr. Brustein asserts,' he said. 'We are Americans trying to fulfill our talents. We are not the servants at the party. We are not apprentices in the kitchens . . . We are Africans. We are Americans.' The aftermath of the debate – something of a tempest in a teapot – still lingers (and is still misconstrued). 'He took that hit for a lot of other people,' McClinton says.

'That's what a champion does – a champion fights.' When Wilson gave me a book of his first three plays, he inscribed it, 'The struggle continues.'

My first sighting of McClinton and Wilson at work was last November, in the rehearsal room of Chicago's new Goodman Theatre, where *King Hedley II* was the inaugural production. They sat shoulder to shoulder at the rehearsal table. McClinton, a heavy man, wore a baggy white T-shirt and a black fedora; he chugged at an economy-sized Dr Pepper. Wilson, in his trademark cap, sat bent slightly forward and absolutely still. His eyes were trained on the figure of Hedley, a former killer trying to make a go of it on the Hill, as he knelt in front of a flower patch demarked in rehearsal by a few stones on the concrete floor. His mother, Ruby, stood nearby, watching him. 'You need some good dirt,' she told him. 'Them seeds ain't gonna grow in that dirt.' Hedley responded, 'This the only dirt I got. This is me right here.' The words – the opening of the play – linked Wilson's newest protagonist to all the other desperate heroes of his cycle, and to himself: men attempting, in one way or another, to claim their inheritance. Wilson leaned across to whisper something to McClinton, who, keeping his eyes on the actors, nodded, took another hit of soda, and stopped the rehearsal to adjust the blocking. 'King don't listen well,' the actor playing Hedley said. 'He's a king,' McClinton replied. 'Kings don't listen.'

At the break, Wilson headed off to the theatre's loading bay for a cigarette. There he brooded about Aunt Ester, the three-hundred-and-sixty-six-year-old character whose death the play announces. 'See, Aunt Ester is the tradition,' he said. 'If you don't value that, then you lose it. So, in 1985, these kids are out there killing one another. Aunt Ester dies of grief. People quit going up to her house. The weeds are all grown over. You can't even find the door no more. So she dies.' He added, 'If you had a connection to your grandparents and understood their struggle to survive, you wouldn't be out there in the street killing someone over fifteen dollars' worth of narcotics. You have to know your history. Then you'll have a purposeful presence in the world.'

As he readied *Hedley* for New York, Wilson had been trying to make a start on his nineteen-hundreds play, in which Aunt Ester is a central character. Like Romare Bearden, Wilson opens himself up to his subjects and communes with them until he finds a pattern: 'I just invite some of the people I know to come into the room and give it an ambience.' *Fences* began with the ending; Wilson says that he saw his hero, Troy Maxson, 'standing out on this brilliant starry night with this baby in his arms, talking to this woman. I didn't know who the woman was.' *Two Trains Running* began in a New Haven restaurant, where Wilson picked up a napkin and wrote, 'When I left out of Jackson I said I was gonna buy me a big Ford. Was gonna drive by

Mr Henry Ford's house and honk the horn. If anybody come to the window, I was gonna wave. Then I was going out, and buy me a 30.06, come on back to Jackson and drive up to Mr. Stovall's house. Only this time I wasn't waving.'

By contrast, Aunt Ester had been balky about making her presence known. 'I said, "O.K., Aunt Ester, talk to me." And she says, "There's a lot of things I don't talk about." And that threw me, because I didn't have anything to write then,' Wilson says. A month later, he tried again. This time, he asked Aunt Ester, 'O.K., what don't you talk about?' 'I don't talk about the trees. The trees didn't have spirits,' she told Wilson. 'What does that mean? What that means is that none of your world is present here. You're looking at this landscape that's totally foreign to you. So I started writing that,' Wilson says. 'Then she started talking about the water, and I find she's talking about the Atlantic Ocean. And she starts talking about a city, a half mile by a half mile, down in there. She has a map to the city,' he adds. 'I think the map is important, so I have to pick the right time to approach that idea about the map. If I do it this afternoon, I get something entirely different than if I do it next week. It's intuition. You have to keep your eyes and ears open for clues. There's no compass.'

In *King Hedley II*, Hedley's sacrifice keeps a dying black tradition alive; in life, Wilson has also made a sacrifice to renew a connection to the past. He seems to know that the price he's paid for his enormous accomplishment is other people; and he has recently begun to take stock of his life and resolve 'to do something different.' He is making noises about retiring. Not long ago, when he returned to Seattle, Wilson, who had been away, by his own admission, 'for the past two years,' was dismayed to discover that Azula didn't know he lived there. 'You live in all the places,' she told him. 'Boston, New York, Pittsburgh.' 'No, I live here,' he said. He took Azula upstairs and showed her his clothes in the closet.

Wilson, who is an insomniac, shares a bed with both Azula and Constanza. At lights-out, Azula will say, 'Don't let the bedbugs bite.' Wilson will reply, 'If they do, take a few,' which leaves his daughter the final word': "Cause I got them from you.' When they wake up, Wilson says, 'Good morning, Sunshine.' Azula replies, 'Good morning, Big Old Dad.' But these moments of connection are only one side of the story. Wilson, who has created a universe of fully imagined characters, whose histories he knows in minute detail, is not as curious about the history of those close to him. 'I've been married before,' Constanza says. 'He's never asked me a single question about that. I mean a lot to him, but what is it I mean to him if I'm not a complete person with history, with wants, with needs?' Constanza met Wilson at Yale fourteen years ago, when she designed costumes for *The Piano Lesson* and she has a kind of clear-eyed fatalism about her life with this ambitious storyteller. 'It's been hard,' she says. 'I don't get the love from him that all of me would like. I don't have a partner through the little things in life. He just doesn't reach that intimate part of everyday life.' She continues, 'In his mind, he's a great father, a great man, a great husband. One time, I was saying to Azula, when she was going to sleep, "I'm going to teach you how to choose a really good husband for yourself." And then August said, "Just like your daddy." And I was thinking to myself, No!'

'Be where you are' – a maxim Lloyd Richards drilled into Wilson – is a habit that Wilson is 'still working at.' When he is at home, Wilson is pretty much wrapped in his own solitude, 'brewing,' as his sister Freda calls it. 'I call him the deepest pool I have ever seen in my life,' Constanza says. 'You can throw a rock inside this man and you'll never see it hit bottom. He's a mystery to me in many ways. He's reachable only in concise sentences.' Wilson's plays are brilliantly furnished with characters and incident, but he hasn't yet managed to furnish his own home. 'It's gone beyond eccentricity,' Constanza says. 'It's an outward symbol of our marriage being so out of the ordinary. We can't even furnish our own house. I mean, that's sad.' Wilson's critical eye and Constanza's conviction that he would disapprove if she took the decoration into her own hands keeps them at a stalemate. 'He's extremely critical,' Constanza says. 'The closer you are to him, the more critical he is. That's a pattern that his mother passed on to him.'

Ordinarily, according to his wife, Wilson 'has a hard time laughing at himself.' But in the presence of his daughter the sombre, self-absorbed Wilson drops away. 'I've seen a different August with Azula,' McClinton agrees. 'She brings out such a playful side of him. He came to the first day of rehearsal in Seattle for *King Hedley II* wearing a bunny mask with the ears sticking up.' Wilson has taught Azula some of the nonsense songs that he learned at the age of five from an uncle: together, they sing, 'Jo and Mo had a candy store / Tellin' fortunes behind the door / The police ran in / Joe ran out / Hollerin' "Run, Mo! / Policeman holdin'' my hand!' Recently, he wrote a story just for her that involved what he calls 'telescoping' – a fusion of the spiritual and the diurnal 'that I'm trying to do in the plays.' The tale starts off in Seattle with a little girl who won't go to bed. 'My aunt in Africa will grant you a wish if you will go to bed at the proper time,' her babysitter says. 'O.K.,' the little girl says. 'My wish is that it be daylight all the time so I never have to go to bed.' The story then moves from reality into a fantastical world of sun gods and kings of darkness and chess games where the pieces come alive. 'I think it's close to what would be an African American world view – tree spirits and all those kinds of things,' Wilson says. 'In this world, you can have a three-hundred-and-sixty-six-year-old woman and you also gotta pay your bills. They exist side by side. They infuse life with a something that lifts it up, almost into another realm. Closer to God.' Even Azula understands that her father's undertaking is somehow special and heroic and big in the world. At the Goodman Theatre, catching sight of him as he walked toward her in the lobby, she threw open her arms and said, 'August Wilson!' Around that time, she also asked him, 'Daddy, why you a writer?' 'To tell the story,' Wilson said.

3

MARY L. BOGUMIL

August Wilson's relationship to black theatre: community, aesthetics, history and race

Before the Harlem Renaissance of the 1920s and 1930s, the Federal Theatre Project (1935–9), and the American Negro Theatre and the Negro Playwrights' Company in the 1940s, where was black theatre? There were minstrel shows conceived by whites and performed by whites in black face in the early nineteenth century, such as E. P. Christy's Minstrels. Then, after the Civil War, black actors were seen on stage performing in such shows as Haverly's Colored Minstrels. Undeniably, however, these, whether performed by white or by black actors, perpetuated derogatory caricatures of African Americans. Before minstrel shows there were plays written by black playwrights, but their titles and creators are not well-known to most American theatregoers: James Brown's *King Shotaway* (1823), William Wells Brown's *Escape, or Leap of Faith* (1858) and Angelina W. Ginkle's *Rachel* (1916). In the 1920s Willis Richardson's *The Chipwoman's Fortune* (1923) and Garland Anderson's *Appearances* (1925) reached the Broadway stage, still the 'Great White Way' (although this was a reference to the lights on theatre marquees, it had a symbolic truth with respect to race), but these, too, were beset by ubiquitous caricatures.[1] In the 1930s, though, Langston Hughes's play *Mulatto* (1935) achieved considerable success, focusing in a serious way on racial identity and establishing a record run for a black play on Broadway not beaten until Lorraine Hansberry's *A Raisin in the Sun* (1959). The latter constituted a crucial moment in black theatrical history, launching the career of a number of black actors and that of a man who would go on to direct August Wilson's plays, Lloyd Richards, the first African American to direct a Broadway play. *A Raisin in the Sun* reflected the civil rights ethos of the period, but times were changing and just a year before Hansberry's death, in 1965, a new mood became apparent in black drama with the emergence of Imamu Amiri Baraka who, as LeRoi Jones, wrote *Dutchman* (1964) and *The Slave* (1964). Baraka founded the Black Arts Repertory Theater (BART) in Harlem in 1965, and it was Baraka who inspired Ed Bullins, among others, to embrace a 'black aesthetic' in American drama.[2] Wilson was one of those who responded to Baraka's lead, founding a black arts theatre in his native Pittsburgh.

Chawley P. Williams, Pittsburgh street poet and close friend of Wilson for forty years, thought that Wilson was popular because he came at the right time, on a foundation built by his predecessors Baraka, Bullins, Hansberry, and Hughes: 'Baraka was very radical but very profound. He stood for no other intrusions; it was his way or the highway, unlike August who thought in terms of inclusion. Bullins was very intellectual, but heartfelt aspects of our struggle Bullins tended to miss. It was in his lyricism and his observations that he was powerful.' Williams portrays Wilson both as a playwright informed by his predecessors and as a writer with a distinctive artistic vision:

> August was light skinned and stood on the backs of Baraka, Bullins, Hansberry, and Hughes and the ground that was prepared for him. Lloyd Richards saw similarities between himself and Wilson; Richards was of that same complexion and had worked in white institutions. He was very black in orientation, receptive to his Africanness, and he knew the American Theatre was ready for a playwright like Wilson.[3]

Wilson did not begin his career with a specific objective in relation to the black theatre. Rather, he began as a writer, a poet first, living and representing the varied experiences of those in the black community. After dropping out of Gladstone High School at fifteen, educating himself at the Carnegie Library, and then working at menial jobs, he began his artistic career as a poet, submitting his poems to black publications at the University of Pittsburgh. As Williams has explained, 'Wilson and I met about 1964, prior to putting together the Halfway Art Gallery in 1967 and before our involvement in theatre.'[4] Williams and Wilson spent time at the Crawford Grill because it provided more to its patrons than its name indicates; it was a haven, a club where those in the neighbourhood came to hear poetry readings, listen to music, particularly jazz, and even see fashion shows. All walks of life would congregate there, from hustlers to lawyers. In other words, at the Crawford Grill one could experience all types of art reflecting the black community. It was located across the street from Pat's, where the older people would gather near the pool room, and a reticent Wilson would bring a yellow pad and sit quietly in the corner to record their aspirations and their lives. Williams and Wilson's friendship, meanwhile, continued as a result of their mutual involvement with the Centre Avenue Poets:

> The Center Avenue Poets included August, Nick Flournoy, Rob Penny, and myself. Back in the early 1960s, before the Halfway Gallery, Carl Smith, a sculptor/painter known as Dingbat, was among our friends and would join in on our plans for the community. We'd talk at the grill about our history,

our lives, our tradition connecting with the [Harlem] Renaissance, the Black Power movement, self-defense, self-determination, self-respect, and how that [related to] our community and affected us as artists in our society. August insisted that our art had to reflect these tenets and how they centered around this community.[5]

For Wilson, community was an expression of the place where one was born, where one was raised, and the values which gave a sense of continuity to African Americans. This community, therefore, ultimately reached out beyond the Hill District of Pittsburgh, since 'any value of love, honor, duty, respect or even betrayal, although universal, had to reflect our history . . . We began in Africa, we were brought from Africa.'

Williams first met Wilson on the corner across from the Crawford Grill. Initially, Wilson recited poetry by Dylan Thomas, but then he read one of his own poems. After hearing him reciting his own poetry and witnessing his skill as a poet, Williams began to meet him on a daily basis. Wilson's shift from poet to playwright occurred when he met Rob Penny. At that time Penny was writing dialogue with poetic intent but wanted to write poetry, and Wilson was writing poetry but trying to write dialogue: 'When I introduced Rob to August, they clicked. Although both Rob and August attended Central Catholic High School neither mentioned knowing one another before.'[6] In 1968 Wilson and Penny founded a theatre company, Black Horizons.

Vernell Lillie, founder of the Kuntu Repertory Theatre, characterizes that period in Wilson's career as 'August prior to Yale and Lloyd Richards'.[7] The August Wilson she fondly remembers was a quiet man, but a gifted story-teller among his friends. Penny, Williams, and Wilson sat for hours in the Crawford Grill. It was a place, Lillie said, where 'all of its patrons were treated with dignity' and a place where these men began to dream about making their community – the predominately black Hill District, its inhabi-tants' voices and experiences, together with its local colour – the subject of their art. They would attempt to reconnect the artists with their community. It was a dream whose foundation was similar to service organizations like the Audience Development Committee (AUDELCO), founded in Harlem in 1973, to garner support from the black community, looking to individu-als, churches and businesses to build audiences for black theatre and dance. Black Horizons staged performances at local elementary school auditoriums, charging only fifty cents. Most tickets were sold as a result of word of mouth just before the performances.

Wilson's characters exist in and through their community and are designed to appeal to a community, a point made by the playwright in an interview for the *Paris Review*: 'I was, and remain, fascinated by the idea of an audience as a community of people who gather willingly to bear witness.'[8] While Lillie acknowledges that some scholars view Wilson as a member of the generation of black artists that includes Baraka and Bullins, who echoed Bullins's sentiment that 'we don't need a higher form of white art in black face', she insists that Wilson's vision, his voice, was less radical. It was, though, no less powerful. When, in 1976, Lillie directed Wilson's play *The Homecoming*, for the Kuntu Repertory Theatre, she heard this voice. The play examines the mystery surrounding the death of Blind Willie Johnson, a character based on blues legend Blind Lemon Jefferson. In that same year Wilson saw a production of Athol Fugard's *Sizwe Banzi Is Dead* at the Pittsburgh Public Theatre and realized that he, too, could become a serious playwright.[9] He learnt that he could address political issues in an artistic medium. As he told David Savran:

> All art is political. It serves a purpose. All my plays are political but I try not to make them didactic or polemical. Theatre doesn't have to be agitprop. I hope that my art serves the masses of blacks in America who are in desperate need of a solid and sure identity. I hope my plays make people understand that these are African people, that this is why they do what they do. If blacks recognize the value in that, then we will be on our way to claiming our identity and participating in society as Africans.[10]

Still considering himself a poet rather than a playwright, Wilson moved to St Paul, Minnesota, in 1978 and, after some coaxing by his friend, director, and fellow Pittsburgh native Claude Purdy, wrote *Black Bart and the Sacred Hills*, originally a collection of poems that became a musical satire in verse loosely based on the infamous cattle rustler turned alchemist Black Bart. Purdy convinced Lou Bellamy, of the Penumbra Theatre, to produce the play in 1981. Meanwhile, to keep financially afloat during this time, Wilson wrote dramatic skits for the Science Museum of Minnesota, adapting Native American folk tales into children's plays, but it was a fellowship, in 1980, from the Minneapolis Playwright's Centre, that afforded him time to devote to writing his own plays. It was in St Paul that he wrote, *Jitney*, a one-act play set in a 1971 Pittsburgh taxi station.[11] *Jitney* had successful engagements at both the Black Horizons Theatre, in 1978, and at the Eugene O'Neill Theatre Centre's National Playwrights Conference, in 1982. (The play, in its revised version, earned Wilson the 2001 Outer Critics' Circle Award for Best Off-Broadway Play.) With the success of *Jitney*, Wilson resumed work on a play he had conceived earlier entitled *Ma Rainey's Black Bottom*.

Ma Rainey's Black Bottom (1984) caught the attention of Richards, then director of the Yale Repertory Theatre. The meeting between Richards and Wilson initiated a creative collaboration that continued through *Seven Guitars* (1995). With *Jitney*, *Ma Rainey's Black Bottom* was the beginning of what would become the playwright's cycle of ten plays chronicling the lives of blacks in America. When Ben Brantley describes Wilson's virtuosity as a playwright, he emphasizes not only the scope of Wilson's project, but also its roots in black culture:

> People talk about an artist having an eye. But with playwrights, it's the ear that counts. Mr. Wilson had a peerless pair. His writing comes closer to the sweep of Shakespearean music than that of his contemporaries [Albee, Mamet, Pinter, Shepard and Stoppard] . . . Mr. Wilson has written plays that sound like grand opera – and it is no contradiction to say that it is opera rooted in the blues.[12]

Such accolades were only enhanced when, shortly before Wilson's death in 2005, Broadway's Virginia Theatre was renamed the August Wilson Theatre, the first theater to be named after a black playwright. However, Wilson's canonization in American drama occurred only after a lengthy debate over the fundamental status and place of black theatre in America, a debate which pitched Wilson against the academic critic Robert Brustein.

Wilson made his position clear in his introduction to *King Hedley II* (1999):

> Before I am anything, a man or a playwright, I am an African American. The tributary streams of culture, history and experience have provided me with the materials out of which I make my art. As an African American playwright, I have many forebears who have pioneered and hacked out of the underbrush an aesthetic that embraced and elevated the cultural values of black Americans to the level equal to those of their European counterparts.[13]

It was a position that would lead him into conflict with Brustein. Whereas he believed that theatre in America should unify rather than segregate, for Wilson expressions of multicultural inclusion, generalizations covering diverse human experience, threatened the integrity and autonomy of black writers. Financially, Wilson warned, African American theatre and its artists would not thrive without funding, but neither would they thrive in an artistic environment eager to strip them of their undeniable, and often cruelly discriminated against, cultural heritage.

In his now-famous keynote address, 'The Ground on Which I Stand', delivered to the Theatre Communications Group's eleventh biennial National Conference held at Princeton University on 26 June 1996, Wilson pointed out that 'we cannot allow others to have authority over our cultural and spiritual products'.[14]

[There are, he insisted,] and have always been two distinct and parallel traditions in black art: that is, art that is conceived and designed to entertain white society, and the art that feeds the spirit and celebrates the life of black America . . . The second tradition occurred when the African in the confines of the slave quarters sought to invest his spirit with the strength of his ancestors by conceiving his art, in song and dance, a world in which he was the spiritual center. (*Ground* 18–20)[15]

In a 1984 *New York Times* interview, Wilson explained that his responsibility as a black playwright was to address and redress black issues of marginalization that his parents' generation of blacks 'shielded' their children from, along with the unrelenting attendant 'indignities they suffered' living in a white society.[16]

Wilson began his address as a response to Brustein's 1993 *New Republic* article, 'Unity from Diversity' (*Ground* 23). For his part, Wilson defines his creative community as one that, while accepting the diverse backgrounds of the American people, must also acknowledge his African and African American ancestors, such as Nat Turner, Denmark Vesey, Martin Delaney and Marcus Garvey, and fellow black artists including Baraka, Bullins, Philip Hayes Dean and Ron Milner. To Wilson, the ground on which he stood became a metaphor for those opportunities available for blacks beyond ball fields and battlefields. The fact that he was invited to be the keynote speaker offered him the opportunity to stand on the platform from which others spoke to those involved in American theatre, a theatre that linked him to the theatrical traditions of the Greeks where theatre began and to which he could assert a legitimate claim. William Shakespeare, George Bernard Shaw, Anton Chekhov, Eugene O'Neill, Arthur Miller and Tennessee Williams were, he insisted, part of his tradition. But beyond that he had another heritage, that of the Black Power movement of the 1960s. He defined himself, like his political ancestor Garvey, as a 'race man' (*Ground* 14). Like Garvey, he insisted on his connection to Africa. For Wilson, the black aesthetic asserted the spiritual presence of the African within the African American experience. To him, Brustein's views smacked of 'cultural imperialism' and 'racial intolerance' (*Ground* 22).

As Harry J. Elam, Jr has explained, those who study Wilson's plays must be cognizant of the fact that 'Wilson seeks to "right" history and remake American History by recuperating African American narratives that have been erased, avoided or ignored. He focuses on the daily lives of ordinary black people within particular historical circumstances.'[17] Their stories become a means of self-authentication in that characters draw on their African cultural identity for spiritual solace. Wilson's stress on an African oral tradition in his plays creates an indelible identity for his characters which lies outside of, if parallel to, a supposedly factual history.

To Wilson, colourblind casting provided no answer. It was 'an aberrant idea'. In a performative context the black actor's body is historically inscribed with the traumatic legacy of maimings, lashings and lynchings, 'and is not for rent.'[18] Its colour represents a history worthy of dignity and its own social discourse and hence 'a play or any other play conceived for white actors as an investigation of the human condition through the specifics of white culture . . . [robs] us of our own humanity, our own history, and the need to make our own investigations from the cultural ground on which we stand as African Americans.'[19] Colourblind casting, he asserted, would lead to an erosion of black theatre, while the abstract category 'people of colour' was one he rejected as a compromise of his blackness and his aesthetic. Instead, he called for more black theatres and for sufficient funding to enable African Americans to have an equal opportunity to develop their potential as writers, directors, company managers, scenic and costume designers. It was a view supported by Lou Bellamy, artistic director of the Minneapolis Penumbra Theatre Company.

According to Chawley Williams, his long-term friend from Pittsburgh, another dimension of Wilson's argument recalled conversations he had had with him many years before when both had been convinced that 'there were no white folks that could direct the cultural experience of our lives on stage, they could not empathize, for it was not part of their history'. Nor were they alert to Africanisms and African American linguistic constructions. Wilson's desire to communicate to his audience a knowledge of vernacular 'Africanisms' derived, then, from the fact that language functioned as nothing more than 'a form of oppression and self-hatred'[20] for those ignorant of their linguistic past.

On 27 January 1997 the actor Anna Deveare Smith initiated a meeting in New York City's Town Hall between Brustein and Wilson. The issue they would address was whether the League of Regional Theatres (LORT), composed of sixty-six professional nonprofit theatres around the country, adequately supported black theatre when at that time, Wilson claimed, only one, the Crossroads Theatre in New Brunswick, New Jersey, could be considered black. Wilson's position was clear. Since LORT represented American regional theatre, funds should go to all those defined as such. But many of the black theatres had closed, forcing their artists to work within Euro-American venues and thus giving rise to the casting of black actors in roles historically Euro-American. Colourblind casting, he insisted, was simply another way to erase colour masquerading as a liberal gesture of inclusiveness. Meanwhile, black theatres were starved of funds and forced out of existence. Although some money had gone to fund regional theatres to help them diversify their audience base, Asian, black and Latino theatres still suffered. Thus money primarily designated to sustain and nurture black theatre companies had simply gone to theatres whose plays featured Euro-American culture which was not, he asserted, 'our own history', and it was that history which Wilson had set himself to record and shape into drama.

Kenny Leon, who directed and also acted in Wilson's plays, explained what seemed to him the importance of Wilson to black theatre:

> I think what he did was to humanize our history. He put a face to many things. After slavery, for instance, there were no jobs [which was] almost worse than slavery . . . [he created] characters and let them tell their stories. He honored our mothers and our grandmothers and out great-grandmothers by putting their rituals, their songs, their myths on stage so that we could hear them.[21]

For Wilson, such stories had to be told in a manner true to the people whose lives they explored. They had to be performed by people who could physically, psychologically and spiritually manifest them. Whatever the race of the audience who witnessed the staging of these stories, whatever the source of funding that ensured those performances, they had to carry with them a certain historical and cultural gravity that should not be ameliorated in order to ensure their place in American drama.

In his response to Wilson, Brustein suggested that their disagreement was not about race, but about philosophy. In particular, he was opposed to what he saw as an 'ideological art', creating a drama of victims. Wilson, though, had no interest in creating a drama of victims. He did not see himself as a historian but as a writer of fiction, poetically rendering the personal lives of his characters while simultaneously placing those characters within a historical context, a distinctly African American context, a context that in essence stretched from the seventeenth century to the present. In order for his plays, or any black writer's plays, to be true to the concept of black theatre, they must be 'one, about us; two, by us; three, for us; and four, near us'.[22] Yet Wilson, born into the revolutionary zeal of the 1960s, would later envision an American theatre of inclusion:

> It's a crazy society. In many ways, again, it's immensely successful, it's able to create some great works of art. And we're moving toward this art being American art – that means being influenced by all the different ethnic groups that make up America – and further and further away from the old, old Western conventions of Europe . . . They're not building on Western convention anymore, but on an amalgam of ideas and thoughts . . . the struggle of all the various ethnic groups in America. Eventually we are going to become an American culture, an American society unlike any other.[23]

What Brustein saw as a flaw in his playwriting, Wilson saw as an achievement not yet fully realized. For Brustein, Wilson wanted to create a drama 'of white culpability and black martyrdom'. This 'single-minded documentation of American racism,' he suggested, 'was a worthy if familiar social agenda, and no enlightened person would deny its premise, but as an ongoing artistic programme it seemed to him 'monotonous, limited, locked in a perception of victimization.'[24] Brustein could not have been further from the truth. Wilson does not write about victims or martyrs. He writes about black people in the American century, living lives whose value does not depend on their political or social roles nor on their historic function but on their human qualities, sustained, as they are, by an awareness of shared myths, a shared language, a shared fate, a shared humanity. Brustein's remarks were wholly beside the point and never blunted Wilson's self-confidence. As he told Suzan-Lori Parks, that confidence never waned. He recalled the words of Romare Bearden, the artist whose paintings informed his creative process:

> It comes from an interior life, and as Bearden said, 'Art is born out of necessity.' So the thing wills itself into being because it has to. Because this is part of your survival, the necessity, the urge to live . . . So, once you do it the first time, and you do sprout wings, it becomes easier to do it a second time. There's no guarantee; it might be the end of it all. But unless you have confidence, you simply cannot do the work.[25]

For OluSegun Ojewuyi, who worked with Wilson during the productions of his plays at Yale, Wilson's stance was straightforward. It was that while white theatres were being given huge sums of money in the name of multiculturalism, just for their once-a-year lip service to black theatre (à la Black History month), black theatres were handed suicide notes for not being mainstream enough. Wilson's argument was that black theatre was as mainstream as the American Dream. His position was that black performance aesthetics are different from the European traditions of white theatre. Different but equal. But the fault did not lie only with those who funded the American theatre. As Ojewuyi remarked, echoing a point made by Paul Carter Harrison, 'The unique, particularized, cultural expression that informs black theatre has been restrained by an historically passive response by blacks to a hierarchal authority of a dominant culture that subordinates the Afrocentric ethos into a conformity with its popular standards of entertainment.'[26]

The central need, therefore, was to raise the consciousness of African Americans and, for Wilson, one way to achieve that was to entrust the staging of his work to those most likely to understand the ideas and values on which he was drawing. White theatres might continue to stage his work 'as long as they did not interfere with [it], but he thought that because of the harrowing experience of slavery, it was most unnatural to have any white director interpret his plays'.[27]

For Wilson, his theatre existed to tell a historic truth. How else to understand the present except through an understanding of the past?

> You have to look at the Reconstruction era to understand the sort of assault that is going on now. Assuming that race relations improved after the Civil War with the abolition of slavery is to hold a naive perspective. That's the role of theater, to make sure the story is told. Write about the history, and the truth will be clear.[28]

The *New York Times* critic Ben Brantley, reviewing *Gem of the Ocean* (2003), identifies Citizen's 'Remember me' response to the incantatory call from his ancestors as central to Wilson's black aesthetic: 'For black Americans to forget their past . . . is to be without a compass in the present and a clear road to the future.'[29]

A comment that Wilson made in an *American Theatre* interview eloquently encapsulates his perspective on his aesthetic as a black dramatist and his relationship to black theatre – and, ultimately, the American theatre. At the time he was working on, thinking about, the completion of his last two plays, *Gem of the Ocean* and *Radio Golf* (2005), and expressed the hope that these would act as an 'umbrella under which the rest of the plays can sit'.[30] He was not only referring to their function in his ten-play cycle. What he was calling for, and through his plays hoped to achieve, was an awareness of the African and African American past and an understanding of the importance of both the black individual and the black community through a troubled century. This was a lesson he had learnt in Pittsburgh's Hill District, a lesson crucially carried forward in a cycle of remarkable plays that constituted a major contribution both to black life in America and to the American theatre itself.

NOTES

1. For more information on black theatre between the 1900s and 1940s, see Christopher Bigsby's chapter 'Black Drama' in *A Critical Introduction to Twentieth-Century American Drama: Volume One: 1900–1940* (Cambridge University Press, 1982), pp. 237–55.

2. See, for example, Amiri Baraka, 'The Descent of Charles Fuller into Pulitzerland and the Need for African-American Institutions', *Black American Literature Forum* 17:2 (1983), pp. 51–4. Baraka asserts that the Pulitzer Prize awarded to Charlie Fuller's play *A Soldier's Play* (1981) represents a 'descent' in the goals espoused by those in the Black Power, Black Arts and Black Theatre movements of the 1960s, namely 'the struggle for democracy, self-determination!' (p. 53). Recognition of Fuller's play, along with Douglass Turner Ward's procurement of the 'bourgeoisie's money' for the Negro Ensemble Company, were counteracting

the tenets of the Black Theatre movement (p. 53). Baraka vociferously claims that 'An oppressed people demand that all their resources be put to the service of liberating them, no matter what these resources are. Certainly art and culture must be seen in such a light. Either we are trying to fashion an art out of liberation, whatever its forms, or we are creating an art that helps maintain our chains and slave status (even high, giggling, or in ecstasy)' (p. 53). For further information on the relationship between the Black Arts movement and the Black Power movement and the poet-essayist Larry Neal's perspective, see W. A. D. Riach, '"Telling It Like It Is": An Examination of Black Theatre as Rhetoric', *Quarterly Journal of Speech* 56 (1979), pp. 177–86. For a list of black theatres and organizations in America between 1961 and 1982, see Andrzej Ceynowa, 'Black Theaters and Theater Organizations in American 1961–1982: A Research List', *Black American Literature Forum* 17:2 (1983), pp. 84–93.

3. Chawley P. Williams, interview, 12 August 2006. The *King Hedley II* dedication page reads, 'For Rob Penny and Nicholas Flournoy – fallen oaks of the Centre Avenue tradition/And for Chawley P. Williams – don't you leave me here by myself.' Williams said that early rumours of Wilson's cancer were circulating that were not true, and this angered Williams and upset Wilson, so they made a bargain that if either had a life-threatening disease they would let each other know before the public. Williams added that Wilson called him about the liver cancer when it was diagnosed as terminal, and that Wilson telephoned him three days before the playwright died to discuss the funeral procession, including the order of the train of cars, the funeral parlour, which undertaker was best and more. In the last book that Wilson sent Williams, a copy of *King Hedley II*, part of the inscription that Wilson wrote included the following words: 'To Chawley Williams who raised me and taught me to how to be a man, forty years, you couldn't ask for a better friend. August.'

4. Interview, 12 August 2006. Williams says that their first community project, 'the Halfway Art Gallery, did not exist at this time; it was in its embryonic stages. Dingbat and I, who spent three years in Washington, brought the concept of an art gallery to Pittsburgh from our experience visiting the many art galleries there. Our benefactor was a renegade white priest from Mount Lebanon, and the location would be Centre Avenue. It was called Halfway because the distance between the two locations would ensure that both whites and blacks could come.' August Wilson mentioned the Halfway Art Gallery when he told Gwen Ifill in a 2001 interview that he attempted to explore the African presence in America by embracing and exploring its musicality: 'See I learned this early on, also, in that when I was writing poetry and we had a place in Pittsburgh, the Halfway Art Gallery, and the musicians and the poets would go down there on Saturdays and Sundays. And the musician would tell us, you could play . . . you could read while we set up. And the people came in and they didn't want to hear the poetry. They came to hear the music. So we were the addendum. So I thought, well, if you're going to do language, if you have the musicality of language, since you're dealing with words, you have to have that. Otherwise, the people are not going to listen, you know' ('American Shakespeare', *NewsHour* with Jim Lehrer, 6 April 2001).

5. Interview, 12 August 2006. 'During our conversations at the Crawford Grill, we played the dozens, we used these call and response techniques in our

conversations. Often Wilson or another member of the group would be the voice of contention. Topics explored were defining community, its leaders, and its differing voices, and Dingbat's words of wisdom always were with us: "Be careful not so much what you accept, but be careful what you reject."' Especially relevant in their minds, during these conversations, was the Harlem Renaissance, for 'it made it clear to us that we as African Americans had a voice of our own, and it spoke distinctly to our lives, and everyone who performed in the Harlem Renaissance represented us, we were no longer the object of conversation but the subject.'

6. Interview with the author, 12 August 2006. Wilson says that he was the only black student in the Central Catholic High School and was confronted with racism on a daily basis. Recalling note after note left on his school desk that said 'Go home, nigger', and the mounting antagonism that led to fights, Wilson stopped attending. At his mother's request, he attended Connolly Trade School, a vocational school. Quickly bored academically, at fifteen he transferred to Gladstone High School, where his history teacher falsely accused him of plagiarism in a paper he wrote on Napoleon. After that, the Hill District, its inhabitants and the public library became the sources of Wilson's education. As for the subject of religion in his plays, Christianity prevails, but not the dogma of Catholicism. For further information, see Michael Feingold, 'August Wilson's Bottomless', in Jackson R. Bryer and Mary C. Hartig, eds., *Conversations with August Wilson* (Jackson: University of Mississippi Press, 2006), pp. 12–18. Williams believes that Wilson's early work is informed by Catholicism: the Wilson family was Catholic, but at some point Wilson rebelled. Wilson acknowledged the strong connection between Africanisms and Catholicisms, in their reverence for rituals and saints, but August did not want religion, he was more interested in spiritualism. It was the power of the spirit, or of spiritualism and the rituals, that gave you a behavioural guide. When Wilson said that he wanted to live life seamlessly, he meant that though his concept of spiritualism came from his early connection to Catholicism, the transition or evolution to spiritualism that he made was informed by his conscious sense of himself as African. Everything is informed by the power of the spirit. Williams asserts that 'such a transition cannot be explained employing a European based ideology that is always invested in a divide and conquer paradigm.' See also John Lahr, chapter 2 'Been here and gone', pp. 28–51.

7. Dr Vernell Lillie, interview with the author, 12 April 2006. Lillie founded Pittsburgh's oldest African American theatre, the Kuntu, in 1974. Its mission was to create and produce theatre that examines the black culture from a historical, spiritual and political perspective. Lillie also discussed some of these ideas in a lecture given at Southern Illinois University on 12 April 2006.

8. August Wilson, 'The Art of Theater No. 14.', *Paris Review* 152 (1999), pp. 3–4.

9. Chawley Williams said that Wilson told him that 'he knew he wanted to be a playwright before he saw Fugard's play or met Penny. Forget that European ideology of either/or playing in your head. What they provided for Wilson were platforms for his own growth as an artist.' When Wilson was asked by *New York Metro*'s Boris Kachka what plays influenced his decision to become a playwright, he named Ed Bullins's *In the Wine Time* and (1968) Athol Fugard's *Sizwe Banzi is Dead* (1972). In Bullins's play Wilson found characters that represented the

underclass on stage. See also Wilson's interview with David Savran in Bryer and Hartig, eds., *Conversations with August Wilson*, p. 23. For a further discussion of Wilson's influences, see www.newyorkmetro.com/nymetro/arts/theater/10176.

10. David Savran, 'August Wilson', in Bryer and Hartig, eds., *Conversations with August Wilson*, p. 37.

11. *The Homecoming* troubled him in what he saw as his inability to come to terms with what he had envisioned, in contrast to *Jitney*, which he started in the 1960s and successfully revised.

12. Ben Brantley, 'August Wilson Revealed Lives as Sagas of Nobility', *New York Times*, 4 October 2005, B1, B7.

13. August Wilson, *King Hedley II* (New York: Theatre Communications Group, 2005), pp. vii–viii.

14. Wilson's keynote address to the Theatre Communications Group in June of 1996. August Wilson, *The Ground on Which I Stand* (New York: Theatre Communications Group, 2001), p. 36. Further quotations will be cited parenthetically in the text. For further discussion on the exchange between Wilson and Brustein, see Mary L. Bogumil, *Understanding August Wilson* (Columbia: University of South Carolina Press, 1999), and Erika Munk, Introduction, 'Beyond the Wilson–Brustein Debate', *Theater* 27:2–3 (1997), pp. 9–41.

15. See also Henry Louis Gates, Jr., 'The Chitlin Circuit', *New Yorker*, 3 February 1997, p. 44.

16. Herbert Mitgang, 'Wilson from Poetry to Broadway Success', *New York Times* (22 Oct. 1984), C15.

17. Harry J. Elam, Jr., *The Past as Present In the Drama of August Wilson* (Ann Arbor: University of Michigan Press, 2006), pp. 3–4.

18. *Ibid.*, p. 30.

19. *Ibid.*, p. 31.

20. Interview, 12 August 2006.

21. 'Remembering August Wilson', *NewsHour* with Jim Lehrer, 3 October 2005.

22. Wilson, 'The Art of Theater No. 14', p. 12.

23. Suzan-Lori Parks, 'The Light in August', *American Theatre* (November 2005), p. 24.

24. Robert Brustein, 'The Lesson of *The Piano Lesson*', *New Republic*, 21 May 1990, p. 28.

25. Parks, 'Light in August', p. 25.

26. Paul Carter Harrison, 'The Crisis of Black Theatre Identity', *African American Review* 31 (1997), p. 457.

27. Ibid.

28. Gloria Goodale, 'Playwright August Wilson On Race Relations and The Theater', *Christian Science Monitor*, 15 May 1998, B4.

29. Ben Brantley, 'Sailing into Collective Memory', *New York Times*, 7 December 2004, p. E1.

30. August Wilson's 'Homeward Bound' *American Theatre* 16 November 1999, p. 16.

4

KIM PEREIRA

Music and mythology in August Wilson's plays

August Wilson has often been described as a dramatic historian because of his quest to document the experiences of African Americans in the twentieth century. In truth, though, he is no more a historian than Shakespeare. Given that he chose to set each of his plays in a different decade of the twentieth century, history clearly constitutes the context in which his characters live their lives, but it is those lives that he places centre stage, not the public events which defined those decades. He had altogether a different version of history in mind, one which sank its roots in mythology. It is there that he looked for the symbols, metaphors and tales that embodied and expressed the hopes, fears, aspirations, and religious and civic yearnings of communities who laid down their true history in legends, poems, songs, prayers and, in Wilson's hands, plays.

Wilson was alive to, and tapped into, African myths, often codified in music. He was a storyteller recounting the history of his people but, as he was aware, he was not alone in that. In some senses he played the role performed by the griot in West Africa whose function it was and is to recount the history of his tribe and thereby to preserve and celebrate it. In an African context history is deeply implicated in storytelling, song and myth.

Wilson was in this tradition. Devoid of their mythological dimensions, his characters, Levee, Troy and Boy Willie, in their separate plays, are merely destructive forces at odds with their world instead of agents of change challenging the status quo and reordering their universe. Within the full context of their cultural ancestry, they are the warrior spirit reincarnations of self-empowered trickster deities, figures which recur in myths from the Yoruban Eshu to the Hindu Krishna, from Bamapana the Australian Aborigine, Prometheus in ancient Greece and Sun Wukong in Chinese lore, to Reynard the French fox, Coyote the Native American, Maui in Hawaii, Susanowo in Japan, Loki the Norse god and even Jacob of the Old Testament.

Wilson was never concerned to chart historical events. Instead, he was committed to capturing the flavour of the period, often through the changing rhythms of the music which reflected black life. As he explained in the Preface to *King Hedley II* (1999):

> From the beginning I decided not to write about historical events or the pathologies of the black community . . . Instead, I wanted to present the unique particulars of black American culture as the transformation of impulse and sensibility into codes of conduct and response, into cultural rituals that defined and celebrated ourselves as men and women of high purpose.[1]

Artistic or political movements develop slowly over time and, although symbolized in the popular imagination by individual historical events, are rarely contained within a single decade. In *Two Trains Running* (1990), set in 1969, there is a short discussion of the death of Malcolm X and a passing reference to Martin Luther King, certainly two significant events for blacks in the 1960s. Those incidents, however, are transmuted into metaphors. The prophets have passed. Music has died (a fact signified by a broken jukebox). At a metaphorical level, Wilson was addressing the complexity of the 1960s, the optimism of the civil rights movement followed by the death of Dr King.

For historians, Jackie Robinson's struggles on and off the field as he tried to make his way through baseball in the 1950s have a special significance. Brown *vs* Topeka Board of Education and the subsequent struggle to implement it are liable to provoke lengthy examination and explication. This is not Wilson's primary territory. He is interested in registering the mythology of the period, in dramatizing the collective struggle of the black community as it is expressed through the lives of individuals. So, he concentrates not on the public events which seem to constitute the history of a given decade but on the struggles of those who endeavour to make sense of their own lives and those of others. So it is that he stages the life of an embittered garbage man whose thwarted baseball dreams have led him into conflict with his son and whose idea of victory lies in moving from the back of the truck into the driver's seat and who becomes an expression of a wider fight for dignity and purpose. He is no more, it seems, than a simple man in a forgotten corner of society who stands in his yard, bat in hand, challenging death's fastball. In the mirror of this human being staving off death, however, are reflected a thousand stories from every back alley of society. Wilson does more than record myths, he creates them; he continued doing so throughout his ten-play cycle from the shiny man in *Joe Turner's Come and Gone* (1986) to a renegade who wrestles with a ghost in *The Piano Lesson* (1987) and a 300-year-old woman in *Two Trains Running, Gem of the Ocean* (2003) and *Radio Golf* (2005).

In Wilson's world spirits can emerge from a piano, the bones of the dead can offer spiritual reunions, and ghosts can walk the earth as easily as humans. Memory itself, an instrument of the oral tradition, becomes a potent receptacle of experiences. Stories and storytelling are the stuff of mythology and together with the blues and the rituals of daily struggles they slip easily into the montagelike texture of Wilson's drama. It is no wonder that he saw in Romare Bearden a kindred artistic spirit; the two work in similar ways.

Bearden's creative style is almost an exercise in musical improvisation as a piece of a poster, a photograph, a painted image, create a collage which captures what Wilson called 'black life presented on its own terms on a grand and epic scale with all its richness and fullness'. A story here, a riff there, some jive talk between men standing in a yard (*Fences* (1985), *Seven Guitars* (1995)) or musicians waiting for a recording session (*Ma Rainey's Black Bottom*), the appearance in the doorway of a man and his child seeking shelter from the dusty road (*Joe Turner's Come and Gone*), are seemingly all Wilson needs to probe the most profound questions of black identity, cultural heritage and familial conflicts. There is a sense in which Bearden and Wilson were musicians, their creative methods as improvisatory as a jazz composition, their craftsmanship reflecting the way black communities constructed themselves. A garbage collector (*Fences*), an innkeeper (*Joe Turner's Come and Gone*), a numbers runner (*Two Trains Running*), or a jitney cab driver (*Jitney* (1982)) all form part of a collage, all constitute aspects of a society in which individual voices sound out like instruments in a band.

Wilson's achievement in the American theatre lies in his ability to transform the stories, myths, language and social rhythms of a particular culture into a vital drama which registered on the national consciousness. Music, as fact and image, is an essential ingredient in this transformative work. As he explained:

> The blues are important primarily because they contain the cultural responses of blacks in America to the situation that they find themselves in. Contained in the blues is a philosophical system at work. You get the ideas and attitudes of people as part of the oral tradition. That is a way of passing along information . . . The music provides you an emotional reference for the information, and it is sanctioned by the community in the sense that if someone sings the song, other people sing the song.[2]

In some instances the blues are an integral part of the subject matter (*Ma Rainey's Black Bottom*); in others they take on a more symbolic role (*The Piano Lesson*). Whatever the precise usage, their dramatic function is to highlight a tragicomic lyricism that survived three and a half centuries of suffering.

The blues developed from African and African American work songs and sorrow songs. Field hollers, shouts, yells, and mournful spirituals provided their structural foundation. As they took shape, they began to reflect the emotional content of the lives of black people, essentially their struggle to deal with and rise above their depressed lifestyles. The blues became a safety-valve to release the tension and pressure precipitated by daily trials. The cathartic lyrics purged anxieties born out of separation, loneliness, love affairs gone sour. Wilson's Ma Rainey says that the blues 'help you get out of bed in the morning. You get up knowing you ain't alone. There's something else in the world. You get up knowing whatever your troubles is you can get a grip on them 'cause the blues done give you an understanding of life.'[3] The blues may not possess the transcendent resolution of spirituals but they struck an emotional chord, generating hope even in the darkest moments. As Ralph Ellison observed in *Shadow and Act* (1964):

> The Blues is an impulse to keep the painful details and episodes of a brutal experience alive in one's aching consciousness, to finger its jagged grain and to transcend it, not by the consolation of philosophy but by squeezing from it a near-tragic, near-comic lyricism. As a form, the blues is an autobiographical chronicle of personal catastrophe expressed lyrically.[4]

The strong emotional overtones in the music find varied expressions in Wilson's plays. In *Ma Rainey's Black Bottom*, Levee's frustration at not being allowed to write a song in his way reaches such a pitch that he kills one of his fellow musicians. In *Joe Turner's Come and Gone*, this sense of the music being inextricably woven into the cultural identity of blacks is given symbolic shape as the characters search for their 'song'. Wilson said that in *Joe Turner's Come and Gone*, the 'song' Loomis seeks is his African identity: 'understanding who you are . . . you can [then] go out and sing your song as an African'.[5] Or, as Bynum tells Loomis in the same play, 'All you got to do is sing it. Then you be free.' In finding his own song – his 'African-ness', his roots – the African American discovers his identity and the value of his true self. In *Seven Guitars* the music is never far away, always present in the jive rhythms of the men in the yard and in their endless stories. Floyd says that 'Even if you don't put the music first . . . it will work its way to the front. I know. I tried many a time. I say, "Let me put this music down and leave it alone." Then one day you be walking along, and the music jump on you. It just grab hold of you and hang on.'[6] In *Gem of the Ocean*, snatches of the blues interpret various situations with Aunt Ester singing a lullaby, while songs accompany Citizen Barlow's journey to and from the City of Bones.

If at first glance the plays appear to be as loosely structured as the lives of their characters, this is merely a reflection of the traditions of the people depicted. Wilson writes out of a black dramatic tradition that inspired such playwrights as Langston Hughes to incorporate in their works the structure of the blues, gospel music, black sermons and storytelling. Closer examination of Wilson's plays reveals a complex form, as an intricate network of motifs and images is unveiled, creating a unique mood and atmosphere for each work. *Ma Rainey's Black Bottom*, for instance, resembles a jazz composition. At the beginning four musicians sit around chatting while they wait for Ma Rainey to arrive. One of them tells a story, then they go back to their conversations until the next story, and so on. Each story is like a solo performance in a jazz quartet which, though it possesses the characteristics of a 'set piece', is related to the major themes on an emotional and imagistic level. As the main thread of the narrative is resumed, we realize that the solo, far from stopping the narrative, has also contributed to the atmosphere of the play, and thus works on a dramatic level as the play moves towards a crescendo.

Personal reminiscences and storytelling, naturally dramatic and in keeping with the black tradition of the spoken word as a transmitter of common values and history, are integral features of Wilson's plays. In *Fences* and *Seven Guitars*, for example, the characters sit around a porch cracking jokes, telling stories and arguing while the plot inches towards a final confrontation. Jive talk is as integral to Wilson's plays as it is to the black community, the patter of conversation, trash-talking, mock and real insults, the exchange of news and opinions, constituting another strategy developed by blacks to make sense of their world and their relationships. It authenticates their self-worth and promotes a sense of community. Like the blues, it gives their lives meaning.

Storytelling, as a form of black expression, derives from an African tradition continued in slave tales, particularly trickster tales, which reflected the same cultural metaphors attested to and preserved by slave songs and spirituals. As Lawrence Levine observes:

> The slaves' ready identification with animals in their tales revealed . . . a tendency to see themselves as part of a unified world in which Man, beasts, spirits, even inanimate objects, were a natural part of the order of things . . . Slave tales no less than slave songs or folk beliefs were fashioned within this world view and derived much of their substance and meaning from it.[7]

Although the tales focused on the more irrational and amoral side of the slaves' universe, they were an integral part of the same folk continuum authenticated by the music, and their impact on black life was complex and varied. They were not just 'clever tales of wish-fulfillment through which slaves could escape from the imperatives of their world . . . [but were also] painfully realistic stories which taught the art of surviving and even triumphing in the face of a hostile environment'.[8] Essentially an artistic distillation of a cultural memory, they afforded blacks an opportunity to witness and comprehend their present affliction. Like the blues and jive talk, the tales were an affirmation, for better or worse, of personal and collective experience. Like the blues, therefore, the performance of the story was as important as the words themselves; indeed, the performance often constituted the narrative.

The breaks, slides and percussive effects used by a blues guitarist to create complex, polyrhythmic patterns, and the reechoing of this sliding technique in the singing of the blues – with its guttural sounds, stretched syllables and inserted pauses – are as important to the emotional content of a blues performance as the semantics of the lyrics themselves. A 'downhome' blues singer's words are often slurred or trailed off, with the music continuing the line, thus underscoring the equal importance ascribed to the instrumental and vocal parts to the melody. This kind of embellishment characteristic of a blues performance is also intrinsic to the raconteur's art. As Levine explains:

> Slave versions of history, like all slave tales, were enhanced by the manner of their delivery. The oral inventiveness of good storytellers . . . was a source of delight and stimulation to their audiences. Their narratives were interlarded with chants, mimicry, rhymes, and songs . . . Nothing, it seems, was too difficult for a storyteller to represent: the chanting sermon of a black preacher and the response of his entire congregation, the sounds of a railway engine, the cries of barnyard animals, the eerie moans of spectral beings, all formed an integral part of black tales.[9]

Storytelling is therefore essential to the form and substance of much black drama, for in it are theatrically codified the experiences and cultural impulses of black Americans. Along with the blues, it takes its place in the 'panoply of expressive strategies that serves as a unifying principle for black identity'.[10] Wilson uses all these strategies in the underlying structure, thematic content and development of his plays.

1927 was a watershed in black music. The Harlem Renaissance was in its tenth year, and black music was rising in popularity on the heels of King Oliver's historic recording session four years earlier. Three of the most important early black musicians came into prominence in 1927 – Duke Ellington launched his Cotton Club engagement in Harlem, Count Basie embarked on his Kansas City career, and Louis Armstrong emerged from the shadow of Oliver's band with his 'Hot Five' and 'Hot Seven' recordings. A new era was dawning – swing and the big band. The significance of this date is apparent in *Ma Rainey's Black Bottom* as the action turns on a conflict between proponents of the old and new forms – between blues and swing.

In the 1950s of *Fences*, the new sophistication of the free jazz of John Coltrane and Charles Mingus, with its emphasis on experimentation and complex harmonic structures, was reflected in the way blacks renewed their struggles for freedom in the courts and streets of America. This new wave of protest represented by the civil rights movement was an intricate balancing act of hope and scepticism. Troy Maxson is a true embodiment of this spirit as he demands job promotions and looks for new relationships, but is made to realize that freedom comes with a heavy price tag as his actions alienate him from his wife and son.

The link between music and identity in Wilson's work grows more tenuous with each passing decade. If the early plays demonstrate a strong connection between the characters and their music, the later plays seem to suggest a loosening of those ties. The long silence, despite the repair of the jukebox (and the revival of music, one may assume), in *Two Trains Running* heralds a shift in this connection. It might seem, therefore, that Wilson is suggesting that with the passing decades the link becomes weaker. On the other hand, we know that black music in the late twentieth century simply found new modes of expression, while retaining its emotional ties to the blues.

At first glance, hip-hop and rap music may not appear to be connected to or influenced by the blues. In his essay 'Hip Hop and Blues', Elijah Wald suggests that a reluctance to accept a connection may be a consequence of inattention:

> Because, looked at in a lot of ways, this is the living blues. There is a direct, obvious line that runs from Robert Johnson or Tampa Red through Louis Jordan, Muddy Waters, Bo Diddley, on to James Brown, Kurtis Blow and Ice Cube. And though there are certainly ways in which Bo or Muddy are more like Mr. Red than like Mr. Cube, in a lot of ways they would sound more at home in NWA than in the Hokum Boys. Both had a tough, electric, urban style that pointed the way towards what has come since. In fact, although he has recently been quoted as opposing the rap scene, I saw Bo give a show in the 1980s that included quite a bit of hip-hop styling, and he sounded like he'd been rapping all his life. Which he had, by any sensible definition – what else was 'Who Do You Love' but an early example of what we now call rap?[11]

While Wilson's later characters do not belong to the hip-hop generation, which has been described as a youthful urban ghetto movement, they are connected by blood and temperament to several of his earlier characters.

As they move towards assimilation in this late twentieth-century urban society (in this case the Hill District in Philadelphia), culminating in *Radio*

Golf, Wilson's characters find themselves engaged in real estate sales, making plans for video stores, running for mayoral office and planning golf outings. The struggle for survival has not ceased, but new strategies have appeared. In America hip-hop has replaced traditional blues and, as pointed out by Wald, the link between the two is imperceptible at best. In his book *The New H.N.I.C.,* Todd Boyd discusses the replacement of the civil rights movement by the hip-hop generation:

> All this is to say that we have a generation of Black people, now defined by the many strands that emerge most visibly through hip hop culture, who have decided to take what they want from the mainstream, while leaving behind what they do not care to embrace. Civil rights often imposed a certain unspoken code of moral behavior, which suggested that one should 'act right' so as not to offend the tastes of dominant White society and so as to speed up one's entrance into the mainstream . . . Hip hop is concerned on the other hand with being 'real,' honoring the truth of one's own convictions, while refusing to bend over to accommodate the dictates of the masses . . . and, as the untimely deaths of many rappers have clearly indicated, they are willing to die for these beliefs.[12]

This account of hip-hop artists could describe the attitudes of all Wilson's 'warrior spirits', from Levee to Troy to Boy Willie and on to King Hedley and Sterling Johnson. But with each passing play they appear to be a dying breed. Although there is no mention of hip-hop in his plays, Wilson can hear that the echoes of the blues are growing fainter. The few bars hummed in *Hedley* and *Radio Golf* come from an Irving Berlin piece, 'Blue Skies', an Arthur Sullivan song, 'Hail to the Gang', and 'Red Sails in the Sunset' by Hugh Williams. Of course, these songs were also made famous by such black musicians as Nat King Cole, Ella Fitzgerald and Sarah Vaughn but where music had been their companion, safety valve and identifying feature, it now appears a reminder of unfulfilled wishes and thwarted dreams. In *King Hedley II* Ruby says, 'I don't sing no more, I quit singing. The people used to like it when I sang. They'd clap and some of them would holler. They'd tell me afterward that I sang real nice. Then I'd go home and lay down and cry 'cause it was so lonely. I thought singing was supposed to be something special.'[13]

But without her singing she is a different person. When asked why he left her, Elmore says, 'You was hard to take. I seen where I wasn't gonna do nothing but fight you. As long as you was singing you was all right. When you wasn't singing you was hard to take.'[14]

Has music lost its redeeming power for Wilson's characters? Have the blues, with their cultural and ancestral associations, lost their central place in the lives of those who struggle to define themselves? Several decades before, in *The Piano Lesson*, Wining Boy had felt the weight of these musical expectations on his identity:

> Go to a place and they find out you play the piano, the first thing they want to do is give you a drink, find you a piano and sit you down . . . They ain't gonna let you get up! . . . You look up one day . . . and you hate the piano. But that's all you got. You can't do nothing else. All you know to do is play that piano. Now, who am I? Am I me . . . or am I the piano player? Sometimes it seem like the only thing to do is shoot the piano player cause he's the cause of all the trouble I'm having.[15]

Black America of the late twentieth century defies a general description. Although the struggles for acceptance and authentication continue, African Americans now make their mark in every field of endeavour, from business, science and technology to education, the fine arts and athletics. They can no longer be defined, literally or metaphorically, by the blues or jazz. They refuse to be contained within or constrained by older paradigms. Wilson's acknowledgement of this is evident in his creation of black businessmen, politicians, golfers and even radio hosts offering golf lessons in *Radio Golf*.

On the other hand, there is, surely, still a music to their lives, subsumed in those lives. In *King Hedley II* Ruby senses the subliminal power of this force when she says to King, 'You don't need no music . . . You got to hear it in your head.'[16] As a stage direction indicates, she then starts waltzing by herself, the music playing in her head, and, for one brief moment, all the possibilities of life are shining. If only for a moment, she is reenergized and begins to sing again, and the song she sings is essentially the song of her life – as it is for so many of Wilson's other characters in a cycle of plays in which music and mythology merge as he tells the story of African Americans who, in a troubled century, survived, flourished and defined themselves through a community whose resources were more compelling and various than perhaps even they realized.

NOTES

1. August Wilson, Preface, *King Hedley II* (New York: Theatre Communications Group, 2005), p. viii.
2. August Wilson, 'August Wilson's America: A Conversation with Bill Moyers', Public Affairs Television Inc., 1988.
3. August Wilson, *Ma Rainey's Black Bottom* (New York: Plume-New American Library, 1985), p. 83.
4. Ralph Ellison, *Shadow and Act* (New York: Random House, 1964), p. 78.
5. Moyers, 'August Wilson's America', p. 16.
6. August Wilson, *Seven Guitars* (New York: Dutton-Penguin, 1996), p. 45.

7. Laurence W. Levine, *Black Culture and Black Consciousness: Afro-American Folk Thought from Slavery to Freedom* (New York: Oxford University Press, 1977), p. 133.
8. *Ibid.*, p. 115.
9. *Ibid.*, pp. 88–9.
10. Paul Carter Harrison, *August Wilson: Three Plays* (Pittsburgh: University of Pittsburgh Press, 1991), p. 294.
11. Elijah Wald, Wald, 'Hip Hop and Blues', at http://www.elijahwald.com/hipblues.html, 2004. Originally published in Wald, 'Various Artists: The Hip Hop Box', *Living Blues* 173 (July–August, 2004), University of Mississippi Press, pp. 82–3.
12. Todd Boyd, *The New H.N.I.C. (Head Niggers in Charge): The Death of Civil Rights and the Reign of Hip Hop* (New York: New York University Press, 2002), pp. 10–11.
13. Wilson, *King Hedley II*, p. 49.
14. *Ibid.*, p. 46.
15. August Wilson, *The Piano Lesson* (New York: Penguin, 1990), p. 41.
16. Wilson, *King Hedley II*, p. 89.

5

HARRY J. ELAM, JR.

Gem of the Ocean and the redemptive power of history

Gem of the Ocean (2003) ends with the benediction and instruction offered by Mr Eli, Aunt Ester's gatekeeper, over the newly deceased body of his friend Solly. As he pours a drink and raises it in a toast, he says, 'So live.'[1] It is a noble petition of hope for the future of the gathered community and a purposeful plea for African Americans to live a life founded on personal integrity and committed to the collective struggle for truth. 'So live.' And so ends the beginning of August Wilson's history plays, the first play in his ten-play cycle, set in 1904 at the dawn of the first migration of blacks from the South to the North. Wilson has situated this play at this precise moment just as he has positioned every work within the cycle at critical historical junctures, key transitional moments in the story of Africans in America. Within such moments Wilson reviews the choices that blacks have made in the past. Yet in *Gem*, as well as his other works, Wilson is not simply reviewing this past and reevaluating history. His project is so much more proactive as he considers how this past now impacts on the African American present.

In *Gem of the Ocean*, Citizen Barlow is haunted by his past. He comes to the home of Aunt Ester, at 1839 Wylie Avenue in Pittsburgh, seeking her assistance. There he finds her tended by Mr Eli, who maintains and watches over her and Black Mary, who cooks and cleans for her. The desperate Citizen has heard that Aunt Ester has the ability to wash people's souls and, racked with guilt, he badly needs some form of spiritual sustenance and moral forgiveness. In order to help Citizen save himself, Aunt Ester, with assistance from Mr Eli, Black Mary and her friend and suitor Solly, a former conductor on the Underground Railroad, takes him on an eerie, symbolic and spiritual journey, back through time and space, to the City of Bones, a place deep down in the middle of the ocean, where, we are told, African slaves who never made it across have built a kingdom of bones. Through the psychic process of travelling to this city, by confronting his past in this site and making his peace, Citizen Barlow is able to move forward.

In Wilson's dramas characters repeatedly return to their history in order to move on with their lives and into their future. Wilson delves into and rewrites the African American past, addressing and righting the wrongs of historical amnesia and social oppression, ritualistically reconnecting African Americans to the blood memories and cultural rites of the African past. For him, black people are not tangential to the central motion of history. He places them at the centre of his attention. His history is not simply a linear line of progression but one that stops and starts. In his plays, and in the construction of his twentieth-century cycle, history is reworked for contemporary purposes. Most significantly, in Wilson's project history becomes redemptive. This concern with the redemptive power of history is critical to *Gem of the Ocean* and to the entirety of the cycle. The idea of going back and confronting the past, as Citizen Barlow must do in *Gem*, initiates redemptive processes. Working through his relationship with history transforms him. Accordingly, history is not simply a lesson. In *Gem* the relationship to history is vertical. Citizen Barlow and the others do not learn from the past in a simple way. Redemption suggests a level of deeper understanding.

The critical figure mediating the redemptive power of history in *Gem of the Ocean* and the cycle as a whole is Aunt Ester, a woman as old as the African American presence in America. Before her appearance onstage in *Gem*, Wilson first mentions her in *Two Trains Running* (1990) and then again in *King Hedley II* (1999). In the final play of the series, *Radio Golf* (2005), set in 1997, Aunt Ester's home is scheduled for demolition as part of a redevelopment project. Born with the arrival of Africans in America, Aunt Ester is the actual site of the African American legacy; history and memory co-mix in her body. In fact, her name, in a riff of aural signifyin', sounds similar to 'ancestor'.[2] 'Aunt Ester' is in fact the 'Ancestor', the connection to the African American past which is both personal and collective, material and metaphysical. Rather than abstract signifier, she is blood, she is family, the aunt of her people. By communing with Aunt Ester, others have the potential to rework their relationship to the past and find redemption.

According to Wilson, 'Aunt Ester has emerged for me as the most significant person of the cycle. The characters after all, are her children.'[3] Yet, in the list of characters for *Gem of the Ocean* Wilson describes Aunt Ester only as 'A very old, yet vital spiritual advisor for the community' (*Gem*, List of Characters) and thus does not simply downplay her advanced age, 285 years, but minimizes the full register of her powers. The idea of the characters all being children of Aunt Ester speaks to the inherent interconnectedness of black people and black lives but also recalls the legacy of slavery and the condition of the mother. According to the slave law, children inherit the mother's condition regardless of the baby's father. As a result, black mothers became the repositories of blackness. Aunt Ester represents such a traditional picture of black womanhood, but she might also be Wilson's most feminist construction, for through her behind-the-scenes presence, through her invisibility before her appearance in *Gem*, Aunt Ester finds and expresses voice and power. She empowers the other characters, including Citizen Barlow in *Gem*, to find the force of god within themselves.

Africanist allusions abound with Aunt Ester, and Wilson is always conscious of an African presence in African Americans. Entrance to Aunt Ester's home is through a red door, and the colour red represents 'the supreme presence of color' for many of Nigeria's Yoruba people.[4] Her 'faith-based practice', her laying on of hands, has a direct relationship to the Yoruba goddess Oshun or Osun, one of the wives of the powerful thunder god Shango, who, when she died, fell to the bottom of the river and became the divinity of the rivers. At the festival for the river goddess Oshun, at Oshogbo in Nigeria, the celebrants praise her by throwing 'flowers into her stream'.[5] In keeping with the river goddess's realm of authority, Aunt Ester asks all those who come to her for counsel to throw their offering into the river. Her city, Pittsburgh, is known for its three rivers, the Allegheny, the Monangahela and the Ohio. Oshun is a spirit of wisdom and generosity. Also known occasionally as the Yoruban 'love goddess', she controls all that makes life worth living, such as marriage, children, money and pleasure.[6] Correspondingly, Wilson's characters come to Aunt Ester when they have trouble over such issues. Going to *see* Aunt Ester requires faith and the engagement of their inner eye. They then come to reconstruct their physical reality and to see the world anew.

In the earlier plays, where she is not physically present, Aunt Ester does not dictate a course of action; she asks that her parishioners be proactive in their lives. As Holloway scolds West in *Two Trains Running*, 'That's what your problem is. You don't want to do nothing for yourself. You want someone else to do it for you. Aunt Ester don't work that way. She say you got to pull your part of the load'.[7] Aunt Ester does not act for the souls who seek her counsel but rather enables them to determine their own way. She explains to Citizen Barlow in *Gem of the Ocean*, before she guides him on his journey to the City of Bones, that she could 'take him to that city, but you got to want to go' (2.1.54). Aunt Ester dispenses advice in parables that compel her supplicants to interpret them, to think and then act. The spiritual and practical healing she initiates is internal, and psychological. She does not provide salve for the external wounds of oppression and racism. 'She make you right with yourself'.[8] This inwardly focused theology is reevolutionary and distinctly Creolized. Only by being touched by the past, by re-membering the lessons of the ancestor, can the characters move forward. The African spiritualism conjoins with the practical American reality.

Aunt Ester's death in *King Hedley II* reverberates loudly. It creates fissures within the community and constitutes a loss of history that requires its own healing. She dies of grief due to the desperate conditions of African American life in the 1980s. More than a testimony to the benign neglect of the Reagan-Bush administration, or the power of external forces corrupting African American existence, her death marks the continued movement of blacks away from their 'songs'. What happens when the spirit of a people passes away, when Aunt Ester, the living symbol of the past, the 'ancestor', or Aunt Ester of all African America, dies? Wilson foregrounds Aunt Ester's death visually and aurally. It causes all the lights to go out in Pittsburgh's Hill District. A voiceover newsflash tells of her passing. Stool Pigeon reports that crowds are lined up inside Aunt Ester's house and outside on the streets below. Following the African tradition, they will remain with the body until she is buried and crosses over to the world of the ancestors. Solly is scheduled to be one of her pallbearers.

Stool Pigeon senses the magnitude of the loss, celebrates her passing and enacts rituals that reaffirm her significance and facilitate her eventual resurrection. The death of Aunt Ester means the evacuation of spirit and Stool Pigeon's rituals over her cat's grave are intended to revive and renew this spirit. As Wilson suggests, through the ceremonies performed by Stool Pigeon at her cat's gravesite, Aunt Ester's is a soul we cannot afford to let die. Her death signals the urgent need for an immediate infusion of social change; it is a call for African American rebirth and reconnection. Her voice – eventually heard in her cat's meow at the play's conclusion – cries out loudly from the grave. The spirit cannot die but must find resurrection through rites of faith and through a ritual return to the past.

In the next play that Wilson wrote after *King Hedley II*, *Gem of the Ocean*, Aunt Ester is quite literally reborn. History is undone and created as Wilson brings a 285-year-old woman on to the stage. How should we read the material presence of the previously invisible Aunt Ester? How should spectators react, for certainly there must be some disjuncture when they see her and hear of her age? In fact, in the earlier draft, and in the first production of *Gem* in Chicago 2004, her age was stated by Aunt Ester and other characters several more times than it is now in the published script, and with each mention the audience laughed, perhaps out of incredulity, perhaps out of nervousness. Does her embodied presence on stage merely require that audience to realize the power of theatre to make possible the impossible and suspend their disbelief? Should they, upon seeing her enacted on Broadway by the beautiful and immensely talented Felicia Rashad, recognize the ageless quality of black skin and the fact that black folk just do not wrinkle like white folk? Does the Chicago audience's unease and laughter reveal that they just did not know what to make of this old, old woman? If Aunt Ester exists symbolically between the world of the spirit and the world of the flesh, can placing her on stage potentially dissolve this imaginative, metaphysical power?

For Wilson, Aunt Ester's power does not simply emanate from the fact that she was previously disembodied. She is far from a static site of remembrance. She is a living force, actively urging spiritual and cultural change. She is a conjure woman with spiritual power and otherworldly authority. She is a woman who has loved and lost, who has been married and given birth. She embodies not only a collective history but also a personal history. Hers is an embodied knowledge, then, that she shares with others. She tells Citizen Barlow, upon his arrival at her home through the upstairs window after she has caught him in the act of pilfering bread, 'You remind me of my Junebug he was the only one of my boys that cause me trouble' (1.1.20). She understands and imagines her new child Citizen Barlow through the eyes of one past, lost and gone. Her point of reference is the past. History and remembrance become a force of authority to enable change in the present and to precipitate an understanding of current circumstances. Her embodiment makes the metaphysical an element of the everyday, and this is critical to Wilson and his drama. Aunt Ester is not merely a spirit unseen but a material force. Her actions have weight.

The City of Bones, the site of Citizen Barlow's redemption, is also a material presence in *Gem of the Ocean*. An actual city below the surface of the water where black souls have come to rest, it is built from the bones of those who perished on the perilous journey across the ocean that was the Middle Passage. Aunt Ester explains to Citizen:

> It's only a half mile by a half mile but that's a city. It's made of bones. Pearly white bones. All the buildings and everything is made of bones. I seen it, I been there, Mr. Citizen. My mother live there. I got an aunt and three uncles live there down there in that city made of bones . . . That's the center of the world. In time it will all come to light. The people made a kingdom out of nothing. They were the people that didn't make it across the water. (2.1.52)

The City of Bones actively remembers the loss of those that did not make it across the water. In a proactive act of reconstructing history at the bottom of the sea, those seemingly forgotten black travellers – those who were too infirm for the journey, those who mounted unsuccessful insurgencies, those who jumped into the cold, uncertain water rather than face the cold uncertainties ahead – have built a city. In a poem in the Africa section of *Wise, Why's, Y's* (1995) Amiri Baraka, one of the most important dramaturgical influences on Wilson, writes:

It's my brother, my sister.
At the bottom of the Atlantic Ocean there's a
Railroad made of human bones.
Black ivory
Black ivory[9]

Baraka's poem notes the loss of black bodies below the sea but, more importantly, suggests that through the image of an underground railroad one can
connect to those lost black family members. The tracks of history are made
out of black ivory. Its construction is an act that reunites or remembers the
collective black body, those old bones making them into a unified structure,
a communal site, a city that joins past to present and that overcomes loss
by recuperating and actively maintaining a living African American history.
Aunt Ester reports that she has relatives who live there, not who rest there
but who live. Thus the City of Bones functions not simply as memorial to
the Middle Passage but as embodiment, a vibrant place, a destination that
Citizen Barlow, the other characters and we, as spectators, can visit. The
Middle Passage has traditionally been conceived as a fixed moment in time,
as a significant event in the collective memory of African Americans that
marks the difficult transition from free peoples to captive Africans in America, but not as a place. In *Gem of the Ocean*, however, the City of Bones is
a locality.

Significantly, Citizen Barlow's journey to the City of Bones occurs at the
beginning of the second act of *Gem of the Ocean*, literally the middle passage
of the play. His journey, then, embodies the idea that it symbolizes, repeating
and revising Wilson's earlier plays, even as it speaks to the specifics of this
play. In addition, the title, *Gem of the Ocean*, is a signifying revision. Aunt
Ester tells us that the 'Gem of the Ocean' was the name of a slave ship but
is also the title of a song, 'Columbia, the Gem of the Ocean', written in
1843 by David T. Shaw. This song was extremely popular during Abraham
Lincoln's Civil War administration and later became a staple of the United
States Marine Corps marching band. Even earlier, back in 1775, the slave
Phyllis Wheatley wrote poems about 'Columbia', celebrating the new nation.
Almost 200 years later, in 1973, Baraka wrote a play called *Columbia, the
Gem of the Ocean* about efforts to free blacks from the psychological tyranny
of white hegemony and to build black solidarity. With its discussions of
slavery, of nation and of spiritual healing, Wilson's *Gem of the Ocean* revisits
and revises the work of Wheatley, Baraka and even Wilson himself. Fittingly,
as they travel to the City of Bones, Citizen Barlow and the others hear the
people singing 'Remember me' (2.2.66). Wilson asks that the trauma of these
Bones People be re-membered, in order to address the unfinished business
of the past within the circumstances of the now.

As Aunt Ester declares that this City of Bones is 'the center of the world' and that 'In time it will all come to light', she enters substantively into contemporary intellectual discourse on the black diaspora and the symbolic capital of black cultural traffic. Paul Gilroy's seminal work of the early 1990s, *The Black Atlantic*, powerfully theorizes how the historical circuit of the Black Atlantic transit makes manifest intersections between the black experience in America and Europe. Most significantly, Gilroy, through his examination of the Black Atlantic, inserts black people as central participants in the creation of the modern world.[10]

More recently, Joseph Roach and others have built on Gilroy in their discussion of a 'Circum-Atlantic', insisting on the centrality of 'the diasporic and genocidal histories of Africa and the Americas North and South' to the creation of a New World.[11] Aunt Ester's proclamation about the City of Bones takes this argument even further. For these scholars who have recognized the significance of the movement between Africa, America and Europe in terms of cultural progress, the Atlantic Ocean functions not as a material site but merely as a transitional passageway connecting these bodies of land. Wilson, on the other hand, through Aunt Ester, plunges down into the water, recovering, reclaiming and reconnecting the bodies discarded there, constructing this liminal site as the 'center of the world'. In this way he refigures not just the black Atlantic but the world by proposing the City of Bones as its centre. This enables him to uncover or, as David Palumbo-Liu phrases it, to 'un-forget' that which had been previously covered up in historical accounts.[12] Not merely the centre of the black world, or seminal just to the collective memory of African Americans, the City of Bones is the place from which the power of the world, its intellectual and cultural thinking, its humanity emanates. Hence black history can no longer be seen only as a footnote or a chapter at the end of the history book. Rather, it must be read as constitutive to all history.

Significantly, the conduit for Citizen Barlow's journey to the City of Bones is a paper boat, modelled after the *Gem of the Ocean*, which Aunt Ester moulds out of her documents of indenture that identify her as a slave. She hands it to Citizen Barlow, who balks at it, complaining, 'This is a piece of paper'. Aunt Ester replies, 'Look at that boat, Mr. Citizen. That's a magic boat. There's a lot of power in that boat. Power is something. It's hard to control but it's hard to stand in the way of it' (2.1.54). Indeed, papers of indenture were very powerful instruments as they declared that Aunt Ester and other black people constituted property that could be bought and sold. The power these papers once had over her life Aunt Ester now employs to her own ends. Her documents of indenture are at once material, symbolic and functional. Part of the historical record of black enslavement and of her personal memory of slavery, the medium of enslavement becomes now the method of transcendence.

Repeatedly in *Gem of the Ocean*, and elsewhere in the cycle, Wilson reminds us that the battle to remove the shackles of slavery is not simply an external struggle but an internal one. Later in the play, when the black constable Caesar brings another piece of paper, a warrant for Aunt Ester's arrest, charging her with aiding and abetting the fugitive, Solly, Aunt Ester asks him to read the same papers that earlier served as Barlow's magical boat:

> I see you got a piece of paper. I got a piece of paper too . . . Sit down there Mr. Caesar I want to show you something . . . Tell me how much that piece of paper's worth, Mr. Caesar . . . That piece of paper say I was property. Say any body could buy or sell me. The law say I need a piece of paper to say I was a free woman. But I didn't need a piece of paper to tell me that. (2.4.78)

Aunt Ester differentiates between the legal authority of these papers to dictate black freedom and the spiritual and psychological power she already possesses to determine her own identity and self-worth.

In *Gem of the Ocean*, the symbol of the white legal system is the black constable, Caesar, who lords his authority over the black mill workers and chastises them for their ignorance: 'People don't understand the law is everything. What is it not? People think the law is supposed to serve them. But anybody can see you serve it. There ain't nothing above the law. You got to respect the law.' (1.3.36). Caesar's claim that nothing functions above the law stands in stark contrast to the figure of Aunt Ester and the portrait of black struggle throughout the cycle. Somehow, Wilson insists, justice can prevail for black America. Caesar's name echoes not only Julius Caesar but the blaxploitation film of 1973, *Black Caesar*, written and directed by the white filmmaker Larry Cohen and featuring Fred 'the Hammer' Williamson, in which the figure of Black Caesar, with the help of a corrupt white police officer, became the power broker, ruling over Harlem. Caesar similarly wields his own form of power but his name also signals his demise and his failure to understand the will of the people. His name recalls as well the legacy of slave naming. Southern masters often gave their slaves ancient Greek and Roman names, such as Pompey and Caesar, as a means of ridiculing slave pretensions and belittling them, preemptively satirizing black attempts at dignity or pride. In the aftermath of slavery, these names were generally rejected by the newly freed blacks as slave designations.[13] Citizen was named after Emancipation. Solly rejected his slave name of Uncle Alfred once free:

I used to be called Uncle Alfred back in slavery. I ran into one fellow called me Uncle Alfred. I told him say 'Uncle Alfred dead.' He say, 'I'm looking at you.' I told him, 'You looking at Two Kings. That's David and Solomon' . . . But my name is Two Kings. Some people call me Solomon and some people call me David. I answer to either one. I don't know which one God gonna call me. If he call me Uncle Alfred then we got a fight. (1.3.27)

Solly thus subverts the former process, finding his identity in this biblical history of greatness, his naming himself King recalling those earlier Wilson kings, King Hedley I and II, who, like Solly, exemplified an oppositional spirit, a warrior energy out of step with the constraints of white hegemony but also out of step with the social status quo. Wilson, who himself grew up as Frederick August Kittel only to become August Wilson after taking his mother's maiden name, as a statement of his affinity to her and his black roots, is profoundly interested in names and the power of naming. His Citizens, Heralds, Kings, Roses all speak to how a name can convey not only a sense of individual identity, but a history, and a culture. In like manner, Negroes became coloureds then blacks then Afro Americans then African Americans, with and without the hyphen.

Caesar exemplifies internalized racism. Unwilling to see the humanity within his black brethren, and settling for the rule of law, he calls Solly by his legal name, his slave name, Alfred Jackson, as he comes to arrest him, rather than Solomon or David. As is evidenced by his relationship with his sister, Caesar has separated himself from his collective history. He tells a story of his personal past but not his ties to family or to a communal spirit. Like West in *Two Trains Running*, he has accepted the rewards of money over the possibilities of collective action and consciousness. He exploits his own people, once selling them magic bread that would supposedly make them twice as full. While West refuses to follow through on Aunt Ester's directives to throw twenty dollars into the river, Caesar takes his alienation from Aunt Ester, the ancestor, a step further. He comes to arrest her and removes her from the house calling the law and the penal code his bible. As a consequence he is bereft of the sort of spirit and spiritual justice that Wilson ultimately promotes. He has no sense of the black spirit necessary to find redemption.

One of the more complex and even contradictory believers in Aunt Ester is the white peddler Rutherford B. Selig, a character we have earlier encountered in Wilson's play set in 1911, *Joe Turner's Come and Gone* (1986). Selig frequents Seth's boarding house and ingratiates himself within black lives even as he capitalizes on them. We learn in *Joe Turner* that Selig, whose surname is German for 'holy',[14] has been nicknamed 'the People Finder' for his skill in retrieving souls presumably lost. Yet, unlike the spiritual meaning of his name, Selig's people-finding skills are based on practical material methods rather than metaphysics. Bertha, Seth's wife and co-proprietor of the boarding house, intimates that Selig's skills at people-finding are built on his manipulation of black lives and their dependence on his white privilege. In *Joe Turner*, and in a room full of black people, Selig proudly and shamelessly announces his family business: 'we been finders in my family for a long time. Bringers and finders. My great-granddaddy used to bring Nigras across the ocean on ships'.[15] In *Gem of the Ocean*, Selig is willing to carry the fugitive Solly back down south hidden in his wagon on the request of Aunt Ester and in the face of the law, as represented by Caesar. 'I ain't never know you to be on the wrong side of anything,' Selig tells her. 'I ain't scared of Caesar' (2.4.75). As a white man of this time, certainly Selig need have no fear of Caesar and his black codes. In his construction of Selig, Wilson underlines his previous history even as he creates a new one. Selig functions as a participant on a redirected Underground Railroad. Rather than heading north, he plans to take Solly south, despite the fact that the roads are blocked and passage will be difficult. The plan is to go back and save Solly's sister. Solly and Selig must go back to move forward, repeating Wilson's central trope. And Wilson himself returns to Selig to chart a new course for the complicated relationships between black and white people within the economics of slavery.

For Citizen Barlow, going to the City of Bones is a ritual act of cleansing in which the spiritual, the political and the historical all combine. He undertakes this journey to cleanse his soul after another man, Garrett Brown, had died for Citizen's crime of stealing a bucket of nails. Accused of the theft and unwilling to go to jail for a crime he did not commit, Brown ran into the river and remained in the cold, potent current until he drowned. In a repetition, with revision, of Christian doxology, he died for the Citizen's sins. Citizen is free because of Brown's fateful action. With the water as his grave, Brown now resides in the City of Bones, a spiritual place of sacrifice, where all the residents have died sacrificial deaths so that others, the Bones People that Herald Loomis describes in *Joe Turner* as rising up out of the water and walking on the land, can survive. While Christianity, in its ritual of communion, remembers the body and blood of Christ, Wilson, in his ritual of remembrance, calls for the souls of Brown and those lost in the perils of the Middle Passage to find eternal life as they are re-membered by the living.

Barlow must confront Brown at the City of Bones, for he is the gatekeeper. 'The gatekeeper . . . the gatekeeper . . . it's Garrett Brown the man who jumped in the river '(2.2.69). And, as Aunt Ester explains, only by confessing his story to Brown can he cleanse his guilt-ridden soul and enter the City of Bones. 'You got to tell him, Mr. Citizen. The truth has to stand in the light' (2.2.69). Barlow must confess. This ritual act of confession is good for his soul. Yet, unlike Catholicism where confession is followed by admonition and acts of contrition, Citizen's confession is linked to the mandate uttered by Solly, to 'live in truth'. The notion of living in truth requires an acknowledgement of the past. This opens up a history to Barlow, the redemptive power of collective history present in the City of Bones. The gates of the city now stand open and, overwhelmed by its glory, he sits down and cries. Citizen Barlow experiences the presence of the past as he goes back to move forward.

Significantly, Wilson brings the African past and African American present into relation with each other in the figure of Citizen Barlow. Overcome by the atavistic power, the emotional weight of his spiritual odyssey, as Wilson's stage direction for an earlier version of the play indicates, he '*begins to sing to himself an African lullaby*'.[16] Wilson provides no information on where this son of a slave would have learnt this lullaby. It is simply part of his blood memory. Similarly, Wilson provides no detail for the actor or director staging the play as to exactly which lullaby from which African country should be sung. In Wilson's work Africa functions as Gunilla Theander Kester suggests, 'as a native soil and empirical abstraction and a metaphorical space'.[17] The idea of Africa as metaphor enables Wilson's 'Africa' to be constructed within the context of the moment or within each different production of a play such as *Gem of the Ocean*.

Africa is also made symbolically present for Citizen when Solly gives him a link of chain to carry with him on his journey. Aunt Ester tells him that he needs to carry a piece of iron for protection, as iron will keep strong. Iron, historically, has been the metal associated with the Yoruba god Ogun. Robert Farris Thompson notes that, Ogun 'lives in the piercing or slashing action of all iron. Lord of the cutting edge, he is present even in the speeding bullet or the railway locomotive'.[18] Fittingly, Pittsburgh, the steel city, the site of all Wilson's plays save *Ma Rainey's Black Bottom* (1984), seems the logical pace for Ogun, the god of metallurgy, to resurface on the shores of America. In fact, the spirit of Ogun, the god of iron, suffuses and infuses the world of Wilson's dramatic cycle. The link of iron that Barlow receives from Solly was one of the pieces of the chain that enclosed his ankles and imprisoned Solly as a slave. He keeps this remnant of the past as 'a good luck piece'. Thus, as he bestows it on Barlow, it functions not simply as a link to Ogun, but as a material connection to the collective memory of African Americans and a synthesis of their history within a single symbol. The ritual journey to the City of Bones at the centre of *Gem of the Ocean* resonates with both African and Euro-Christian rites of communion. In its unique syncretism and in its social and symbolic meanings, it represents an act that is decidedly African American.

Wilson's characters embody spirit and spirituality, as evidenced in Barlow's confession and redemption. This proves crucial to his dramaturgy and its processes of cultural healing and regeneration. Citizen's journey is itself an embodied ritual. He sees himself as reacting to the forces around him but also as shaping these circumstances. His embodied rite produces a complex interaction with systems of power, history and knowledge. He is linked to powerful external spiritual forces but also locates the force of god, of spirit, within. For Wilson, such spiritual salvation as that of Citizen Barlow is not antithetical to but a necessary component of a progressive historicism and a revolutionary politics. Invoking rites which connect the spiritual, the cultural, the social and the political does not simply serve to correct the past but also serves to interpret it in ways that impact powerfully on the present.

For Citizen Barlow, redemption through history and spiritual cleansing is a step to self-empowerment. In its aftermath he determines to take revolutionary action. He will travel down south with Solly and Selig in the reverse Underground Railroad pilgrimage, to reach Solly's sister and aid Solly in escaping Caesar. With a new recognition and appreciation of the need to be right with oneself, Citizen tells Black Mary, 'Black Mary, is you right with yourself? Cause if you is I believe when I come back from down Alabama, I'd come by and see you. If I was still right with myself. Then maybe we could be right with each other' (2.4.76). Their budding relationship is, then, to be built not simply on the mutual desire expressed earlier in the play, but on an awareness of the power of self-realization. Black Mary has taken steps in this direction when she stands up to Aunt Ester for the first time, asserting that after trying to please her and follow her will for three years she will now do things her own way. Aunt Ester responds, 'What took you so long' (2.3.74)? Through a form of tough love, Aunt Ester has moved Black Mary, too, towards self-empowerment.

Perhaps the leading advocate of black self-determination in the play is Solly, the former conductor on the Underground Railroad, who lives out the principle of Fredrick Douglass that without struggle there is no progress. For Solly, his life is a constant battle not only to live in truth but to realize the hard-earned freedom that he and other slaves have achieved. 'You got to fight to make it mean something' (1.3.28). Thus Solly is willing to burn down the mill in the name of justice and as a strike against oppression. Ultimately, he is willing to die for his beliefs. For Solly, a willingness to risk death rather than continue to endure oppression is built on his experience in slavery and the understanding by the enslaved that nothing, not even death, is worse than slavery. 'Ain't nothing worse than slavery! I know. I was there' (2.2.56). The choice of death does not represent an act of Western rationality, or acceptance of the present social reality, but rather a revolutionary action aimed at a utopian vision of a liberated future. For Wilson, the key to defining a new liberatory vision lies in the steps his black figures take towards self-determination.

Freedom by itself is not enough. Early in the play, Solly asks, 'What good is freedom if you can't do nothing with it?' (1.3.28)? This question informs Solly's own determination to resist as he recognizes that for African Americans the new condition of freedom poses new challenges. The play makes clear that the act of Emancipation by itself did not make black people free. The task for Solly and the other characters is to find a way to make the word freedom have concrete meaning. Unfortunately, Solly is killed for his efforts. Gunned down by Caesar, he attempts to commit one final act of civil disobedience.

Solly's death near the end of the play, and the trajectory of *Gem of the Ocean* as a whole, suggests that this question, 'what good is freedom?', is not simply one left in the past. For Wilson, in this play and throughout his canon, asks that this question continually be reconsidered. Throughout Wilson's interrogation of the conditions of African American freedom there is a recognition of the racism that persists and keeps blacks at the bottom of the economic system in America. He asks, however, how responsible blacks are for their own condition, how complicit they are in their own oppression. He wonders what actions African Americans can take in the present that will change their future. How are black people to redefine themselves and determine their own history? In many ways *Gem of the Ocean* can stand as a paradigm for Wilson's entire ten-play cycle in which he explores the psychological, emotional, political and spiritual dimensions of this struggle for freedom. And so the cry goes out from *Gem* and from Wilson's canon to black America past, present and future: 'So live'.

NOTES

1. August Wilson, *Gem of the Ocean* (New York: Theatre Communications Group, 2006), p. 85. Further quotations will be cited parenthetically in the text.
2. I thank Margaret Booker for bringing this to the class's attention during our seminar at Stanford University on August Wilson in spring 1997.
3. August Wilson, 'Sailing the Stream of Black Culture', *New York Times*, 3 April 2000, Section 2, p. 1.
4. Robert Farris Thompson, *Flash of the Spirit: African and Afro-American Art and Philosophy* (New York: Vintage Books, 1983), p. 6.
5. *Ibid.*, p. 79.
6. Sharon Holland, *Raising the Dead* (Durham: Duke University Press, 2000), p. 55.
7. August Wilson, *Two Trains Running* (New York: Plume, 1993), p. 76
8. *Ibid.*, p. 22.
9. Amiri Baraka, *Wise, Why's, Y's* (Chicago: Third World Press, 1995).

10. Paul Gilroy, *The Black Atlantic: Modernity and Double Consciousness* (Cambridge, MA: Harvard University Press, 1993).
11. Joseph Roach, *Cities of the Dead* (New York: Columbia University Press, 1996), p. 4.
12. David Palumbo-Liu, 'The Politics of Memory: Remembering History in Alice Walker and Joy Kugawa', Amritjit Singh, Joseph T. Skerrett, Robert Egan and Appaduria Arjun, eds., in *Memory and Cultural Politics* (Boston: Northeastern University Press, 1996), p. 215.
13. See Herbert G. Gutman, *The Black Family in Slavery and Freedom 1750–1925* (New York: Pantheon Books, 1976), pp. 185, 186.
14. Observation from Margaret Booker in May 2000.
15. August Wilson, *Joe Turner's Come and Gone* (New York: New American Library, 1988), p. 41.
16. August Wilson, *Gem of the Ocean*, unpublished playscript, 6 December, 2004. Act 2, scene 2, p. 69.
17. Gunilla Theander Kester, 'Approaches to Africa: The Poetics of Memory and the Body in Two August Wilson Plays', in Marilyn Elkins, ed., *August Wilson: A Casebook* (New York: Garland Press, 1994), p. 108.
18. Thompson, *Flash of the Spirit*, p. 53.

6

SAMUEL A. HAY

Joe Turner's Come and Gone

August Wilson created a structural challenge for himself in writing *Joe Turner's Come and Gone* (1986), the story of some 'footloose wanderers', as the poet and playwright Amiri Baraka called the displaced ex-slaves who, during the early twentieth century, tried to make sense of their social and cultural problems.[1] Critics almost uniformly praised the play but condemned its structure as 'sprawling',[2] 'off the track',[3] and 'confusing'.[4] One was more graphic: 'Wilson's elemental power continues to overwhelm the basic structure of his dramas. His efforts remind you of a large man trying to squeeze into a suit two sizes too small. Every now and then, you hear the fabric ripping.'[5] Implicit in these judgements was the idea that Wilson had wished to link episodes causally through characters, mood association or collage. A close study of the play, however, reveals that Wilson used signature elements from almost every major movement in African American theatre history, intent 'to engage in refiguration as an act of homage', to borrow a Henry Louis Gates, Jr. phrase.[6] They came from German Expressionism, first introduced by Langston Hughes's *Don't You Want to Be Free?* (1938)[7] and from the choreopoem, pioneered by Ntozake Shange's *for colored girls who have considered suicide/when the rainbow would be enuf* (1976); from the kitchen table, in William Wells Brown's *Escape; Or A Leap for Freedom* (1858), to talking winds in Loften Mitchell's *A Land Beyond the River* (1957); and from the Non-Objectivism of black theatre in the 1960s and 1970s[8] to Keith Antar Mason's performance text *From Hip-Hop to Hittite and Other Poetic Healing Rituals for Young Black Men* (1985).

Wilson used language, as the scholar William W. Cook explained, as a device for 'narrative sequencing – the telling of the self through stories'.[9] Plot, as he said, grew out of character without having the play 'flow from plot point to plot point'. It emerged, instead, 'from the seemingly aimless banter of the characters'. If one dismissed this 'as so much excessive verbiage', then one simply missed the point.[10] The 'banter' told stories that, in addition to developing plot and character, also stated, enlarged and crystallized the theme.

The themes of worth and self-sufficiency lie at the heart of *Joe Turner's Come and Gone*, both casualties of that rootlessness which Wilson regrets and deplores. It was a concern that he found in Ayi Kwei Armah's *Two Thousand Seasons* (1973), one of his favourite novels. Wilson so admired the novel that he used it to pay overdue royalties to Ed Bullins, who recalled;

> On October 23, 1993, at Chicago State University's Gwendolyn Brooks Center for Black Literature and Creative Writing, where I was receiving an award, I met August Wilson. We spent a warm two days together, discussing a range of topics. I was especially interested in his stories about producing my plays in Pittsburgh in the sixties and seventies. I remember him joking to me before we parted that 'the check is still in the mail'. On the last day of the meeting, he gave me *Two Thousand Seasons* .[11]

This, it turned out, was the cheque. As the Nobel Laureate Wole Soyinka remarked, the novel reconstructed the Ghanaian people's Akan past not for the sake of nostalgia or sentimentality, but 'as a state embodying a rational ideal'.[12] The premises of the novel were that a 'people losing sight of origins are dead. A people deaf to purposes are lost. Pieces cut off from their whole are nothing but dead fragments'.[13] Such convictions lie at the centre of *Joe Turner* and of Wilson himself.

Wilson often repeated the story of having his 'worth' severely damaged at Pittsburgh's Gladstone High School by an African American teacher of English, who accused him of plagiarizing a paper on Napoleon. Even as a teenager, he was proud of his writing skills. The teacher's charge so disturbed him that, like Garret Brown in *Gem of the Ocean* (2003), he saw himself as confronted by a choice between living with the accusation or jumping into the river, and the idea of jumping into the river recurs as a motif in *Joe Turner's Come and Gone* as it also recalls the desperate acts of those who experienced the Middle Passage. Natives of St Simons Island, Georgia, the Cleveland Browns All-American Jim Brown[14] and recent historians have all spoken of the nineteenth-century Igbo, who, while being offloaded at Dunbar Creek on the island, got so angry and desperate to get away from their captors that some broke free and, according to Cornelia Walker Bailey, a salt-water Geechee native, 'turned and walked into the water, *straight* into the water, like they were going to walk back to Africa. They had to have known they couldn't make it back to Africa'. 'They knew how far away Africa was. In the end, they chose the water as their grave, rather than live out their lives as slaves'.[15] For his part, Wilson chose the symbolic walk away from school rather than live with the unearned guilt of stealing.

Wilson returned to the incident with his teacher throughout his life for two reasons. Like Aunt Ester in *Gem of the Ocean*, he wanted to 'live in the truth' that people were worth more than a bucket of nails – or a paper on Napoleon. A man or a woman was the product of his or her own actions rather than other people's opinions. Typically, he recalled his alleged plagiarism at events that celebrated his mastery as a writer, for instance at the ceremony awarding him the prestigious Heinz Award in Pittsburgh in 2003. He told the audience that the dais stood 'but a few steps from the Carnegie Library, where, as a fifteen-year-old high school dropout, I sought refuge from the school system that had failed me'.[16] The second reason for recalling this incident was that he thereby offered a solution to those who had been similarly failed by the education system. Although his formal education had been terminated by an unjust accusation, he had set about educating himself, reading more than 300 library books on everything from sociology, anthropology and theology to fiction. He read for up to five hours a day for four years, he later told the critic John Lahr.[17] He wrestled with the revolutionists Nat Turner and Denmark Vesey; the soldier and physician Major Martin R. Delaney; the pan-Africanists W. E. B. DuBois and Marcus Garvey; the spiritual leader the Honourable Elijah Muhammad; the novelists Ralph Ellison, Langston Hughes and Richard Wright; and the poets/playwrights William Shakespeare and John Berryman. Ironically, his high school teacher had inadvertently directed him along the path to his own self-worth.

Crucially, however, in a highly politicized decade in which the idea of black consciousness had been promulgated by Baraka and others, the poet and playwright Rob Penny (1941–2003) invited Wilson to help found the Black Horizons Theatre (1968–71) at the A. Leo Weil Elementary School.[18] It was here that he became aware that he 'was the carrier of some very valuable antecedents'.[19] The local Black Arts movement – with its programmes in self-reliance, self-determination and self-defence – became not only, as Wilson explained, a 'part of my consciousness',[20] but also a 'brilliant explosion' that remained for him the 'hallmark and the signpost' pointing 'the way to our contemporary work on the same ground'.[21] The movement, then, laid the foundation for the African premise and structure of *Joe Turner*. It was Black Power that enabled him to see the parallel needs for both Africans and African Americans to link themselves to their common African past in order to locate what Soyinka called the 'matrix of a philosophy' for the future.[22]

The story of *Joe Turner* is straightforward enough. Herald Loomis, with his daughter Zonia, entered Seth and Bertha Holly's boarding house in Pittsburgh in search of Martha, Loomis's wife, whom he had not seen in ten years because of her move from Memphis to Pittsburgh while he was serving a seven-year peonage. He wanted to find her because he believed that seeing her face was the only thing that would help him to restart his life. Loomis, on conjure-man Bynum Walker's advice, hired Selig Rutherford, a peddler and 'people finder', to locate his wife. Selig returned with Martha after seven days, then Loomis gave her their daughter and left. That original 'scheme of action', however, was complicated by unexpected shifts of direction, causing unanticipated outcomes.[23] There are, indeed, a series of subplots.

Wilson found his inspiration for the play in part in Romare Bearden's collage *Mill Hand's Lunch Bucket* (1978),[24] which features a hunched-over man sitting sideways in a chair in front of a table with a child – a man, Wilson concluded, who was dejected;[25] in part from W. C. Handy's song *Joe Turner's Blues* (1915). The Tennessee governor Pete Turner, wrote Handy, charged his brother Joe to take black prisoners from Memphis to the Nashville penitentiary. A kangaroo court had convicted them for playing craps. But Joe Turner took them, instead, to farms along the Mississippi River where they were needed because of the loss of more than 37,000 area blacks to Pittsburgh alone during the 1910–20 period of the Great Migration.[26] Turner's prisoners worked off their 'debt to society' for seven years. Handy said that as local women missed their man, they asked a neighbour what had become of him, and they likely received 'the pat reply, "They tell me Joe Turner's come and gone".'[27] Handy's blues, interestingly, turned Joe Turner into a 'masculine victim of unrequited love, who sang sadly but jauntily".[28] Wilson replaced the Handy blues storyline with the traditional story, but kept the masculine victim as the subject of unanswered love. The significance of the coalescing of the man at the table and the man on the road was that it enabled Wilson to progress what might otherwise seem an almost static storyline as, from the audience's point of view, Loomis gradually changes. Initially, Wilson presents him as a man who is 'possessed' and 'driven'.[29] Seth suspects that he robs churches because he 'owes the devil a day's work' (34). This view was modified, however, when Wilson added the third influence, from the Book of Job.

Loomis, like Job, feared God and eschewed evil, so much so that his fellow men looked up to him for spiritual guidance. God blessed both men with sufficient comforts, as well as a virtuous family, which helped them to know what God and ancestral tradition expected of them. Each, however, suffered seven demoralizing losses. Job lost servants, sheep, camels and children, along with health, wife loyalty and knowledge. Loomis's wounds came from the losses of wife, faith in God, ability to walk, freedom, knowledge and self-worth, capacity to love a woman, and the will to supplicate himself. The damage caused by what Loomis called the 'desertion' by his wife Martha was so insurmountable because she had seemed a paragon of African American womanhood: a 'trustworthy, Christian woman' (34); a totally lovable and dutiful mother; and a five-foot, brown skin beauty with 'pretty long hair'(16, 37). The evidence of her devotion to Christ lay in her walking with the members of her church from Memphis to Pittsburgh in order to found a church in a safer place, having left her child in the care of her mother. She had been equally devoted to Loomis, so much so that upon hearing of his capture by Joe Turner, her 'whole world split half in two' (90). After five years of mourning, however, she had taught herself to stop loving him. Loomis's seven-year search for such a person showed the extent to which she was his compass, as well as his reason for living. It was fitting, therefore, that Martha, like Job's friends (Eliphaz, Bildad and Zophar), later intervened and led Loomis back to himself and salvation.

Loomis had not only been separated from Martha, however, but also from God, a breach whose significance can only be gauged in the context of the central role played by religion in turn-of-the-century America. Deacon Loomis, as an elected church layman, would have been part of a complex social world which linked a rural low-income people to the Memphis-area food-and-shelter programmes, burial societies and fraternal orders – all financed by black churches. He would have had to work with the deacon associations at such sister churches as the Beale Street Baptist Church (founded in 1864), now First Baptist Church of Memphis, where white politicians courted black votes. Loomis, as church fundraiser, would have solicited from the freedman and black millionaire Robert R. Church, Sr. and newspaperwoman Ida B. Wells. Had Deacon Loomis had the chance to contact Edward Shaw, Memphis's leading black politician in 1901, he might have escaped his peonage because he had stature, as evidenced by his assigned mission to convert public gamblers. It was unthinkable, therefore, that such a man, only a decade later, could have interrupted a worship Juba, a dance reminiscent of the 'Ring Shouts' of African slaves:

> You all sitting up here singing about the Holy Ghost. What's so holy about the Holy Ghost? You singing and singing. You think the Holy Ghost coming? You singing for the Holy Ghost to come? What he gonna do, huh? He gonna come with tongues of fire to burn up your woolly heads? You gonna tie onto the Holy Ghost and get burned up? What you got then? (52)

The Deacon Loomis of 1901 would have entered the lion's den before allowing this outburst to degenerate into blasphemy:

> Why God got to be so big? Why he got to be bigger than me? How much big is there? How much big do you want? (LOOMIS *starts to unzip his pants.*)

Seth stops him: 'Nigger, you crazy! . . .You done plumb lost your mind!' (52)

Loomis's loss of health parallels Satan's smiting Job with boils from the sole of his foot to the top of his head. His physical collapse, now followed by a mental collapse, had been triggered by revelation of the fate of his ancestors during the Middle Passage, a revelation which takes the form of a vision of their bones rising up out of the sea and, now fleshed, being washed on the land where they are fated to minister to those who had chosen slavery. A prostrate Loomis had watched this, breathless until the wind put breath into his body:

> LOOMIS The ground's starting to shake. There's a great shaking. The world's busting half in two. The sky's splitting open. I got to stand up. (LOOMIS *attempts to stand up.*)
> BYNUM Everybody's standing and walking toward the road. What you gonna do, Herald Loomis?
> LOOMIS My legs won't stand up . . . I got to stand up. Get up on the road . . . My legs won't stand up! My legs won't stand up. (55–6)

Why had God blessed him with this revelation if He did not want him to be one of their number? Such wickedness, Loomis reasoned, proved God to be nothing less than a trickster.

The relating of the Middle Passage trauma provokes Loomis to speak of his fourth tragedy, the loss of his freedom. For Wilson, this story was so pivotal that he made the narrative reflect Loomis's fractured mind: 'Joe Turner catched me when my little girl was jus born', he explains. 'Wasn't nothing but a little baby sucking on her mama's titty when he catched me'. He then introduces details of the number of people captured (forty), along with the dates on which they were caught (1901) and released (1908), followed by alternating fragments of story ('I was walking down this road in this little town . . . Come up on these fellows gambling') and personal history ('I was a deacon in the Abundant Life Church. I stopped to preach to these fellows to see if maybe I could turn some of them from their sinning, when Joe Turner . . . swooped down on us and grabbed everybody there'). His lost purpose and psychological dislocation are thus mirrored linguistically. Ironically, however, it is the telling of this broken narrative that initiates the process of healing, not only of Loomis but also of Seth, who, for the first time, abandons his self-absorption and offers an assistance not tied to financial returns: Seth tells Loomis that Joe Turner just wanted 'you to do his work for him' (73).

Loomis, like Job, wondered why God was punishing him. Throughout his service to God, he had lived by the ancestral belief that blessings flowed from individual or communal good deeds and that destruction resulted from wickedness.[30] It was precisely this, however, that made Loomis lose his bearing because, unlike Memphis in *Two Trains Running* (1990), he had never disavowed ancestral powers, or, like Becker in *Jitney* (1982), voiced wariness of 'waiting for God to decide to hold my hand'.[31] His family's long devotion to God meant that he could not be suffering because of inherited sins. His family had never lied, like Turbo in *Jitney*, or dishonoured fathers, like Cory in *Fences* (1985), or fornicated, like Canewell in *Seven Guitars* (1995). Yet Loomis suffered so much that it destroyed his vision of self, which more than matched the sixth and seventh losses of forgetting how to love a woman and of knowing how to humble and cleanse himself. The dramatic importance of the parallel between Loomis and Job lies in the structure of both parables: by the end, both men come to understand that God destroys the good as well as the wicked.

Wilson created Bynum as a one-man chorus, which, for the playwright and director Paul Carter Harrison was a way of personifying the community of the living and the dead and signified the spiritual imperatives of the community's moral universe.[32] Viewed from an Igbo perspective, Bynum would symbolize the collective African ancestors, called Ndi Ndushi, who made sure that people obeyed ancestral traditions of good and evil, and cleansed themselves of all abominations. The ancestral spirits chose Bynum, then, to protect the living from 'death', by which, Soyinka said, the Igbo meant 'not simply the curtailing of existence but the more terrible loss of self'.[33] Bynum was an apt choice to save Loomis, who believed him to be 'one of them bones people' (73). Loomis also believed that Bynum had caused his three-year journey to find Martha: 'It was you [Bynum]! All the time it was you that bind me up! You bound me to the road!' Bynum, like Aunt Ester, has a way of expanding questions into insights: 'I ain't bind you, Herald Loomis. You can't bind what don't cling' (91). Had Bynum, in fact, been paving the way for Loomis to gain real worth and sufficiency through supplication and cleansing even ten years before it occurred? Bynum lived in the Memphis area around the same time that Joe Turner captured Loomis: 'That song ["Joe Turner's Come and Gone"] the women sing down around Memphis. The women down there made up that song. I picked it up down there about fifteen years ago.' Bynum, additionally, had preceded Martha to Seth and Bertha's boarding house and had counselled the distraught Martha there almost three years before Loomis arrived. Bynum, like Hedley in *Seven Guitars*, immediately started working feverishly, sacrificing fowl. Was he appeasing the ancestors in preparation for Loomis's arrival? Had Bynum, in fact, even delivered Loomis to Joe Turner in order to show the ex-slaves the way back to self?

Wilson raised the possibility by mirroring the Loomis-Job connection with the conversions of Bynum and the apostle Paul, found in Acts 9:1–28. Saul walked the road to Damascus to bring disciples of Jesus to Jerusalem to be slaughtered. On the way, light from heaven felled and blinded him. God led him to Damascus, where he stayed for three days without food before God sent the disciple Ananias to lay hands on him, to baptize and anoint him, and to restore his sight. Saul walked with Jesus in the desert for three years, leaving as Paul to preach to nonbelievers that they must accept Jesus as the Son of God.[34] In like manner, Bynum walked the road to Johnstown, Pennsylvania, where he met a man asking where the road led and, in the Igbo tradition, if he could have food to break a three-day fast. The man, after eating an orange, laid hands on Bynum, causing blood to appear. He told Bynum to rub the blood over his body in order to cleanse himself. Light erupted from the man, causing Bynum to shield his eyes 'to keep from being blinded' (9). The man left Bynum, who encountered his father, who took him to the City of Bones in the ocean to show him how to find his song of binding people to the truth of themselves. Bynum, like the apostle Paul, preached the Word: 'You'd have thought I was a missionary spreading the gospel the way I wander all around [Blawknox, Clairton and Rankin]' (42).

The importance of the comparison lies in the fact that from the point of view of African philosophies and religions, Bynum would represent what the apostle did for Christian theology. He understood the apostle Paul's creed that nonbelievers should accept Jesus as the Son of God because Bynum, like Loomis himself, had used the creed in his mission work. He also understood the African beliefs and practices because, as a disciple of the City of Bones, he had rescued scores who had chosen slavery over watery graves, thereby becoming Christian Africans. Bynum was fully equipped, therefore, to help Loomis solve his dilemma of whether or not he should abandon Joe Turner's God in favour of the chi (providence) and the Chukwu (supreme deity) of the Igbo. Bynum made Loomis face his quandary with Juba, which, like the blues – to interpolate Wilson – stirred the 'emotional response' of African beats into the 'information' of Christian words.[35] Bynum, significantly, controlled the beats. His success with Loomis might be attributed, in part, to each of the nine residents of the boarding house, whom Bynum called upon to help him teach his seven principles: (a) Some things are worth going to jail for; (b) people should be very clear about what they want fixed before seeking people to fix it; (c) if a person is in the wrong place with the wrong person, then both people are lost; (d) spread the word about your salvation; (e) a man needs a woman to make something out of himself; (f) nobody can bind you to anything that you do not cling to; and (g) your song of worth and self-sufficiency is in your throat. All you have to do is sing it.

Wilson told Professors Sandra G. Shannon and Dana A. Williams in an interview that *Joe Turner's Come and Gone* was his 'signature play' because most 'of the ideas of the other plays are contained in that one play'.[36] In many ways the dominant ideas in *Joe Turner* were represented by its minor characters, who illuminated aspects of Bynum's teachings or Loomis's character. Seth and Bertha Holly, the stable and hardworking owners of the boarding house, represented the brunt of the ideas, which were the needs for economic planning and development by blacks in the black community, owner-workshops to teach saleable skills to anyone who wanted them, a prevailing black work ethic, exemplary black behaviour based on African ethics and philosophy, collective decision-making, and obedience to ancestral customs and traditions. It was ironic – and instructive – that Seth, a highly skilled craftsman whose parents were free northern small business people, delivered these laws. He, single-minded and self-centred, was suspicious (he said that Loomis probably robbed churches), unprincipled (he believed that Jeremy had erred by not paying a bribe to keep his job) and class-conscious ('I ain't never even seen no cotton') (70). Wilson showed that Seth's flaws were attributable, in part, to his overbearing individualism, which the political scientist John T. McCartney said was considered 'a form of evil' by the Black Power movement. The movement, which Wilson said had shaped his consciousness and his artistic method, held that the 'collective voice of the black community set the parameters for its members'.[37] Seth, then, was Wilson's characterization of the potential for class-conscious individualism to run amok if not tempered by a Bertha, Seth's wife and the epitome of grounded wisdom and humanity. She was, to that extent, an exception to Harry J. Elam, Jr.'s view that the female characters in *Joe Turner* function 'within the patriarchy and traditional gender roles'.[38] Bertha, in fact, was the synapse through which the blood's memory flowed, manifesting itself in her centuries-old dance to celebrate Africa not as a distant time and space but as an ever-present compass.

Jeremy Furlow, a livewire boarding house tenant who believed that he had 'the world in his hand' and that he could 'meet life's challenges head on' (12), represented another key aspect of Wilson's teachings. He showed through Jeremy that the black man, in general, might be so very complex because he, as the critic Clayton Riley said of Luke in James Baldwin's *Amen Corner* (1968), was the classic figure in historic 'flight, maligned and emotionally lacerated by the very fact of that flight; oppressed by personal doubts and often stunted into enraged helplessness'.[39] Jeremy's dualities, however, were, if anything, more pronounced. He behaved, on the one hand, like one of several 'foolish-acting niggers' with an 'old backward country style of living', of which Seth continually complained (5–6); but, on the other hand,

Jeremy was principled and intelligent enough to recognize and resist shyster promoters and race-bribers. Although Wilson tilted the characterization in favour of Jeremy the trickster, there was a tragic element to a man whom Bynum described as an example of death waking up in the wrong bed, a tragedy undoubtedly suffered by Jeremy himself when he discovered that the stunning Molly Cunningham, a newly arrived roomer to whom he had transferred his attention from Mattie Campbell, distrusted all men, hated procreating and refused to work.

Mattie, a desperate seeker for love, symbolized the belief that, regardless of past losses, recovery was there just for the asking. Her losses were almost as staggering as Loomis's: two of her babies had died in infancy, and her husband, Jack Carper, had abandoned her because he believed that she had a 'curse prayer' on her. Mattie's recovery steps included following Bynum's advice to 'let him go find where he's supposed to be in the world'. She then accepted on faith Bynum's prophecy that there was 'somebody searching for your doorstep right now' (23). She continued loving, trusting, needing and serving people, which made her Molly Cunningham's foil. Loomis, after his resurrection and cleansing, so admired Molly's 'good heart' that he took her as his woman, thereby making Mattie's loss of family the very instrument for reviving family.

Rutherford Selig, a white peddler and people finder, was also a healer. A descendant of slaveowners, he now dedicated his life to reuniting those separated by time and space, a function he also played in terms of the narrative. Loomis hired Selig to find his wife Martha Pentecost, who had been separated from him and had adopted her last name as a symbol of resurrection – Pentecost being the name given to the coming of the Holy Spirit to God's disciples after Christ's resurrection. Wilson made Selig the evidence that regardless of how despicable past sins might be, forgiveness, like recovery, was but a word away. Selig, notwithstanding the fact that he was the progeny of a slave trader great-grandfather and a runaway-slave-hunter father, gained the trust of all the residents in Seth and Bertha's boarding house. Wilson apparently used Selig to say that gaining worth and self-sufficiency required blacks to forgive past racist transgressions and form workable alliances.

Loomis's daughter, Zonia, projected the concerns of the play forwarded into the next generation with her rope-skipping ditty, 'Pullin' the Skiff', which lamented mistakes, frustrated intentions and creeping-but-never-arriving tomorrows.[40] Reuben, a child who lives next door to the boarding house, echoed the faults of his elders but readily accepted the supernatural, being visited by a ghost, thereby fusing the different elements of a play in which daily life and ancestral myths were never seen as being mutually contradictory.

The ideas in *Joe Turner*, like its structure, were unprecedented in the history of American theatre because, like jazz, blues and the Negro spiritual, they were uniquely American but rooted in African beats and cultural systems. The ideas startled people with the notion that African Americans could – and must – resurrect themselves from watery graves and walk back to the purposes and ideals and places that were already in them waiting to be brought back to life. So big was this motion that its representation on stage, as the director and Wilson-mentor Lloyd Richards said, was difficult because it 'took you deeply into a place where you had never been before. It made you work'.[41] That in turn posed a challenge to critics for whom its subtly interwoven stories spanning time, its structure, its complex mythologies, dissolving the clear line between an apparently hard-edged reality and a more expansive version of the real, were unfamiliar.

NOTES

1. LeRoi Jones, *Blues People* (New York: William Morrow and Company, 1968), p. 62.
2. William A. Henry III, 'Exorcising the Demons of Memory,' *Time Magazine*, 11 April 1988, pp. 77, 79.
3. Frank Rich, 'Panoramic History of Blacks in America in Wilson's "Joe Turner"', *New York Times*, 28 March 1988, C15.
4. Clive Barnes, 'O'Neill in Blackface', *New York Post*, 28 March 1988. Reprinted in *Contemporary Literary Criticism Yearbook* (Detroit: Gale Research Company, 1984), pp. 450–51.
5. David Richards, 'The Tortured Spirit of *Joe Turner*', *Washington Post*, 9 October 1987, B1, p. 12. Cited in Sandra G. Shannon, *The Dramatic Vision of August Wilson* (Washington, DC: Howard University Press, 1995), p. 128.
6. Henry Louis Gates, Jr., *The Signifying Monkey: A Theory of African -American Literary Criticism* (New York: Oxford University Press, 1988), p. xxvii.
7. See my *African American Theatre: An Historical and Critical Analysis* (New York: Cambridge University Press, 1999), pp. 24–5.
8. See Jahnheinz Jahn, *Muntu: An Outline of the New African Culture* (New York: Grove Press, 1961), p. 49. The critic Larry P. Neal might be credited with first suggesting that the then nascent Black Arts movement in America carefully examine Jahn's *Muntu* with an eye towards 'extending' and using some of the concepts as 'instruments in the black revolution that is now in the process of developing' ('Review of Jahn's *Muntu*', *Liberator* (March 1965), pp. 29–30). The concept of Non-Objectivism arose from the subsequent symposia in Philadelphia and New York, as well as other cities, where writers and scholars heeded Neal's suggestion. Paul Carter Harrison followed up on these sessions with his seminal works, *The Drama of Nommo* (1972) and *Kuntu Drama* (1974).
9. William W. Cook, 'Members and Lames: Language in the Plays of August Wilson in Paul Carter Harrison, Victor Leo Walker II and Gus Edwards, eds., *Black Theatre: Ritual Performance in the African Diaspora* (Philadelphia: Temple University Press, 2002), p. 390.

10. George Plimpton and Bonnie Lyons, 'The Art of Theater: Interview with August Wilson', *Paris Review* 14 (2005), p. 20.

11. Ed Bullins, 'An African Connection between the Plays of August Wilson and Ed Bullins – Based upon a Comparative Read of Ayi Kwei Armah's *Two Thousand Seasons*'. Paper presented at the First Annual Symposium on African American Theatre: August Wilson, held at North Carolina Agricultural and Technical State University on 14 October 1994. Ed Bullins was the first American playwright to write an extant seven-play cycle, which included four published plays: *In New England Winter* (1969), *In the Wine Time* (1969), *The Duplex* (1971) and *The Fabulous Miss Marie* (1974). See my *Ed Bullins: A Literary Biography* (Detroit: Wayne State University Press, 1997) for an analysis of the unpublished plays in the cycle: 'Home Boy' (1976), 'Daddy' (1977) and 'Boy x Man' (1995). Only Eugene O'Neill, prior to Bullins, had written a longer cycle (nine), but he destroyed all but one manuscript, *A Touch of the Poet* (1957).

12. Wole Soyinka, *Myth, Literature and the African World* (New York: Cambridge University Press, 1976), p. 112.

13. Ayi Kwei Armah, *Two Thousand Seasons* (Portsmouth, NH: Heinemann, 1979), pp. xiv, 1.

14. See Spike Lee, *Jim Brown: All-American* (New York, Home Box Office Video, 2003).

15. Cornelia Walker Bailey with Christena Bledsoe, *God, Dr. Buzzard, and the Bolito Man: A Saltwater Geechee Talks About Life on Sapelo Island, Georgia* (New York: Anchor Books, 2000), pp. 280–1.

16. Wilson's extemporaneous comments were transcribed by the Heinz Centre. The remarks can be found at www.heinzawards.net/speechDetail. asp?speech ID=59.

17. John Lahr, chapter 2, 'Been here and gone', p. 38.

18. I am indebted to Dr Vernell Lillie, director of the Kuntu Repertory Theatre at the University of Pittsburgh, for giving the actor Stephen McKinley Henderson and me on 7 June 2006 a four-and-a-half-hour lecture/tour of the August Wilson-Rob Penny stomping grounds in Pittsburgh. We are also grateful to bluesman Leroy Wofford for treating us to a classic black breakfast at the L & M restaurant in Homewood, a Wilson hangout.

19. August Wilson, cited in Lahr, chapter 2, 'Been here and gone', p. 40.

20. August Wilson, *The Ground On Which I Stand* (New York: Theatre Communications Group, 2001), pp. 12–13.

21. *Ibid.*, p. 21.

22. Soyinka, *Myth, Literature*, pp. 114–15.

23. *Ibid.*

24. See Calvin Tomkins, 'Profiles: Putting Something over Something Else', *New Yorker*, 28 November 1977, pp. 53–77.

25. Shannon, *Dramatic Vision*, p. 125.

26. Peter Gottlieb, *Making Their Own Way: Southern Blacks' Migration to Pittsburgh, 1916–30* (Chicago: University of Illinois Press, 1997), p. 65.

27. W. C. Handy, *Father of the Blues* (New York: Collier Books, 1941), pp. 151–2.

28. *Ibid.*

29. August Wilson, *Joe Turner's Come and Gone* (New York: New American Library, 1988), p. 14. Further quotations will be cited parenthetically in the text.

30. Onuora Ossie Enekwe, *Igbo Masks: The Oneness of Ritual and Theatre* (Lagos: Federal Ministry of Information and Culture, 1987), p. 48.
31. August Wilson, *Jitney* (New York: The Overlook Press, 2001), p. 36.
32. Paul Carter Harrison, *Kuntu Drama: Plays of the African Continuum* (New York: Grove Press, 1982), p. 19.
33. Soyinka, *Myth, Literature*, p. 91.
34. I am indebted to my brother, Deacon Joseph McNeil Hay, chair of the Deacon's board at Beulah Baptist Church in Augusta, Georgia, for his insights about the apostle Paul.
35. Sandra G. Shannon and Dana A. Williams, 'A Conversation with August Wilson', in Shannon and Williams, *August Wilson and Black Aesthetics* (New York: Palgrave Macmillan, 2004), p. 189.
36. *Ibid*, p. 194.
37. John T. McCartney, *Black Power Ideologies: An Essay in African-American Political Thought* (Philadelphia: Temple University Press, 1992), p. 186.
38. Harry J. Elam, Jr., 'August Wilson's Women', in Alan Nadel, ed., *May All Your Fences Have Gates* (Iowa City: University of Iowa Press, 1994), p. 173.
39. Clayton Riley, 'Review of *Amen Corner*', *Liberator* (May 1965), p. 26.
40. Wilson must have researched widely to find a children's song with lyrics so appropriate for his theme: 'I went downtown/To get my grip/I came back home/Just a pullin the skiff./I went upstairs/To make my bed/I made a mistake/And I bumped my head/Just a pullin the skiff./I went downstairs/To milk the cow/I made a mistake/And I milked the sow/Just a pullin the skiff. Tomorrow, tomorrow/Tomorrow never come/The marrow the marrow/The marrow in the bone' (Wilson, *Joe Turner*, pp. 26–7). Wilson got the song from a John A. Lomax recording made in Drew, Mississippi, on 24 October 1940. The song, sung by the ten-year-old Ora Dell Graham, is on *A Treasury of Library of Congress Field Recordings*, selected and annotated by Stephen Wade (Cambridge, MA: Rounder DC 1500, 1997).
41. Lloyd Richards, cited in Shannon, *Dramatic Vision*, p. 133.

7

ALAN NADEL

Ma Rainey's Black Bottom: cutting the historical record, dramatizing a blues CD

Ma Rainey's Black Bottom (1984), Kim Pereira points out,

> resembles a jazz composition . . . [each musician's story at the outset] is like a solo performance in a jazz quartet that, though it possesses the characteristics of a 'set piece', is related to the major themes on an imagistic and emotional level . . . As the play moves along easily, its improvisatory cadences contain ever-quickening impulses that gather force toward a cataclysmic ending, like a shattering crescendo.[1]

Pereira's description, however, applies not only to *Ma Rainey* but, more generally, to Wilson's approach to drama. As I have written elsewhere, because his plays resemble

> a jazz set as much as they do a Euro-American play, we are confronted not with protagonist and antagonists, but rather with the tension of interpretive energy, as a community of players play off one another's solos. If they tend at times to play variations on recognizable themes, the synergy of the interaction creates unexpected and exciting results rather as in a piece by Duke Ellington or John Coltrane.[2]

Nor is it only a matter of style. Wilson's use of the blues instantiates an alternative form of historiography so that a blues rendition can have the same status for African American culture as a history text. 'The thing about the blues', Wilson has said, 'is that there's an entire philosophical system at work. And whatever you want to know about the black experience in America is contained in the blues.'[3] If Wilson's drama is fundamentally structured by blues performance, his ten-play cycle can be thought of as a record (or CD) album that orchestrates and arranges the American twentieth century as ten versions of African American blues, played by a combo with one to three singers.

The early Wilson combo includes the warrior, the historian, the earnest young man, the trickster, the pragmatist and the man-not-quite-right-in-the-head. With the addition, in *Joe Turner's Come and Gone* (1986), of the magician/healer and a spectrum of female soloists, the full array of Wilson's styles and arrangements becomes evident, providing a blues history and a history of the blues that reconciles the styles of African American blues to the events and traditions that produced them. At the same time, the variegated forms of the blues delimit the possibilities for reconfiguring the community produced by those historical and aesthetic conditions.

From this perspective, *Ma Rainey's Black Bottom* becomes the paradigmatic play in the Wilson canon, by openly identifying his dramatic structure with the arrangements of a blues band, and the kinds of characters instrumental in those arrangements. The play takes place during an afternoon recording session in 1927. First, three members of Ma Rainey's band, Toledo, Cutler and Slow Drag, arrive, then the fourth, Levee, a belligerent, cocky trumpeter who is proud of his expensive new shoes and what he thinks may be the possibility of securing a recording contract. Eventually, Ma Rainey arrives with her friend Dussie Mae and her stuttering nephew Sylvester. The recording session is delayed several times while Ma Rainey exerts her prerogatives and the members of the band verbally spar with one another. After the session and the resolution of a dispute over payment, Levee learns that instead of offering him a contract the recording studio will simply buy the rights to his songs at five dollars apiece. When Toledo accidentally steps on Levee's new shoes, that trivial incident becomes the focus for Levee's frustration, disappointment, and rejection. In a furious and self-defeating attempt to assert his self-worth, he stabs Toledo fatally. Thus the play ends in a tragedy that never finds its way out of the rehearsal room and on to the stage of history. In a very literal way, the band becomes the embodiment of the blues.

While not all Wilson's plays end in tragic deaths, in *Ma Rainey's Black Bottom*, as in all his plays, his blues orchestrations reconfigure the notes, the time and the key of the dominant society to produce a blues variation. Dependent on orchestration rather than crisis and resolution, the play establishes the community as the locus of dramatic action, recognizing that a community constitutes a critical mass that is not a fixed unit or a painted backdrop on the stage of history. For Wilson, a community is an ever-changing set or series of arrangements and rearrangements of melody and time.

For the record

In 1982, after the Eugene O'Neill Theatre Centre's Playwrights Conference workshopped *Ma Rainey's Black Bottom*, Wilson was offered $25,000 to take the play to Broadway. At the time, since he was still making only $88 a week as a cook, the offer seemed tempting compared with Lloyd Richards's more modest offer to produce the play at the Yale Repertory Theatre. The

Broadway contract, however, gave control of the script to the producers, who could bring in other writers and turn the play into a musical. When Wilson complained, one producer told him, 'It doesn't matter what the contract says . . . A lot of things in this business are done on faith', to which Wilson responded, 'Okay – if it doesn't matter what the contract says, let's make it say what I want it to say.'[4] This ended the negotiations and brought Wilson back to Richards, who did produce the play at Yale before taking it to Broadway.

The fact that history (as this anecdote illustrates) might have been very different informs all of Wilson's works, which manifest an acute awareness of the plasticity of the official record. Consider, for example, the role in *Fences* (1985) of the home run records 'earned' by white baseball players who did not have to face black pitchers, the historical record inscribed on the surface of the piano in *The Piano Lesson* (1987), the criminal records of so many of Wilson's characters, including Floyd Barton, Troy Maxson, Herald Loomis, Sterling Johnson, Lymon and Levee. Records, Wilson makes clear, are not facts but interpretations. In *The Piano Lesson*, for example, Lymon had been given an exorbitant fine for not working, so he fled, rather than allow that fine to turn him into an indentured servant. Whereas his official criminal record means that he is a fugitive from justice, from his and from Boy Willie's perspective it means that he is a fugitive from injustice. The meaning of Lymon's criminal record, in other words, is determined by the record keepers; history, as I have argued elsewhere, belongs to whoever owns the erasers.[5]

This point is made early in *Ma Rainey's Black Bottom* when Toledo wins a bet with Levee about the spelling of the word 'music' but cannot collect because everyone else is illiterate. 'I done won the dollar,' he states, in a way that articulates the problem that Troy Maxson has with baseball records, which is the quintessential problem of black history: 'But if don't nobody know but me, how am I gonna prove it to you?'[6] The problem of history, in other words, is how the record is produced, whose voices it includes, what arrangements it uses, and who has the rights to control its distribution and accrue its revenues. Although the historical record is being cut and recut in all Wilson's plays, that process provides the explicit content of *Ma Rainey*. If, as many have noted, the play is about recording the blues,[7] it is also about versions of the blues and the conditions that produce them.

Changing the notes

For Wilson, the blues thus comprise an alternative history encoding the African American experience ignored by official historical documentation.

As Ma Rainey points out, 'White folks don't understand the blues. They hear it come out, but they don't know how it got there. They don't understand that's life's way of talking' (82). 'Life's way of talking', of course, is a vernacular name for history, a vernacular name for vernacular history, and Ma Rainey is acutely aware that she does the work of the historiographer: 'This be an empty world without the blues. I take that emptiness and try to fill it up with something' (83). Exactly because she regards the blues as history, Ma Rainey understands that she is necessarily as much their inheritor as their producer. 'They say I started it,' she explains, 'but I didn't. I just helped it out' (83).

In this moment she is footnoting herself as purveyor of history in a play replete with historical footnotes. Toledo, the piano player – who is the only literate member of the band – constantly attempts to create historical contexts. When the bass player, Slow Drag, and the guitarist, Cutler, bond through naming, he explains that they are performing an African ancestral retention ritual, a bond of kinship. Calling attention to the diasporic aspects of African American culture, he insists, 'We done sold Africa for the price of tomatoes' (94). Toledo's role in the band, in other words, is to supply the notes, not just the melody; he retrieves the historical circumstances that have brought Ma Rainey, her band and her entourage to this time and this place.

The tragedy *Ma Rainey* foregrounds, however, is that although the band can supply the notes, none of them, not even Ma Rainey at the peak of her power, can control the record. For the record to be produced, in fact, Ma Rainey must sign away her voice. The play thus pivots around the historical moment when her song, in its unique moment of production, becomes the property of the white company. As the play represents it, that moment comes in such a way as to reduce 'art' to 'labour' in that Ma Rainey is paid a fee for the session rather than receiving contractual residuals. This effacement of her labour, by reducing it to *merely* labour, makes her song ahistorical. In other words, it is the history of its own production. The unavoidable self-consciousness with which Ma Rainey and her band participate in this moment of erasure renders that moment an unmistakable site for the blues.

Thus Wilson's conflict with the Broadway producer over the meaning of the contract to produce *Ma Rainey's Black Bottom* replicated the conflict in the play between establishing a recording of Ma Rainey's art and transferring the rights from the maker of the music to the producers of the recording. In both instances the official record is circumscribed by the historical conditions that give it meaning, that is, that multiply its meanings. In the short term, Ma Rainey's authority prevails because nothing can progress until she makes the recording and until she records her signature relinquishing her rights to that recording. In that interim, her song and signature comprise a form of extortion, empowering her to control the music's orchestration and even to make the studio accommodate her stuttering nephew, who, she insists, must not only introduce her but also be paid for his performance commensurate with the amount paid to the other members of the band.

In the long run, however, the contract will be more powerful than the signatory, and the control of the physical record will merge with the control of the artistic record and the historical record. In that process the rest of the play's events will be omitted so that the events and the black people who enact them will be what Toledo calls 'leftovers':

> The colored man is the leftovers. Now, what's the colored man gonna do with himself? That's what we waiting to find out. But first we gotta know we the leftovers. Now, who knows that? You find me a nigger that knows that and I'll turn any whichway you want me to . . . The problem ain't the white man. The white man knows you just a leftover. 'Cause he the one that done the eating and he know what he done ate. But we don't know that we been took and made history out of. (58)

In this sense *Ma Rainey's Black Bottom* not only explicitly articulates the position of the historical subject in general, and of the African American historical subject in particular, but also plays out the fate of the leftovers in direct contrast to those who make and keep the records. Inverting the hierarchy of power that official history demands, Wilson's play foregrounds those most marginalized by the process, playing out an arrangement in the time measure of those in the margins.

The only performance of the song 'Black Bottom' that the audience hears, moreover, is the *un*official version, because the play skips the actual recording session, moving directly from the failed attempts to the moment when the lights come up in the studio as the 'the last bars of the last song of the session are dying out' (100). Wilson intentionally dramatizes what preceded and followed the dying of the music, that is, everything the session did not resolve: the conflict over Ma Rainey's withheld signature, over the band's delayed payment, over Levee's delayed rejection first by Ma Rainey and then by the studio, and finally the delayed confrontation between Toledo and Levee, ostensibly over Toledo's stepping on Levee's shoes, but more basically about the accuracy of Toledo's sense of history as the instrument that steps on Levee's aspirations. In this sense the play culminates in the moments when Levee has run out of time, when Toledo's time is up, and when Ma Rainey's time has passed.

Changing the tempo

From both a musical and a historical perspective, therefore, it is not surprising that so much of *Ma Rainey's Black Bottom* deals with time and who controls it. Sandra G. Shannon and Sandra Adell have both noted the importance of waiting in the play.[8] For Shannon, the waiting is crucial to the play's structural tensions. It gives meaning to the multiple conclusions of the play: the completion of the session, the completion of the compensation negotiations, the recording of Ma Rainey's signature, the culmination of Levee's employment in Ma Rainey's band, the (unsatisfactory) conclusion of Levee's negotiation with Sturdivant to record his own songs in his own style, the conclusion of Toledo's life at the point of Levee's knife. For Adell, the waiting comprises the presence of Ma Rainey, a presence that is at odds with the action of the play, in that the recording session is precisely designed to replace the real woman with a mechanical reproduction. Paradoxically, Wilson creates a play in which the very vibrancy of the central character serves to underscore the process of her elimination as her talent, her cultural truth, is appropriated by a white world which understands little and cares less about her or the world she embodies and expresses.

When the play opens, two white men, Ma Rainey's agent, Irvin, and the director of the recording studio, Sturdyvant, are preparing for the session and implicitly preparing the audience for the problems they foresee with Ma Rainey and the future of her style of blues. Even before the band arrives, Sturdyvant tells Ma Rainey's manager that he is worried Ma Rainey will not be on time, that the session will take too long. Because Sturdyvant thinks that Ma Rainey wastes his time, the only way she can refute him is to make him wait for her, in other words to demonstrate that, despite his claims to the contrary, he thinks her recordings are worth the time it takes.

This is the first of numerous occasions in which scenes of waiting organize the time. Next, the four members of the band arrive and kill time while they wait for Ma Rainey who, it turns out, has been detained by a policeman after a melee following a car accident. The band then waits for Irvin to cajole (and bribe) the officer; then they wait in the band room to rehearse. At the same time, Ma Rainey waits in the studio to begin the recording session. More waiting is necessary, however, while Ma Rainey's disputes the song list and the arrangements. Not until the second act, in fact, does the session actually start, but this turns into a false start because Ma Rainey insists that, despite his stutter, her nephew, Sylvester, introduce the song 'Black Bottom', and, when he fails to do so without faltering, she makes everyone wait again while Sylvester and the bassist, Slow Drag, go out to get her a Coca-Cola. As Ma

Rainey waits for her coke, and the producers, the band and the audience wait for Ma Rainey, the trumpeter, Levee, seduces Ma Rainey's friend Dussie Mae in the band room. Even after the coke arrives, however, and the recording session resumes, we wait through several more starts before Sylvester can complete the brief introduction without stumbling on the words.

This dispute over time is manifest not only in the procrastination effected by Ma Rainey's refusing to record until someone buys her a bottle of coca-cola, but also by Sylvester, who challenges authorized time in several ways. As a stutterer, he speaks his words according to his own time and rhythm, not those of his audience. Each time he stutters in the introduction, moreover, means one more time that the recording has to be made. It also means additional delays while the band or the producers argue over whether Sylvester can be used on the record. 'He don't stutter all the time,' Ma Rainey insists, to which Irvin replies, 'Ma, we don't have time' (74).

Irvin, of course, is right. People *do not* have time; time has them and they make of that condition what they can. To put it another way, the historical record is what people make out of our captivity by time. Within the parameters of that captivity, everyone is a slave, and slavery thus is the definitive historical condition. From this perspective, Toledo is wrong: the black man is not the leftover but the quintessence. Thus Ma Rainey states an irrefutable truth when she responds to Irvin, 'If you wanna make a record, you gonna find time' (74).

But even after Sylvester finally makes the introduction smoothly and we hear Ma Rainey sing *her* song according to *her* arrangement, the producers discover that, because of a mechanical failure, they have to start again. If Sturdyvant and Irvin have to make time for Ma Rainey, she has to make time for the recording because the mechanical device wields more authority over the song than she does, reducing her excessive displays of power to a meaningless performance in the face of the official record and all its attendant apparatus.

Learning the blues

Because the play is about people who are waiting for their lives to be put on the record, only to find out that the record will render those lives superfluous, it is structured around the ways that people tell the stories of their lives while they are waiting for the significant moments. In this sense, it can be viewed as an initiation rite, one which focuses especially on Levee, the warrior turned killer, and Toledo, the historian reduced to fatal victim.

Levee has, as Wilson puts it, a warrior spirit, that is, he refuses to accept the limitations society imposes. Because, for African Americans, this constitutes rejection not just of personal circumstances but of history itself, his assault on Toledo is, in one sense, inevitable and, in another sense, self-defeating. Levee, Wilson points out, 'does a tremendous disservice to blacks by killing Toledo, because he's killing the only one who can read, he's killing the intellectual in the group. That's a loss we have to make up . . . It's a progression towards the wrong target, but I salute [Levee's] willingness to battle, even to death.'[9] What is at stake, in many ways, is change which is simultaneously necessary and threatening. These characters and their music are the carriers of the past, and in that sense cultural historians, recorders of past sufferings and the transmutation of those sufferings into art. Yet they are also aware that the times are changing and that certain changes are necessary not simply for their survival but for their growth. It is the tension between those conflicting necessities that constitutes Wilson's drama as it was those tensions that he registered in the world he set himself to capture.

In *Ma Rainey's Black Bottom*, there is a tension between Ma Rainey's voice and those who record it, as there is a tension between Levee's materialism and Toledo's literacy, and we become aware of this, and of the centrality of change as an issue, even before Ma Rainey and her entourage arrive or Levee and Toledo engage in an argument. When Levee complains about changes in the rehearsal room, Toledo notes that everything is changing all the time, to which Levee responds, 'I ain't talking about no skin and air. I'm talking about something I can see!' (24). In a sense both men have a vested interest in the given, in the world that has shaped them and the music they play, but they also have an interest in change, their social and artistic positions putting them in thrall to the white world. It is precisely this paradox that drives the play. Levee wants to change his music, and thereby his life, but can do so only by undermining Ma Rainey's authority and appealing to the white record producers. As Toledo warns him, 'As long as the colored man look to white folks to put the crown on what he say . . . as long as he looks to white folks for approval . . . then he's never gonna find out who he is and what he's about. He's gonna find out what white folks want him to be about' (37).

The inevitable collision between Levee and Toledo results from a musical, historical and ontological conflict about the nature of change, but they are also at odds when it comes to language, Toledo favouring metaphor, Levee the immediate, the material. When Toledo remarks to Levee, 'Things change. The air and everything. Now you gonna say you was saying it. You gonna fit two propositions on the same track . . . run them into each other, and because they crash, you gonna say it's the same train' Levee replies, 'Now the nigger talking about trains! We done went from the air to the skin to the door . . . and now trains' (25).

One of the play's ironies, though, lies in the fact that however much of a materialist he seems to be, Levee, too, sees the world in symbolic terms. He has bought a pair of new shoes, shoes that will prove the source of contention between himself and Toledo, a seemingly trivial dispute which nonetheless leads to Toledo's murder. These shoes have come to be a sign of Levee's ambition, a mark of his self-esteem, a symbol of his hope for an expansive future in which his life will be transformed. When Toledo accidentally scuffs them, it is a minor incident but one, to Levee, which seems to bear on his sense of himself. An assault on his property is an attack on himself, and property, in its various guises, turns out to be crucial in *Ma Rainey's Black Bottom*. Beyond that, indeed, it has also been crucial to the African American experience, to a people who were themselves once regarded as property and whose access to property was subsequently curtailed, not least because property rights have always been intertwined with human rights. Wilson recalled the story of his mother's winning a new washing machine by phoning in the correct answer in a radio give-away competition. 'When they found out she was black, they wanted to give her a certificate to go to the Salvation Army where she could go down and get a used washing machine.' Refusing the used machine, she got no prize at all, but 'she didn't want no used washing machine because she was due a brand new machine'.[10] Forced to choose, Wilson's mother showed that she considered the figurative value of her human rights more important than tangible property.

This is the same struggle enacted by Ma Rainey as she deals with efforts to control her art and her life and, through both, the history which that art and that life embodied. No matter how she asserts her rights, however, in the end she cannot prevent herself becoming a commodity for sale in a competitive market that has distant echoes of the slave auction block, except that the slave had no voice and she does. To be sure, on one level that voice is appropriated but on another it captures all those conflicting emotions that we see as the various musicians come together to create an art which finally resists co-option. To the white record company, she is property and her music no more nor less than a piece of entertainment. For Wilson, she contains and expresses the history of the African American, a history which provides the context for music rooted in the black community. Her song is her life as it is the life of that community, often divided in its vision of the future but united in a common sensibility and apprehension of the past.

Wilson's characters figuratively form a band throughout his cycle in the same way that they do literally in *Ma Rainey's Black Bottom*. The musicians are individuals, with their own distinctive ways of playing, their own voices, their own dreams, and there are moments in which they dominate the stage, play their solos. But when they play together, no matter how briefly, they express what is shared rather than what divides and in the end, as in *Ma Rainey'*, it is the black musicians, real and symbolic, not the whites who exploit them, who demand and receive his and our attention.

The pragmatist, the earnest neophyte, the trickster, the magician, the madman, the maternal nurturer, the independent woman, and the dependent woman,[11] each discrete, with their own personal histories, needs, urgencies, all come together to express a community which is an expression of history but which is something more than a simple product of that history. In *Ma Rainey's Black Bottom*, Wilson orchestrates those individual artists as he does in all ten of the plays in his cycle. In *Ma Rainey* the music is literal, as it is on occasion in some of the other plays. But, literal or symbolic, what he creates is a dramatic blues, in doing so laying explicit claim to the significance of lives excluded from the American Dream but not from their own dreams of becoming. Each voice is clear and distinctive but, taken together, they tell a story of the struggles, defeats and victories which have defined the experiences of those invited to live on the margins of American life but who have done so much more than merely survive.

NOTES

1. Kim Pereira, *August Wilson and the African American Odyssey* (Champaign-Urbana: University of Illinois Press, 1995), p. 10.
2. Alan Nadel, ed., *May All Your Fences Have Gates: Essays on the Drama of August Wilson* (Iowa City: University of Iowa Press, 1994), p. 5.
3. Jackson R. Bryer and Mary C. Hartig, eds., *Conversations with August Wilson* (Jackson: University of Mississippi Press, 2006), p. 58.
4. *Ibid.*, p. 135.
5. Alan Nadel, *Invisible Criticism: Ralph Ellison and the American Canon* (Iowa City: University of Iowa Press, 1988), p. xiii.
6. August Wilson, *Ma Rainey's Black Bottom* (New York: Plume Books, 1985), p. 28. Further quotations will be cited parenthetically in the text.
7. See Eileen Crawford ('The B$^\flat$ Burden: The Invisibility of Ma Rainey's Black Bottom', in Marilyn Elkins, ed., *August Wilson: A Casebook* (New York: Garland, 1994), pp. 31–48); Harry J. Elam, Jr., *The Past as Present in the Drama of August Wilson* (Ann Arbor: University of Michigan Press, 2004); Pererra, *August Wilson and the African American Odyssey*; John Timpane, 'Filling the Time: Reading History in the Drama of August Wilson', in Nadel, ed., *May All Your Fences Have Gates*, pp. 67–85; and Craig Werner, 'August Wilson's Burden: The Function of Neo-Classical Jazz', in Nadel, ed., *May All Your Fences Have Gates*, pp. 21–50.
8. Sandra G. Shannon, 'The Long Wait: August Wilson's *Ma Rainey's Black Bottom*', *Black American Literature Forum* 25:1 (1991), pp. 135–46, and Sandra Adell, 'Speaking of Ma Rainey/Talking about the Blues', in Nadel, ed., *May All Your Fences Have Gates*, pp. 51–66.

9. Bryer and Hartig, eds., *Conversations*, p. 78.
10. *Ibid.*, p. 47.
11. I do not mean to suggest that Wilson reuses the same characters from play to play or that these types comprise rigid categories. I am arguing, in fact, exactly the opposite. These types do not represent themes but rather instruments arranged and rearranged to play the blues in its infinite variations.

8

FELICIA HARDISON LONDRÉ

A piano and its history: family and transcending family

What time or period is the setting for *The Piano Lesson* (1987)? That was the first question asked by the late great Chinese actor and director Ying Ruocheng (1921–2003) after he read the play in 1991.[1] The question surprises those who know that each play in August Wilson's ten-play cycle depicting African American experience is set in a different decade of the twentieth century. If the historical period is part of the basic concept underlying each play, the temporal setting should be evident. Indeed, a stage production communicates the time of the action to the spectator almost immediately through period-specific details like the appliances in the kitchen and the dresses the women wear. Wilson's printed text, however, is curiously reticent in conveying such information. The reader of the play does have an advantage over the theatre spectator. He or she can pause and calculate, as Ying eventually did, using the data woven into Doaker's story about the piano. Doaker's older brother, Boy Charles, 'would have been fifty-seven if he had lived. He died in 1911 when he was thirty-one years old.'[2] If the action of the play occurs twenty-six years after 1911, it must be 1936 or 1937.

A reference to 1930s America usually conjures images of the Great Depression: breadlines, Hoovervilles, the Dust Bowl, WPA projects. That Wilson sets his play in the latter part of the decade and hoists none of those cultural flags is surely deliberate. The economic depression of the 1930s hit hardest those who had bought into the prosperity of the 1920s, but African Americans – not having experienced much, if any, of that prosperity – moved into the 1930s under already familiar financial constraints. The view from inside the Charles home in Pittsburgh is one of cultural continuity; there is no reason for them to talk about changes that affect people outside their culture.

Apart from Doaker's story supplying the 1911 touchstone, the play's allusions hinting at historical context may be briefly summarized: the settlement house where Maretha gets extra schooling; Doaker's railroad work; coffee that costs a nickel; the boogie-woogie that Boy Willie plays on the piano; the

Gulf building, a 'skyscraper' with steel elevator cables in downtown Pittsburgh; aeroplanes; Wining Boy's having called on the Ghosts of the Yellow Dog in July 1930; picture shows with 'speakers outside on the sidewalk'; and the need to watch for cars when crossing the street.[3] For those who know the history of the blues, the songs may serve as additional clues. Some allusions are oblique but unerring, like the fact that Wining Boy has been living in Kansas City, which was indeed wide open for black musicians in the 1930s.

If *The Piano Lesson* was written as part of a history cycle, why would an initial reading create the impression that some obvious contextual markers are missing? The answer may lie in Wilson's comment in an interview with Kim Powers: 'The importance of history to me is simply to find out who you are and where you've been. It becomes doubly important if someone else has been writing your history.'[4] In fact, there is plenty of history in *The Piano Lesson*; it is simply not the kind of history we learn in school. Each major character in the play is a repository of family and community history, and these histories augment one another, sometimes conflicting in the details, but collectively preserving through storytelling an awareness of elements of the past that contributed to the lives they are presently living.

The action begins with the pre-dawn arrival of Boy Willie and his friend Lymon at the Pittsburgh home of Boy Willie's sister Berniece and his uncle Doaker. They have a truckload of watermelons from Mississippi to sell, after which Lymon plans to start a new life in the northern city, but Boy Willie wants to return home and buy the land that is up for sale because the owner, James Sutter, had fallen down his well and died three weeks earlier. The point of contention throughout the play is that Boy Willie needs to sell the carved piano from Berniece's parlour and use his share of the cash – along with his savings and the watermelon money – to buy the land that he wants to farm, but Berniece believes that the piano should be kept in the family. The hostilities between brother and sister are complicated by Berniece's blaming him for the circumstances that led to the death of her husband and by the appearance of the ghost of Sutter. Their uncle Doaker is forced into the role of mediator. The arrival of Doaker's brother Wining Boy puts the household into a family reunion mode with ghost stories and other reminiscences as a backdrop to the ongoing contest of wills between brother and sister.

Perhaps the most significant historical allusion is 'back to slavery time' in one of Doaker's stories (42). The characters in the play are only seventy-two years away from slavery. Their grandparents – and even a parent – had been enslaved, and the stories told by parents and grandparents survive in the living memories of Berniece and Boy Willie and their uncle Doaker. From the various stories recounted, we can piece together parallel histories of two families, one white, one black. The white Sutter family is traced back to the slaveowner Robert Sutter who acquired the piano for his wife, Miss Ophelia, in exchange for two slaves. That would have been in the early 1860s. Robert Sutter was the grandfather of James Sutter whose ghost now haunts the black family. Significantly, while this history covers three generations of white Sutters, the black Charles family has an oral history spanning six generations. Their history can be traced back to the first Boy Charles, who married Mama Esther and fathered Willie Boy. It was Willie Boy who carved the family history into the piano after Willie Boy's wife Berniece and their nine-year-old son were traded away to a man named Joel Nolander from Georgia. Willie Boy's son was emancipated and returned to Mississippi where he became the "daddy" of three boys: Boy Charles, Wining Boy and Doaker. The eldest, Boy Charles, married Mama Ola and had two children, Berniece and Boy Willie. Berniece's eleven-year-old daughter Maretha, by her late husband Crawley, is thus the sixth generation of the Charles family in this history.

With the first three generations represented in the carving on the piano, that piano stands as an objective correlative of a family history marked by blood and tears. Maretha practises on the piano every day yet knows nothing of its story. The images carved on it must be supplemented by the words of the storyteller in order for those carved portraits to become meaningful. The family history recorded on the piano is incomplete. Objectively, one must admit that as a permanent record of family history the piano's importance is minimal.

Yet the piano is the object of contention in a sibling rivalry so serious that Berniece fetches a gun to stop Boy Willie taking it, while he knowingly risks being shot rather than give it up. Both siblings recognize that family history is part and parcel of that piano. Where they differ so acrimoniously is over how the historical past should be allowed or used to impact on the present. As Wilson expressed it, 'What do you do with your legacy? How do you best put it to use?'[5]

By any democratic definition of property rights, the piano has always belonged to the Sutter family. But for Berniece that piano was unequivocally purchased from the Sutters by suffering. She recalls her Mama Ola's seventeen years of daily rubbing the piano with her own blood and tears to polish it (52). While carved family portraits decorate the piano's exterior, the horrors of slavery are symbolically contained within. Although Berniece refuses to play the piano because she does not want to wake the spirits of her tormented ancestors, she senses that it would be a betrayal to sell off a possession for which so much family blood was shed.

For Boy Willie, the piano's value is purely pragmatic. If Berniece were using the piano to give lessons and generate income, he would be happy to have it stay in the family. Since she does not play it, it stands in the living room like a mere 'piece of wood' (50) and it could be better used being sold to provide money to put towards building his future. Just as the first Boy Charles was killed for stealing the piano from the Sutter home and Crawley was killed for stealing some wood to sell, so Boy Willie could be killed for taking 'that piece of wood' from his sister's house. The irony is that in order to get the money for the piano that will enable him to realize his dream, Boy Willie must sell it to a white man.

For the white man, the piano has monetary value because the carvings raise it to the status of folk art. In that respect the piano is a manifestation of what Eric Lott has called 'love and theft': 'the quite explicit "borrowing" of black cultural materials for white dissemination'.[6] Pianos are European in origin and long associated with a wealth of European music literature. With black hands on the keyboard, the instrument produced a whole new world of musical material – blues, jazz, boogie-woogie – that was loved and appropriated or commodified by white musicians and entrepreneurs. Wining Boy's experience as a black musician is emblematic:

> 'Go to a place and they find out you play the piano, the first thing they want to do is give you a drink, find you a piano, and sit you right down. And that's where you gonna be for the next eight hours. They ain't gonna let you get up! . . . You can't do nothing else. All you know how to do is play that piano. Now, who am I? Am I me? Or am I the piano player?' (41).

Wining Boy's very sense of identity is threatened by the phenomenon of love and theft, while in a larger sense the intertwining black and white history bound up in the carved piano embraces all Americans in the legacy of slavery.

Boy Willie is not content to let the ghost of a descendant of slave owners affect his future. From his first entrance until the resolution of the play, he holds fast to his vision of how he wants to live a life of integrity and personal fulfilment. He repeatedly articulates his goal, which is clear and simple and, given his persistence, even possible. He wants to own and work the land on which his forebears slaved. He is not afraid of hard work as long as it involves the pride of ownership. To achieve economic independence by making a living on the very land to which his enslaved great-grandfather was bound is what Boy Willie envisions as a way of redeeming the history of the family. Selling off a wooden relic that has fallen into disuse seems to him a small sacrifice in return for honouring his ancestors through the realization of his dream.

Boy Willie's hunger for the land sounds almost visceral. Land is 'something under your feet. Land the only thing God ain't making no more of. You can always get you another piano. I'm talking about some land. What you get something out the ground from' (50). His repeated evocations of the land gather force throughout the action: 'If you got a piece of land you'll find everything else fall right into place. You can stand right up next to the white man and talk about the price of cotton' (92). One of Wilson's most effective dialogue devices is the orchestration of sequences in which the words 'piano' and 'land' are alternated. Sometimes the effect occurs subtly in the dialogue of several characters, as in the three lines when Doaker and Wining Boy question the viability of Willie Boy's plan: 'land . . . piano . . . land . . . land . . . piano . . . land' (36). The most remarkable sequence occurs in the dialogue between Boy Willie and Berniece that culminates in Boy Willie's 'aria' following his attempt, near the end of Act 1, to move the piano: 'piano . . . piano . . . land . . . piano . . . land . . . piano . . . land . . . land . . . piano . . . land . . . piano . . . piano . . . piano . . . piano . . . piano . . . piano . . . land . . . piano . . . piano . . . piano . . . land . . . piano . . . land . . . land . . . land . . . land . . . piano . . . piano' (50–1).

Boy Willie's dream of farming his own land also carries intertextual mean- ings that may provide some sense of historical context for *The Piano Les- son*. Most filmgoers know that *Gone With the Wind* (1939) was made in the 1930s, and they remember Gerald O'Hara's line that later echoes through Scarlett O'Hara's memory of her father: 'Why, land is the only thing in the world worth workin' for, worth fightin' for, worth dyin' for, because it's the only thing that lasts.'[7] Boy Willie understands the importance of the land in the same way, whereas Lymon, in contrast, is eager to avail himself of urban amenities like available women, picture shows, fancy shoes (despite their uncomfortably tight fit) and a silk suit. Avery and Wining Boy have already situated themselves in city life, but their ways hold no appeal for Boy Willie. Popular literature of the 1920s abounded with tropes of city versus country, and to an extent this carried over into the 1930s. Numerous plays and films depicted city dwellers who escape the urban rat race to rediscover the joy of living close to nature in a country cottage and raising chickens.[8] Indeed, Boy Willie envisions having chickens when he tells Maretha about his future farm (20). Even the theatregoer who initially apprehends Boy Willie's plan to buy land as analogous to Walter Lee Younger's ill-conceived plan to buy into a liquor store in Lorraine Hansberry's *A Raisin in the Sun* (1959) is likely to be won over by Boy Willie's awareness of obstacles to be overcome and his unswerving dedication.[9]

Both the piano and the land are associated with Sutter, a 340-pound man who died when he fell (or was pushed) into his well about three weeks before the action of *The Piano Lesson* begins. Although this Sutter never owned slaves, he represents that legacy, especially as his ghost is aroused largely in relation to the piano with carved portraits of his grandfather's slaves. We learn that Doaker saw Sutter's ghost seated at the piano about three days after his death. Four of the six manifestations of the presence of Sutter's ghost during the action relate to the piano: first, when Boy Willie talks of finding the man who will buy the piano (12), then when Boy Willie and Lymon start to move the piano in Act 1 and twice again in Act 2 (50, 82, 103). Although Boy Willie occasionally alludes to 'Sutter's land' as the land he plans to buy, Sutter's ghost does not seem to be at all concerned with the land; the piano is his concern. Sutter's brother is reportedly eager to sell the land to Boy Willie. Without slaves to work the land, white men are gravitating to the cities, leaving openings for African Americans like Boy Willie who are willing to take on the hard work of farming. The final apparition of Sutter's ghost is spurred neither by the piano nor by the land, but by Boy Willie's personal challenge to Sutter.

In the powerful sequence that ends the play, Boy Willie calls his challenge to Sutter's ghost and starts up the stairs, but is 'thrown back by the unseen force, which is choking him'. As soon as he has struggled free, he dashes up the stairs and is heard wrestling with Sutter's ghost, 'a life-and-death struggle' (106). Thrown back down the stairs again, Boy Willie rises and dashes up again. At that point Berniece begins to play the piano and to call upon the ancestors to help her brother.

A combination of factors may be signalled in the exorcism of Sutter's ghost from the house, beginning with the brother and sister at last overcoming their mutual antagonism and uniting in a joint effort to defeat their common foe. Boy Willie's physical combat with the ghost may be a belated coming into manhood for the thirty-year-old braggart; having taunted the ghost, he must now live up to his words with deeds. In Devon Boan's analysis Boy Willie's ascending the stairs – or 'going to the mountaintop' – to engage with Sutter is an act of self-realization by which he can square himself with his ancestors whether or not he ever owns the land.[10] Berniece's piano playing and ritual invocation have been analyzed in terms of African traditional religious practices[11] and call-and-response folk traditions.[12] While most critics see Avery's Christian blessing of the house as a futile gesture, certainly by comparison with African spiritualism, one might also posit the combined effect of Christian and African religious ritual as necessary for the defeat of racism as a legacy of slavery. At least subliminally, Boy Willie's showdown with Sutter's ghost recalls the biblical Jacob's wrestling all night with an angel and ultimately obtaining a blessing. Finally, there is the power of art to exorcise demons. As a musical instrument on which an artist has carved portraits, the piano necessarily becomes a symbol of art, and it is situated within a work of art: Wilson's play from which slavery's racist ghost takes a lesson.

The use of the ghost in *The Piano Lesson* was a particular point of interest to Ying in 1991, because ghosts are a staple of Chinese classical theatre. Whereas Chinese ghosts always seek vengeance, however, Sutter's ghost could not be seeking vengeance, in Ying's view, since 'the Sutters were to blame in this whole history of conflicts. They were the oppressors. I think most people would feel that.'[13] Vengeance could be a motive for the ghost's visitations if Boy Willie did indeed push Sutter into the well, as Berniece believes, but that view would belie the epic sweep of what happens in this play. Again, the key concept is 'history': a whole history of conflicts. Wilson himself addressed the point in a 1991 interview with Sandra G. Shannon: 'The idea of ghosts and the idea of supernatural phenomena in black American life is a very real phenomenon that is quite different from . . . what, in essence, may be an accusatory play in which you simply come back to accuse someone for murdering you.'[14]

The audience of *The Piano Lesson* never sees Sutter's ghost, but several characters do see it and hear it. They describe what they saw in very specific terms. Yet a ghost is presumably incorporeal. How does one grapple physically with a ghost? The struggle between Boy Willie and Sutter's ghost is not seen by the audience, but the sounds of the struggle are 'heard from upstairs' (106). Whatever may be happening up there, we know that a ghost cannot be knocked out. To Ying, Boy Willie's fight with Sutter's ghost could be emblematic of black frustration, grappling with something that most people do not see at all. Since slavery is no longer real, the struggle to overcome its legacy is like wrestling with a ghost. The scar is deep, but there is no closure.[15]

Although the television miniseries based upon Alex Haley's *Roots* (1976) had not been publicly broadcast in China by 1991, there were so many copies in circulation that *Roots* had a formative effect on Chinese people's understanding of race relations in the United States.[16] A Chinese person reading or seeing *The Piano Lesson* would readily side with the 'fighter' Boy Willie as opposed to the 'conformist' Berniece.[17] But the introduction of the ghost takes the play to another level, according to Ying, beyond the Marxist doctrine that privileges struggle over acquiescence. Now the fighter and the conformist both face the loss of identity and tradition. The ghost forces an awareness that would not have been possible if the play had been written in 1937. 'It needed all the history in between, the healing of the wounds, racial hatred and antagonism. It took a world war. It took people like Martin Luther King [and] the whole sixties, and now we see the problems in another light. You cannot solve the problems like a fighter, by shooting all the Ku Klux Klan, or in the conformist way, by turning all blacks into middle-class professionals. The important thing is the piano that cannot be chopped in two.'[18]

The late twentieth-century Chinese historical understanding that is implicit in Ying's remarks may be seen as a dialectic, tracing the interplay of opposing forces. Embodying thesis and antithesis, Boy Willie and Berniece finally achieve synthesis, and the piano will not be chopped in half, as Boy Willie had threatened. Ying's original interest in finding some historical marker that would pinpoint the period of the play's action is emblematic of a Western sense of history (with which Ying was also fully imbued) that chronicles events in linear progression, often correlating them to external data. A third type of historical sensibility, the one most applicable in *The Piano Lesson*, derives from an African awareness of what Jay Wright has called 'the communal significance of experience'.[19] The spiritual element permeates a vast web of interrelationships, encompassing the animate and the inanimate, and this is why the piano – that 'piece of wood' – can harbour spirits. The African sense of history emphasizes 'continuity of experience' that is often cyclical,[20] and, like black storytelling and song, involves repetitions, variations, polyrhythm and musical vamps.

The all-embracing nature of the black aesthetic allows for apparent digressions like Doaker's monologue about 'trains going every whichaway' (19). The fact that his story seemingly has no point is exactly the point; life is not about the destination but the continuity, even with its unplanned detours. Similarly, the truck that keeps breaking down injects the unplanned into the plan. The play's earliest character note about Boy Willie is spoken by Lymon with reference to the truck: 'Boy Willie have his door open and be ready to jump when that happens' (3), and it turns out to be a false pointer. It sets up the audience to view Boy Willie as Berniece does, as an irresponsible and disruptive force. Boy Willie's gradual earning of the spectator's respect is dramaturgically unerring.

All the little stories within the larger story intertwine and merge into the whole. Citing the black storyteller's 'resistance to static exposition and fixity of conclusion', Paul Carter Harrison signals 'a creative process with a plurality of meaning, its significance changing as the experiential context shifts'.[21] In *The Piano Lesson*, for example, the heavy load of watermelons that contributes to the truck's breakdowns works both metaphorically and ironically. The old cliché that associates African Americans with watermelons is a burden, for an individual subjected to caricature by stereotype is, like the truck, unable to function at full capacity. Yet the stereotype is playfully inverted when we hear how white folks turned out in droves to buy the watermelons from Boy Willie and Lymon at inflated prices. One lady actually believed Boy Willie's story about putting sugar in the ground along with the watermelon seed: 'Them white folks is something else' (59).[22] The joke will undoubtedly become embedded in the Charles family history.

All the male characters in *The Piano Lesson* have done time on Parchman Farm, the penal institution that 'parches' a man's soul. Water references function as a subliminal antidote, especially in the tales of men who fell into their wells and drowned. The response to the first appearance of Sutter's ghost is to get Berniece a glass of water (13). In subsequent scenes she heats water for a bath and puts water on for tea. As typically multivalent symbolism, her association with water could refer to purification or to washing her hands of responsibility for the hauntings. After Avery sprinkles water to bless the house, Boy Willie mockingly throws water from a pot: 'Sutter! Come on and get some of this water! You done drowned in the well, come on and get some more of this water!' (105). Thus, water is part of the challenge to the figure associated with 'parching' him.

Although Boy Willie is the one who engages in direct combat with Sutter's ghost, all the characters except Grace, his woman, feel its presence at some point. Grace's obliviousness to the ghost makes sense in that she is not a member of the family, nor does she have the south as a point of reference. It could further be posited that Grace's urban upbringing has kept her less immediately aware of the legacy of slavery, while the impact of slavery across the generations is one way of understanding the ghost. Of course, the ghost could also be explained in psychological terms, or what Ying called 'collective hallucination'.[23] Some spectators, on the other hand, would be inclined to take the ghost quite literally. Ying commented:

> I don't think whether the ghost is real or imagined is the point. It is real in the sense that it is real to these people . . . The ghost is so woven into the interrelationships of the people and their history that it is there with good reason. It's not a *deus ex machina*. It's not something the playwright suddenly invokes to mislead us or to get us out of the impossible argument between brother and sister. It is simply there, part of the organic whole, every bit as integral as the ghost of Hamlet's father is to *Hamlet*.[24]

The telling insights about this play by a Chinese artist hint at a universality of meaning and audience appeal. Although the story of *The Piano Lesson* and its presentation are deeply rooted in African American culture, it speaks to white audiences as well. Wilson's comment to the *New York Times* writer Mervyn Rothstein shortly before *The Piano Lesson* opened on Broadway is pertinent: 'Blacks and whites do all the same things, they just do them differently.'[25] We may preserve our histories differently, but those histories can still be appreciated by families of different cultural backgrounds. As a repository of history, the piano is the family and it also transcends family.

NOTES

1. Transcript of a three-hour recorded discussion of *The Piano Lesson* between Ying Ruocheng, the designer John Ezell and the dramaturg Felicia Hardison Londré in Beijing, China, on 31 December 1991. (Patricia McIlrath Centre for Mid-American Theatre, University of Missouri-Kansas City), p. 1.

2. August Wilson, *The Piano Lesson* (New York: Dutton, 1990), p. 45. Further quotations will be cited parenthetically in the text.

3. These allusions appear on the following pages in corresponding order in ibid.: pp. 10, 18, 19, 21, 23, 34, 61, 87.

4. Kim Powers, 'Theater in New Haven: An Interview with August Wilson', *Theater* 16:1 (Fall/Winter 1984), p. 52.

5. Mervyn Rothstein, 'Round Five for a Theatrical Heavyweight', *New York Times*, 15 April 1990, Section 2, p. 8.

6. Eric Lott, *Love and Theft: Blackface Minstrelsy and the American Working Class* (New York: Oxford University Press, 1995), p. 3.

7. The quotation appears, with slight spelling variations, in websites devoted to famous lines of dialogue from motion pictures as well as on some *Gone With the Wind* websites. For example, www.fiftiesweb.com/movies/gone-with-wind.htm.

8. A few examples of plays that demonstrate the redemptive power of farming or country life are *Adam and Eva* (1919) by Guy Bolton and George Middleton, *Beyond the Horizon* (1920) by Eugene O'Neill, *Nice People* (1921) by Rachel Crothers, and *Beggar on Horseback* (1924) by George S. Kaufman and Marc Connelly. Many others depict urban stress; for example, *Ambush* (1921) by Arthur Richman, *To the Ladies* (1922) by George S. Kaufman and Marc Connelly, *Chicago* (1926) by Maurine Watkins, *Machinal* (1928) by Sophie Treadwell, *Mr Moneypenny* (1928) by Channing Pollock, *The Front Page* (1928) by Ben Hecht and Charles MacArthur, *Meteor* (1929) by S. N. Behrman, *Subway* (1929) by Elmer Rice, and *Women at Four O'Clock* (1929) by Dawn Powell.

9. For an insightful comparison of *The Piano Lesson* and *A Raisin in the Sun*, see Harry J. Elam, Jr., 'The Dialectics of August Wilson's *The Piano Lesson*', *Theatre Journal* 52:3 (October 2000), pp. 363–7.

10. Devon Boan, 'Call-and-Response: Parallel "Slave Narrative" in August Wilson's *The Piano Lesson*', *African American Review* 32 (Summer 1998), p. 269.

11. See discussions of this idea in Harry J. Elam, Jr., *The Past as Present in the Drama of August Wilson* (Ann Arbor: University of Michigan Press, 2004), chapter 5, 'Ogun in Pittsburgh: Resurrecting the Spirit', pp. 166–214; Michael Morales, 'Ghosts on the Piano: August Wilson and the Representation of Black American History', in Alan Nadel, ed., *May All Your Fences Have Gates: Essays on the Drama of August Wilson*, (Iowa City: University of Iowa Press, 1994), pp. 105–15; and Amanda M. Rudolph, 'Images of African Traditional Religions and Christianity in *Joe Turner's Come and Gone* and *The Piano Lesson*', *Journal of Black Studies* 33 (May 2003), pp. 562–5.

12. See Boan, 'Call-and-Response', pp. 263–71.

13. Ying Ruocheng discussion, p. 16.

14. Sandra G. Shannon, *The Dramatic Vision of August Wilson* (Washington, DC: Howard University Press, 1995), p. 206. The interview is reprinted in Jackson

R. Bryer and Mary C. Hartig's *Conversations with August Wilson* (Jackson: University of Mussissippi Press, 2006), pp. 118–54.

15. Ying Roucheng discussion, p. 10.
16. *Ibid.*
17. *Ibid.*, p. 11.
18. *Ibid.*, pp. 7–8.
19. Jay Wright, quoted in Paul Carter Harrison, 'Mother/word', in Harrison, *Totem Voices: Plays from the Black World Repertory* (New York: Grove Press, 1989), p. xii.
20. *Ibid.*, p. xxvi.
21. *Ibid.*, p. xiv.
22. Karen Sotiropoulos in *Staging Race* (Cambridge, MA: Harvard University Press, 2006) cites a Bert Williams joke in which a black character refers to watermelons as apples, and the black peddler with his wagonload of watermelons replies, 'Dem ain't apples. Dem's goose berries.' As she explains, 'With this joke, whites may have been secure in witnessing "darky" ignorance, but blacks would have understood the feigned ignorance as a conscious refusal to recognize watermelon and an implicit critique of the stereotype of watermelon-eating "darkies"' (pp. 66–7).
23. Ying Ruocheng discussion, p. 11.
24. *Ibid.*, pp. 12–15.
25. Rothstein, 'Round Five', p. 8.

9

BRENDA MURPHY

The tragedy of *Seven Guitars*

August Wilson described the creative process that produced *Seven Guitars* (1995) in a 1996 interview with Jan Breslauer. Fundamentally, he said, 'the basis is character'. He suggested that the characters occurred to him first in the form of a speech, or a turn of phrase, noting that although 'they're all different aspects of my personality', they are all also 'voices of the black community.'[1] He described his creative work as analogous to that of a collagist, piecing the voices together to make a whole. In the case of *Seven Guitars*, this is particularly important, for, as he told Carol Rosen, Wilson conceived of the seven characters in the play as instruments themselves: 'They are the seven guitars. They each have their individual voices and their individual characters. And if they're the guitars, then I guess I'm the orchestra.'[2] It took Wilson some time to arrive at the design for the play. He explained later that it began its life in his imagination with four characters, none of them women, set in a turpentine camp in Georgia. Lacking any knowledge of turpentine camps, he had the idea of moving the play to Chicago, 'the natural place for a bluesman', and found that he was 'writing a play set in the 1940's that was supposed to be somehow representative of black American life, and I didn't have any women in there. And I knew that wasn't going to work.'[3]

In the play as Wilson finally wrote it, there are seven characters, the blues musician Floyd Barton, his two sidemen, or supporting musicians, drummer Red Carter and harmonica player Canewell, Canewell's girlfriend Vera, and three people who live in Vera's house: Louise, a middle-aged single woman whose beautiful young niece Ruby comes to stay with her, and King Hedley, a West Indian who lives in his dreams.

Wilson told the story of how the three female characters entered the play many times, with the variations that enter an oft-told tale.[4] Essentially, he said that Vera entered his writer's imagination and demanded her own space, which turned out to be the back yard that was ruled over by Wilson's mother,

Daisy Wilson Kittel, at his boyhood home in Pittsburgh, and that became the setting for the entire play. The other two women just walked in behind her. Wilson also said that the play 'started with an image of seven men with guitars on stage'. Floyd Barton has been killed, and 'these men were in a lineup and they were responding to this unheard and unseen voice, this disembodied voice. "No, sir," "Well, I know Floyd for however many years,"' etc.' ('Bard' 190).

In the early stages of writing, he spoke of the play as a murder mystery that would reveal the 'social content' of Floyd's life through a series of flashbacks within flashbacks. Explaining that all the male characters in the play were blues musicians, he said that 'it's about their relationship to society, to white society and to black society. Whereas in black society they are carriers of the culture . . . in white society they are vagrants, drunkards . . . So there are two different values at work here.'[5] Later, he added that he 'wanted to expose – sort of look behind – the songs, to the interior psyche of the individuals who create the songs so you see how the blues are created and where in essence they come from' ('Bard' 191).

As in his earlier plays, Wilson's method of composing *Seven Guitars* required a long process of development and revision. His longtime collaborator Lloyd Richards, who had recently had a heart attack, was not available for the first production, at Chicago's Goodman Theatre in January 1995, which instead was directed by Walter Dallas. Richards joined the production in Boston for its opening with the Huntington Theatre Company in September 1995 and stayed with it for its runs in San Francisco and Los Angeles and its Broadway opening in March 1996. The change of directors made for a particularly drawn out and stressful production process for this play, but it led to some discoveries on Wilson's part, as he learnt to work with Dallas and the actors on revisions during the rehearsal process rather than between productions, as was his custom with Richards.[6] In the course of bringing *Seven Guitars* to light, Wilson cut its running time from more than four hours, when it was first read at the playwrights' conference at the Eugene O'Neill Theatre Centre in Waterford, Connecticut, to just about three hours in New York. Asked about the process of the writing, he said that 'some things may appear to be extraneous to the plot line . . . But if you start pulling things away, you take away the field of manners and ritual intercourse. All of the things in the play are very necessary, but they all appear to be quite unnecessary. If you take something out, the structure will fall down'.[7]

Nevertheless, during those fourteen months of development, the script changed constantly. Zakes Mokae, the South African actor for whom the role of King Hedley was originally intended, was replaced after the opening night in San Francisco because Wilson and Richards did not think he was able to do justice to the West Indian rhythms of Hedley's dialogue. Ruben Santiago-Hudson, who as Canewell was generally considered by critics to give the strongest performance of the cast, saw his part cut repeatedly during the development process, as Wilson decided that Floyd was the central character of the play and Canewell, originally a rival, was a sideman in every way. After having his most powerful speech cut in Boston, he refused to speak to Wilson for three days and told a reporter, 'I don't know if I'll do another play for a while. It's too hard, too painful'.[8] The most significant change was the splitting of the final scene into what are now the opening and closing scenes of the play. Originally, *Seven Guitars* had ended with Floyd's death and the postfuneral scene. Splitting the latter into a beginning and an ending turned the play into something of a 'murder mystery', while it did not undermine what the play had become, a classical tragedy.

Seven Guitars opens in 1948 with six of the seven characters gathering in the back yard of the house where Vera, Louise and King Hedley live after the funeral of the electric blues guitarist Floyd 'Schoolboy' Barton. Joined by Floyd's two sidemen, Canewell and Red Carter, they talk about Floyd and the six figures, who may have been angels or employees of the funeral home, but who, Vera says, carried Floyd up to the sky after the funeral. The next scene takes place a few days earlier in the same place, and the rest of the play unfolds the events leading to Hedley's stabbing Floyd, before the final scene completes the action of the first scene. In the course of the play, it is revealed that Floyd has just emerged from the workhouse, where he was confined for ninety days for vagrancy, and that a record he had recorded in Chicago some time before has just become a hit on the radio. He is determined to get back to Chicago to record some more songs but, to do so, he first has to get his wages from the workhouse, use them to retrieve his electric guitar from the pawnshop, talk his sidemen into going with him to Chicago to record, and win back Vera, to whom he has been unfaithful.

All six of the other characters also have their concerns, and their voices are heard throughout the play, creating a rich sense of life as it is lived in this Pittsburgh neighbourhood in 1948. Vera, who, as Canewell says, makes her bed up high but turns her lamp down low, wonders whether she should continue to resist Floyd or go with him to Chicago. Canewell, the most gifted raconteur of the group, nurses a hopeless love for Vera, and also serves as a wise counsellor for Floyd, insisting that Floyd needs to stand up to his manager and the white music producers to ensure that he is not cheated again. Red Carter is a gentler, more genial voice than Canewell. Hedley is the shamanistic character often found in Wilson's plays. He is in touch with blood rituals from his West Indian heritage and sees and hears things in his dreams that are more significant to him than waking reality. Hedley kills, cooks and sells chickens for a living. Louise, the most modern of the group, lives across from Hedley, and is anxious for him to get tested for tuberculosis. She is a middle-aged woman who is reasonably content to have a hand gun instead of a man in her apartment. Her beautiful niece Ruby comes to visit, pregnant, escaping man trouble back home in Alabama, and turning the heads of all the men who hang around in the yard.

As the play progresses, Floyd becomes so frustrated in his quest that he engages in a robbery with another young man, Wilford Ray Tillery, getting him killed, and buries the money in the garden. Floyd seems to be succeeding as the band members get their instruments and play for a very successful Mother's Day dance. But Hedley, who has dreamed that his father is sending the musician Buddy Bolden to him with the money to buy a plantation, sees Floyd in the garden with the money and demands it. When Floyd refuses to give it to him, Hedley cuts his throat. Meanwhile, Ruby has accepted Hedley as her man and has decided to name her child after him. The community comes together after Floyd's death, and although Canewell, for one, knows who killed him, there is no suggestion in the play that anyone is going to give the assailant up to the authorities. It is important to note this ending of *Seven Guitars*, for in the sequel to the play, *King Hedley II* (1999), it becomes clear that Canewell has eventually turned Hedley in. He has been given the name Stool Pigeon by Ruby, though he insists he should be called Truth Sayer.

Wilson has acknowledged that *Seven Guitars* is rooted in Aristotelian tragedy. Describing it in a 1996 interview, he said, 'you'll see a proscenium [and] a Western-style drama based on Aristotle . . . It is not based on African concepts of theater and ritual' (Breslauer 8). Speaking specifically of Floyd Barton as tragic hero, he said that

> Floyd has to assume the responsibility for his own death, his own murder. Had he not been standing in the yard with the money, then Hedley never could have assumed that he was Buddy Bolden, etc . . . . whatever events conspired to have him standing in that yard at that precise time, he has to himself bear the responsibility for that. ('Bard' 193)

The nature of Floyd's tragedy is related to Wilson's revisiting of the issues he had first raised in *Ma Rainey's Black Bottom* in 1984. Harry Elam, Jr. has noted that *Seven Guitars* 'repeats and revises both the image of a misguided blues musician from *Ma Rainey* and the trope of white exploitation of the black song'.[9] Reading the play as a tragedy arising from the commodification of the black musician and the racism of the white music industry, Elam focuses on Wilson's inversion of the tragically displaced violence that ends *Ma Rainey*. In the earlier play the younger jazz musician Levee kills the older blues musician Toledo for stepping on his shoe because he is seething with rage over a white record producer's breaking his word and casually dismissing him. In *Seven Guitars* Hedley kills Floyd because he mistakes him for Buddy Bolden, sent by his father to give him the money to build his plantation yet refusing to give it to him. Elam suggests that Toledo is a spokesman for black nationalism, and that his murder 'functions as a performance of tragic, unfulfilled promise, a loss of black activism that needs to be reclaimed through the triumph of the blues voice', while in *Seven Guitars* 'the representative of black militancy is Hedley, and it is he who kills the misguided bluesman, Floyd. Thus the tragic action is inverted.'[10]

This is certainly a significant element of both plays, but both are as much concerned with the generational relationships among the black musicians as with the white music industry. Toledo, for example, is a spokesman for the values of race pride and independence, but also a representative of the past, and the blues of the rural South, in contrast with Levee's ambition to move into the future, embracing the new jazz just then entering the music scene. For *Seven Guitars* Wilson carefully chose another pair of musicians to represent two generations, and two different music cultures, Buddy Bolden and Muddy Waters. 'King' Buddy Bolden, for whom King Hedley is named, was a cornet player and band leader who is credited with creating the sound that became New Orleans jazz at the turn of the twentieth century. His popularity lasted only from 1900 until about 1907, when he was confined to a state asylum for the insane, spending the rest of his life there. The jazz he played was picked up by better-trained musicians such as Louis Armstrong and Sidney Bechet, who brought it into the mainstream by way of Chicago and New York in the early 1920s. But Bolden remained the stuff of legend in the jazz world, partly because his music was never recorded and thus could only be imagined by those who had never heard him play. Muddy Waters, who was known as 'the King of the Electric Blues', came from Mississippi and grew up playing Delta blues on the harmonica and the guitar. He moved to Chicago, however, and changed the face of the blues in 1948 when he released two blues songs on the electric guitar which became enormous hits, establishing Chicago-style electric blues as the dominant new blues form of the late 1940s and 1950s.

In *Ma Rainey's Black Bottom*, set in 1923, Wilson plays out the generational conflict between the older 'pure' country blues musicians and the new jazz musician Levee. In *Seven Guitars* the conflict is between the culture of the turn-of-the-century New Orleans jazz musician Buddy Bolden and that of the young electric blues guitarist Muddy Waters, who is Floyd 'Schoolboy' Barton's idol. As Floyd says, the first time he heard Waters playing in a club in Chicago, he took off his hat: 'I didn't know you could make music sound like that. That told me say, "The sky's the limit," I told myself say, "I'm gonna play like that one day." I stayed there until they put me out.'[11] Hedley's father, a trumpet player, had had the same experience with Bolden at the beginning of the century.

Hedley associates Bolden and his nickname King with both his pride and his difficulties with living in the world the way it is. 'It is not a good thing he named me that' (67), he says, remembering that he has killed a black man for refusing to call him King. He also believes that he is destined to be 'the father of someone who would not bow down to the white man' (68), and perhaps of the messiah. It is the connection between Bolden and his father that dominates Hedley's imagination, however, and that finally results in Floyd's death.

Throughout the play, Hedley sings variations on 'Buddy Bolden's Blues', a traditional blues song with the phrase 'I thought I heard Buddy Bolden say' repeated, and the second part of the line improvised in several different ways. The first time Hedley sings it, Floyd insists that Buddy had said, 'Wake up and give me the money' (23), Floyd's obsession with getting the money he needs to get to Chicago dominating his every thought. Hedley corrects him, saying that Buddy had actually said 'Come here. Here go the money' (23). When Floyd asks what he gave him, he replies, 'He give me ashes' (24). Three times during the play, the line is sung by either Floyd or Hedley. The first time, Floyd asks, 'What he say?' and Hedley answers, 'He didn't give me nothing' (39). The second time Hedley sings the whole line, 'I thought I hear Buddy Bolden say/Soon I be a big man someday' (65). The third time, he again sings the line, 'I thought I heard Buddy Bolden say,/Here go the money, King take it away' (70).

This image is reprised and fully realized at the end of the play, after Hedley has killed Floyd, with Canewell, who has taken over Floyd's line, 'Wake up and give me the money' (106). Again Hedley insists that Buddy's line is 'come here, here go the money' (106), but when Canewell asks what Buddy gave him, Hedley says, 'He give me this' and holds up a *handful of crumpled bills. They slip from his fingers and fall to the ground like ashes* (107). Hedley's thrice-repeated truncated line from the song, 'I thought I heard Buddy Bolden say . . .' (107), makes up the final dialogue of the play, with no attempt to complete the statement. The implication is that Buddy has neither told him anything nor given him anything that he can use. The significance of the Bolden song is its connection to the story of Hedley's father, to which he alludes three times in the play. The first is in Act 1, when he tells Louise that he is going to be a 'a big man' when he gets his plantation, for 'that is the day my father forgive me . . . and my father is a strong memory' (2). More is revealed in Act 2, when he tells Floyd that the money Buddy will be bringing him is from his father, whom he has forgiven for kicking him in the mouth, and who has come to him in a dream and told him he is sorry he died without forgiving him. To show his forgiveness, Hedley's father sends Bolden with the money to buy the plantation 'so the white man not tell you what to do'. He says that once Buddy had come with the money, and he had taken it, it had fallen like ashes, 'ashes to ashes and dust to dust to dust. Like that. It all come to nothing' (70).

Later in Act 2, Hedley reveals the insult to his father that had caused him to 'kick me with him boot in my mouth' (86–7): asking him, at the end of a hard day's work, why he did 'nothing' because he was not like Toussaint L'Ouverture, fighting the white man. Through the dream and Bolden, he and his father have forgiven each other, but action remains to be taken. This is precipitated by Louise when she lets the public health authorities know that Hedley needs to be tested for tuberculosis and he gets a notice to appear. Determined that he is not going to be taken and locked up by the white men, Hedley obtains a machete, signifier of the plantation, to defend himself against the white men. The tragic irony is that he uses the machete not on the white men but on Floyd, whom he drunkenly mistakes for Bolden refusing him the money.

If Hedley is obsessed with his father and the ghost of Bolden, Floyd 'School-boy' Barton, with his one hit record, is fixated on getting back to Chicago and the electric blues of his hero, Muddy Waters. Like Hedley, he is defined by one song in the play, his hit record 'That's All Right'. Like many a blues musician of his generation, Floyd has been cheated out of his royalties on the record. True to his nickname, he has a childlike sense of the music business. Canewell tells him that they were played for fools when they recorded the record, with the white producers paying Floyd a flat fee for the song instead of a royalty, and even trying to cheat the musicians out of their agreed-upon fee. When Canewell says that everything has to be clear from the outset the next time, Floyd says ingenuously, 'that's the way the recording business work. You ain't gonna change that. The main thing is to get the record out there. Let the people hear it. Then come back and ask for more money. Then you can get double if it's any good' (46).

Everything Floyd does in the play is meant to be a step towards his goal of getting his guitar, his sidemen and Vera to Chicago, which is synonymous for him with 'opportunity', a concept he can articulate only in terms of the material status symbols of a Buick or a Cadillac, a telephone and expensive furniture: 'The white man ain't the only one can have a car and nice furniture' (80). During the play, Floyd is schooled in the ways of the record business when his white manager, T. L. Hall, makes off with his advance money and is then arrested for selling fake insurance policies. In fact, each action that Floyd takes towards his goal is thwarted by some white person: by the clerk refusing to pay him for his time in the workhouse because he does not have the letter he was sent; by the pawnshop owner who will not redeem a ticket that is two days overdue; by his lying, thieving, manager.[12] Hedley fingers Floyd as a man of destiny when he says, 'You are like a king! They look at you and they say, "this one . . . this one is the pick of the litter" . . . The white man got a big plan against you. Don't help him with his plan' (71).

Feeling his avenues of escape closing inexorably one after the other, Floyd tries to assert his will against fate as executed by the white power structure. Starting with 'seven ways to go', he sees them cut to two, but insists, 'I am going to Chicago. If I have to buy me a graveyard and kill everybody I see. I am going to Chicago. I don't want to live my life without . . . Floyd Barton is gonna make his record. Floyd Barton is going to Chicago' (81–2). Floyd engineers the robbery that gets Tillery killed but allows him to get the band instruments out of the pawnshop, to buy a dress for Vera, to buy tickets to Chicago, and, most importantly, to buy a brand-new electric guitar, 'the same kind of guitar as Muddy Waters got. Same color and everything' (90). Floyd's goal is within reach, until his desire comes up against Hedley's dream in the garden. Seeing Floyd in the moonlight with a fistful of money, Hedley takes him not for the brand-new electric blues musician, Muddy Waters, but for the ghost of the jazz musician Buddy Bolden. He demands the money, insisting, 'It's my father's money. Give it to me' (104), and when Floyd refuses, he cuts his throat with the machete, as he had the rooster's at the end of Act 1. In killing Floyd, with one blow, Hedley becomes the instrument of death for both the dream of the past represented by his father – the plantation life of the West Indies and Bolden – and Floyd's dream of a future filled with opportunity for the black man, signified by Waters's electric blues and all the latest conveniences of modern life.

Unlike Levee, whose tragic stabbing of Toledo means his own destruction, too, Hedley pays no price for the killing of Floyd in *Seven Guitars*. Wilson's final scene makes it clear that the community continues to embrace Hedley even as it mourns Floyd. The police have been around asking questions about Floyd's death, but there is no indication that they will discover who the killer was, even from Canewell, who seems to be their chief suspect and knows it was Hedley. Amid the talk of angels bearing Floyd up into the sky, the warm tones of the everyday life of the community as it comes together and goes on with life are what dominate the first and last scenes of the play. The other six of Wilson's 'seven guitars' form a tragic chorus commenting on the significance of Floyd Barton's life and acting as a community that must accept the loss and continue.

There is also a strong suggestion of possibility and hope for the future in this play. Hedley voices a prophecy of doom as he kills Miss Poochie Tillery's rooster at the end of Act 1. The characters have been riffing on the rooster, and the various voices express attitudes ranging from Canewell's claim to privileged knowledge of all the roosters in the rural South to Louise's disdain for someone who would keep a rooster in the city when she can buy an alarm clock at Woolworth's to wake her up. The basic theme is the link between the rooster and the unsophisticated country people who would bring him to a city like Pittsburgh or Chicago as part of the Great Migration in the early part of the twentieth century. Hedley insists, 'The rooster is the king of the barnyard. He like the black man. He king' (61), but the others pay no attention. When Hedley slits the rooster's throat, he prophesies the doom of the black man along with the death of the rooster, or the culture of the rural South:

> God ain't making no more roosters. It is a thing past. Soon you mark my words when God ain't making no more niggers. They too be a done thing . . . You hear this rooster you know you alive. You glad to see the sun cause there come a time sure enough when you see your last day and this rooster you don't hear no more. (*He takes out a knife and cuts the rooster's throat.*)
> That be for the living. Your black ass be dead like the rooster now. You mark what Hedley say. (64)

Hedley performs a ritual, scattering the rooster's blood in a circle and then throwing the rooster on the ground, saying, 'this rooster too good live for your black asses' (64). This ritual killing severs the connection between the urban black community in this Pittsburgh back yard and its rural southern roots, reaching back further through the West Indian and African traditions on which Hedley is drawing.

If Hedley kills off the old culture with the rooster, he would seem to be killing off the new when he severs Floyd's windpipe with the machete. But Wilson offers another suggestion for the future of the community in the person of the pregnant Ruby. Exuding a sexuality that literally stops the men in their tracks at times, Ruby functions as a fertility symbol in the play. When Hedley is at his lowest point, believing he will be taken away to the asylum by the white men, she inspires him to offer himself: 'I am a man, woman. I am the man to father your children. I offer you a kingdom!' (89). Once Ruby *'gives herself to him out of recognition of his great need'* (90), the couple begin to form some sort of promise for the future. Ruby goes to church with Hedley and he agrees to go with her to the sanitarium so that he can be tested for tuberculosis. Ruby decides that she will tell him that her baby is his because 'He wants to be the father of my child and that's what this child needs' (95). She says, 'I don't know about this messiah stuff' (95) but she decides to name the baby King after him, a suggestion that the future will be rooted in the traditions of the past.

Floyd's dream of the future was a dream of material gadgets and empty status symbols, uprooted from the community that had nurtured and supported him. Even his music was played on an electric guitar that he sold his old acoustic guitar to acquire and, at a further remove, on the radio. In being so eager to get to Chicago and leave his community behind, Floyd was in a sense cutting himself off from the people and floating off into the sky, as the image of the funeral angels suggests. Hedley's deed simply gave concrete existence to the action. The tragedy of *Seven Guitars* is ultimately the tragedy of a life wilfully cut off and a hope for the community's future which subsists in the lives and traditions that continue without it.

NOTES

1. Jan Breslauer, 'He Types Only on the Blue Keys', *Los Angeles Times*, 14 January 1996, p. 8.
2. Carol Rosen, 'August Wilson: Bard of the Blues', *Theater Week* 9 (27 May 1996), in Jackson R. Bryer and Mary C. Hartig, eds., *Conversations with August Wilson* (Jackson: University Press of Mississippi, 2006), p. 192. Futher quotations will be cited parenthetically in the text. For commentary on the significance of the number seven in the play, see Peter Wolfe, *August Wilson* (New York: Twayne, 1999), p. 132, and Mary Bogumil, *Understanding August Wilson* (Columbia: University of South Carolina Press, 1999), p. 151 n. 13.
3. Bruce Weber, 'Sculpturing a Play into Existence, *New York Times* (late edition), 24 March, 1996, p. 7.
4. See, for example, Rosen, Bard of the Blues', p. 191; Weber, 'Sculpturing a Play', p. 7; and Ben Brantley, 'The World that Created August Wilson,' *New York Times* (late edition), 5 February 1995, p. 2.
5. Richard Pettengill, 'The Historical Perspective: An Interview with August Wilson', in Marilyn Elkins, ed., *August Wilson: A Casebook* (New York: Garland, 1994), pp. 219–20.
6. See Joan Herrington, '*I Ain't Sorry for Nothin' Done': August Wilson's Process of Playwriting* (New York: Limelight, 1998), pp. 116–19.
7. Breslauer, 'He Types Only', p. 8.
8. Weber, 'Sculpturing a Play', p. 7. Santiago-Hudson has long since recovered. Ben Brantley wrote that he directed the 2006 revival of *Seven Guitars* by New York's Signature Theatre 'with the intimacy and warmth of a fraternal embrace' ("Weaving Blues of Trying Times and Lost Dreams", *New York Times* (late edition), 25 August 2006, p. E1).

9. Harry Elam, Jr., *The Past as Present in the Drama of August Wilson* (Ann Arbor: University of Michigan Press, 2004), p. 48.

10. *Ibid.*, p. 51.

11. August Wilson, *Seven Guitars* (New York: Plume, 1997), p. 11. Further quotations will be cited parenthetically in the text.

12. For an interesting commentary on the importance of the papers and reading in the plays, see Bogumil, *Understanding August Wilson*, p. 121.

10

MATTHEW ROUDANÉ

Safe at home?:
August Wilson's *Fences*

> 'Some people build fences to keep people out . . .
> And other people build fences to keep people in.'
> Jim Bono, *Fences*

August Wilson was one of America's most gifted storytellers. His plays read like fiction, the narrative drive, symbolic settings, evocative stage directions, music, and characters themselves propelling the action with a sparkling performativity. This sense of storytelling is nowhere more evident than in *Fences* (1985). No wonder Lloyd Richards, who directed so many of Wilson's plays throughout their careers, suggested one year before its Broadway premiere, on 26 March 1987, at the Street 46th Theatre, that the playwright was 'one of the most compelling storytellers to begin writing for the theater in many years'.[1] Following the success of his first Broadway play, *Ma Rainey's Black Bottom* (1984), *Fences*, which in 1987 won the Pulitzer Prize, the Tony Award and the New York Drama Critics' Circle Award, confirmed the arrival of a theatrical voice of genuine originality.

Fences concerns the lives of the Maxsons, an African American family whose struggles are chronicled from 1957 to 1965. The dates, of course, encompass a key period in the civil rights movement, but this was also the time in which Wilson was a teenager and high school student, and experienced the full force of white racism. Ostensibly a fairly straightforward domestic drama, *Fences*, by the final blackout, has expanded into an enabling fable of rebellion and recovery, of myth and history, and of confrontation and expiation. Asked two years before his death if he considered *Fences* his 'signature play', Wilson commented that that accolade would go to *Joe Turner's Come and Gone* (1986). But, most theatregoers and critics feel, *Fences* remains one of his finest achievements.[2]

Such achievement, what John Barth calls 'passionate virtuosity,' took Wilson years to perfect. In 1968 he helped to establish the Black Horizons Theatre Company in Pittsburgh, a liaison that gave him a chance to hear his language live on a stage. He was not pleased. He subsequently admitted that at that time he did not respect the ways his fellow blacks talked and therefore tried to alter and, in a sense, falsify the linguistic sources that lay before him. In 1978 he moved to St Paul and began writing scripts for the Science Museum of Minnesota, and it was during his stay in the Twin Cities that he became associated with the Penumbra Theatre in St Paul. His early plays, *Black Bart and the Sacred Hills* (1981), *Fullerton Street* (1981) and *Jitney* (1982), show Wilson struggling, with uneven results, to transmute craft into art. The limitations of these early plays, *Jitney* aside, lay in their language, in Wilson's unwillingness to tap into the musicality and unique rhythms of his black linguistic heritage and culture. In effect, he denied himself access to the very subjects that would become the greatest resource for *Fences* and his subsequent works: history, or what Suzan-Lori Parks often refers to as the holes in American history, and the language deployed to bring that history and the African American experience to life in performance.

Their unimpressive debuts notwithstanding, these first plays were important to the development of Wilson's career, and, more specifically, to the development of his stage language. For it was during their writing and production that he began to attend to the linguistic and theatrical possibilities implicit in black dialect. Rather than devaluing the black idiom he knew so well, as he had done in his first compositions, he now began to appreciate, indeed to celebrate 'voices I had been brought up with all my life'. As he told one interviewer, 'I realized I didn't have to change it [black dialogue]. I began to respect it.'[3] Those 'voices' beautifully fill the stage in *Fences*.

This play extends Wilson's exploration of the African American experience within the twentieth century. Troy Maxson, the protagonist, is a former baseball player, a talented athlete whose prowess on the field never received the attention or recognition it deserved because, in part, he was imprisoned during his prime playing years (though, ironically, this is when he learnt the game) and, of course, blacks were not then allowed to play in the Major Leagues. Thus Troy, now a 53-year-old garbage collector, has collected his share of dreams deferred and hopes deflected. Wilson animates the play with a host of characters whose intersecting lives contribute to its rich plot. Every scene of the play, Wilson has pointed out, features Troy, and audiences watch as Rose, Troy's powerfully steady and loving wife of eighteen years, and Cory, their son, debate each other's dreams and desires against the backdrop of a rundown inner-city neighbourhood.

It is, in part, a play about a father who emerged from a battered past and who once dreamed of swinging for the fences – playing professional baseball – only to be consigned to being a garbageman. It is equally a play about two sons' thwarted dreams. Lyons, Troy's son from a previous marriage, has struggled for years, with little success, to establish a musical career, while Cory, Troy and Rose's younger son, finds his hopes of attending college on a football scholarship sabotaged by his father and himself consigned to join the Marines. Jim Bono emerges as Troy's best friend, an accepting man who is a kind of *raisonneur* in the play and who offers sound advice throughout. Troy's brother, Gabriel, meanwhile, was severely wounded in the Second World War and until very recently lived in the Maxson home on a government pension.

As the play develops, we learn about these characters and their aspirations, their attenuated options, difficult pasts and immediate predicaments, including the fact that Troy has a newborn baby girl, Raynell, the product of his ongoing affair with Alberta, to raise. Wilson adds yet another layer of tension and loss to the plot when we learn that Alberta has died in childbirth. *Fences*, a play about family, love, friendship, betrayal and human desires, and what happens to individuals whose private needs jar with their outer world of limited possibilities, spans an eight-year period, culminating with Troy's death and funeral scene. In its richly symbolic exploration of the home life of the Maxsons, it is now regarded as an important contribution to the ongoing narrative history of the American stage.

The title of this chapter, 'Safe at home?', is ironic, for 'Safe at home' is the baseball term that every player trying to score yearns to hear from the home-plate umpire. Within the language of American popular culture, it is a term instantly recognizable to nearly all Americans. Troy dreamed of playing in the Major Leagues and hearing the umpire bellow 'Safe at home,' as he scored but, of course, never had the opportunity to enjoy such an experience. Further, in the world Wilson constructs for his protagonist, Troy is hardly 'safe' and secure and fulfilled at home. The home he inhabits harbours a paradoxical mixture of refuge and tension, shelter and rejection, love and indifference. It is a home that may not appear as depressing as Lincoln and Booth's squalid apartment in Parks's *Top Dog/Underdog* (2001), but it is a place from which a son is physically and emotionally evicted and where a husband has damaged his marriage immeasurably through his trespasses.

Wilson initially spotlights the idea of Troy's deferrals and deflections visually with the physical set of the play. When theatregoers settle into their seats, they see a stage that at first glance seems fairly unremarkable. As a framing device, though, James D. Sandefur's set, in the original production, provided a richly symbolic point of entry into Wilson's play. The drama unfolds within the fenced yard surrounding the home of Troy and Rose Maxson, an 'ancient two-story brick house set back off a small alley in a big-city neighborhood' (n.p.). Their small yard lacks grass, the wooden porch is 'badly in need of paint', and fence-building equipment and a pile of lumber are plainly visible, as is a baseball bat propped against a tree. From one tree hangs a baseball made of rags. Stage right are two oil drums that the Maxsons use for garbage cans. Wilson works carefully to ensure a semiotic of play space that reveals much about the challenging life of its occupants. It is not for nothing that Wilson specifies that the newly constructed wooden porch, though solid, 'lacks congruence'.

Wilson foregrounds the action with copious stage notes preceding the play. These are of crucial importance. They become, textually and symbolically, part of the performance, part of what Michael Issacaroff and Robin F. Jones call a 'performing text'.[4] His stage notes chronicle the successful immigration of Europeans whose 'capacity for hard work' ultimately certified their financial and cultural security in America. By contrast, 'the descendants of African slaves were offered no such welcome or participation'. Their lives are filled with 'quiet desperation and vengeful pride', a description that certainly fits Troy's life. Interestingly, Wilson ascribes to Troy many of the terms employed to characterize the Europeans, for he is a large man whose 'honesty, capacity for hard work, and . . . strength' inspire his friends and family and, despite his considerable faults, define his not always dignified dignity.

Troy has challenged his employer about the unfair working conditions under which he and other blacks labour. A lifetime of missed opportunities plague him and at his age he demands a reckoning; on one level he wins, however minor and ironic such a victory may seem. He is granted his wish not to do the heavy lifting of the garbage but instead to drive the garbage truck. This is a Troy who in 1941 struggled with pneumonia, an illness that nearly killed him, and who survived fifteen years of prison life. He emerges as a survivor, a warrior whom Bono, his dear friend, and Rose, his wife, admire and love.

Indeed, Wilson has said that he is fond of presenting in his plays a man who has 'a warrior spirit'. This 'warrior' figure is a strong, ambitious man who, frustrated with outer injustices, seeks, if possible, to precipitate social change. Levee, in *Ma Rainey's Black Bottom*, Boy Willie in *The Piano Lesson* (1987), and Sterling in *Two Trains Running* (1990) approximate this warrior image, as, to a degree, does Troy, who, like Levee before him, also embodies the problems of someone challenging the dominant culture. But both men are also figures whose flaws stem from an inability to harness frustration with reality, and reality with constructive private and public change. Like Walker Vessels in Amiri Baraka's *The Slave* (1964), or Sergeant Waters in Charles Fuller's *A Soldier's Play* (1982), Troy Maxson seems fated to destroy, or at least tear down, the many metaphoric fences within his life. Frustrated by being barred (in many senses of that term) from the Major Leagues, haunted by generations of racial disenfranchisement, rejected by a brutalizing father,

Troy, in 1957, has come to fence out those spiritually and culturally closest to himself.

Troy Maxson emerges as a man savagely divided against himself. He is a figure who is clearly at odds with those who come within his orbit, but he is also a man who is equally at odds with his own very being in the world. He fences himself in. Although Wilson has resisted comparisons between *Fences* and Arthur Miller's *Death of a Salesman* (1949), there is a similarity between the houses of the Lomans and Maxsons; a similarity both in architectural and symbolic terms; a similarity in the fathers' respective infidelities, and, more compellingly, in the father-son tensions. Indeed, the tension between Troy and his teenage son Cory underscores just how entrapped these characters are. Cory yearns to play football; his father wants him to mend fences, and to secure a vocational job rather than attending college, like Biff Loman, on a football scholarship. Cory exudes youthful enthusiasm; Troy, perhaps sensing something of himself within his son, and perhaps subconsciously wanting to deny his son the sporting and educational opportunities he had been denied himself, resents the boy's youthfulness. Cory feels that the racial injustices suffered by his father do not fully apply to him. Troy has suffered profoundly from the white world that has fenced him in athletically, professionally and emotionally. Cory sees no reason why this should define his own possibilities. If Biff Loman saw his father as a fake, Cory sees Troy as a paternal oppressor.

Wilson himself believed that the father-son conflict within American culture was 'actually a normal generational conflict that happens all the time'.[5] He told David Savran that such conflicts are healthy and positive, and that Troy's attitude and actions towards his son throughout the play are motivated by love. As he explained:

> Troy is seeing this boy walk around, smelling his piss. Two men cannot live in the same household. Troy would have been tremendously disappointed if Cory had not challenged him. Troy knows that this boy has to go out and do battle with that world: 'So I had best prepare him because I know that's a harsh, cruel place out there. But that's going to be easy compared to what he's getting here. Ain't nobody gonna whip your ass like I am going to whip it.' He has a tremendous love for the kid. But he's not going to say, 'I love you,' he is going to demonstrate it. He's carrying garbage for seventeen years just for the kid. The only world Troy knows is the one that he made. Cory's going to go on to find another one, he's going to arrive at the same place as Troy.

Wilson further explained that 'There aren't many people who ever jumped up in Troy's face' and that the father is so 'proud of the kid at the same time that he expresses a hurt that all men feel. You got to cut our kid loose at some point'(*Conversations* 32–3). It is difficult to agree fully with the playwright. On the one hand, most in the audience understand the concept of parental tough love, the necessity to teach life lessons to children. This would be especially true for Cory, who is about to enter a Bigger Thomas-like naturalistic cosmos in which the individual is reduced to an insignificant speck in a universe over which he has little or no control. This is equally true for Lyons, whose musical aspirations are temporarily put on hold when he is imprisoned for three years for cashing 'other people's checks' (94). We have to accept Wilson's thought that Troy is expressing his love for his son throughout the play. On the other hand, in virtually every scene with his son Troy emerges as a model of pent-up rage, his anger and inability to understand his son's point of view barely held in check. He also appears disdainful of most others, and he reduces his conception of mortality to little more than a clichéd baseball analogy. 'That's all death is to me,' he patronizes Rose. 'A fastball on the outside corner' (10). He had rejected his own father years earlier because he regarded him as 'the devil himself' (52). In the climactic fight scene between father and son, Troy accuses Cory of having 'the devil in you' (87), but much the same could be said of Troy himself at that moment. At times it appears as if Troy experiences the self-alienation Julia Kristeva theorizes about when discussing the fear of the other, and which leads to a sense that we may become 'foreigners to ourselves.'[6]

Thus fences, in this play, do not make good neighbours; they divide. Fences symbolize separateness, otherness, an inability to communicate with the self and the other. Significantly enough, the nearly fatal father-son battle at the end of Act 2 scene 4 occurs in the front yard, near the fence. After Cory has tried to bash in his father's head with the baseball bat, Troy screams, 'Get your black ass out of my yard!' (87) and a rejected and defeated Cory tells his father that he will be back to get his belongings, to which Troy replies, 'They'll be on the other side of that fence' (89). This is one of several key emotional highpoints in the play, a moment in which Troy severs the bonds between father and son (as he had done, if we can believe his older son, with Lyons). Like Robert Frost's fences, Wilson's represent something that distances Troy from the other, and from the self. Although there is a somewhat sentimental and predictable Lorraine Hansberryan reconciliation at the play's end, when Cory relents and agrees to attend his father's funeral, from this confrontation near the fence on, Cory retreats from his family, joins the Marines, and tries, the text implies, to make a productive life for himself. Wilson claims that Troy loves his son – and ultimately the audience detects that love – but that same audience may also detect much resentment, misunderstanding, and ignorance within that love.

Despite Troy's shortcomings – his estrangement from his son, his affair with Alberta and his fathering of their child, Raynell, his pent-up anger, his sexism, and so on – Wilson mythicizes his protagonist. He necessarily bestows upon him an antiheroic status, but many in the audience see a man whose spirit radiates from his core being until his death, in 1965.

The source of much of his antiheroic status, and anger, is in a traumatic, transformative experience when he was fourteen years old. His father had discovered him with a thirteen-year-old girl, 'real cozy with each other' (52). His father had beaten him, but his real purpose, we learn, was less to discipline Troy than to rape the young woman: 'But I see where he was chasing me off so he could have the gal for himself. When I see what the matter of it was, I lost all fear of my daddy' (52). Troy sees in his father nothing less than the devil. In his account of his father's attack, Wilson works carefully to construct an Oedipal texture to the struggle between father and son, for Troy suffers, if not a Sophoclean blinding, then a beating so savage, as Troy recalls, that

> I thought I was blind. I couldn't see nothing. Both my eyes were swollen shut. I layed there and cried. I didn't know what I was gonna do. The only thing I knew was the time had come for me to leave my daddy's house. And right there the world suddenly got big. And it was a long time before I could cut it down to where I could handle it. (52–3)

This assault by his father transforms Troy, especially in terms of his being forced to stand up to authority figures, by thrusting him into a malevolent and racialized world.

Unsafe at home, Troy, as a young teenager, becomes a cosmic waif, drifting with little discernible purpose in a malevolent universe whose white values and culture systems remain inimical to a black boy walking 200 miles to Mobile, Alabama, in 1918. It is here that a homeless and jobless Troy turns to robbery, and then murder, which lands him in prison for the most formative years of his young life. Although the ever sensible Rose reasons, with reference to Raynell, whose mother Alberta has just died giving birth to her, that 'you can't visit the sins of the father upon the child' (79), we also see, in the world Wilson constructs, that the sins of the past may very well be replicated in the present, if not the future. Hence Troy, with his sons Cory and Lyons, can only ponder the inevitability of their biological and spiritual destiny. These are men who remain vaguely aware that a replicating process ensures that the heritage propagated by their fathers and their fathers before them has been transferred to the sons through a seemingly ungovernable Darwinianism. The threat to future generations, Wilson implies, is a given:

'There's that sense of loss and separation. You find out how Troy left his house and you see how Cory leaves his house. I suspect with Cory it will repeat with some differences and maybe, after five or six generations, they'll find a different way to do it.' (*Conversations* 33).

Despite Troy's formidable presence within the play (Wilson's character descriptions relate all the other figures to Troy, i.e., Troy's friend, Troy's wife, Troy's brother, and so on), Rose occupies the most central and civilizing role in the play. Although Troy's circuitous language can be specific, that language also descends to the level of baseball banalities and clichés. Rose's language, however, cuts through Troy's rationalizations and highlights the truth. Linda Loman, in *Death of a Salesman*, cannot tell the truth directly to her husband. Rose Maxson can. She shows no evidence of evasion. Early in Act 2 in a scene that revolves around Troy's affair with Alberta, Troy tells Rose that when he saw Alberta, 'I got to thinking that if I tried . . . I just might be able to steal second . . . I stood on first base for eighteen years and I thought . . . well, goddamn it . . . go for it!' Rose responds, 'We're not talking about baseball! We' are talking about you going off to lay in bed with another woman' (70). Clearly Rose sets her sights on coming to terms with her husband's dreams and his rhetoric of equivocation. More tellingly, the scene signals a key power shift in their relationship, a shift characterized by Rose's assuming matriarchal control over her husband and extended family. It is a feminine control born out of an accepting love. As Rose says, 'Okay, Troy . . . I'll take care of your baby for you . . . 'cause like you say . . . you can't visit the sins of the father upon the child. A motherless child has got a hard time' (79). Troy's affair with another woman and the fathering of an illegitimate child, however, render him a 'womanless man' for the rest of his life (79).

James Earl Jones and Mary Alice, who played Troy and Rose in the 1985 Yale Repertory Theatre production, later recalled the cathartic effect that acting in *Fences* had on them. 'The first time I watched the rehearsal of the last scene, I was crying – not just for what I should have been crying about,' Jones related. 'I was crying for all the times that I should have been watching it and hadn't. There are three moments that trigger the ending catharsis: the moment when Rose acknowledges Troy has died, Cory's tribute, and Gabe's blowing the trumpet.' Alice added, 'Unlike Jimmy, I think I *have* a catharsis. I have mine at the top of the second act. I don't feel it in the evening, but more when I wake up the next morning – then I feel drained.' Finally, Jones concluded, 'I think this play, this story, demands all of what this man is, and it asks its actors to make a commitment larger than you would make even in a Shakespeare play.'[7] Wilson's catharsis produces a celebratory ending.

Wilson tempers the celebratory, however. He suggests that, despite the vitality of Rose and Troy and the reconciliation of Troy and Cory at the funeral which ends the play, there is a sense that the Maxsons remained entrapped. Indeed, as the playwright explained, each of the major characters in *Fences*

> is institutionalized. Rose is in a church. Lyons is in a penitentiary. Gabriel's in a mental hospital and Cory's in the marines. The only free person is the girl, Troy's daughter, the hope for the future. That was conscious on my part because in '57 that's what I saw. Blacks have relied on institutions which are really foreign – except for the black church, which has been our saving grace.' (*Conversations* 33)

Despite allusions to the institutionalization of the characters, however, Wilson ends the play with a sense of affirmation. In the final scene he mixes gestures of reconciliation, forgiveness and understanding to produce an image of family unity – and love. Music and song fill the stage. Gabriel adds a magical realism to the action in the final scene. An estranged son, thanks to motherly advice shorn of cliché, honours his father. This extended family unites, and, Wilson implies, despite his considerable flaws, Troy must be regarded, finally, as a noble, even heroic figure, a man who, despite his irresponsibility, understands the importance of self-reliance and social responsibility. His rise to heroism, Wilson said, 'may be nothing more than his willingness to wrestle with his life, his willingness to engage no matter what the circumstances of his life. He hasn't given up despite the twists and turns it's given him. I find that both noble and heroic' (*Conversations* 172). The epigraph the playwright provides at the start of the published version of *Fences* contextualizes the spirit of the play's final sense of compassion, affirmation and forgiveness:

> When the sins of our fathers visit us
> We do not have to play host.
> We can banish them with forgiveness
> As God, in His Largeness and Laws.

Thus, by the play's end, an earlier Barakian rage has yielded to a Hansberryan sense of renewal and hope. The family accord their flawed but finally heroic, noble, and lovable patriarch a proper and honourable funeral. Gabriel brings the play to its celebratory close when he blows into his trumpet. The trumpet produces no sound, yet Gabriel feels so passionately that Troy deserves full entry into heaven that, though baffled by the lack of sound, he wills Troy into salvation with his hypnotizing dance. For Wilson, Gabriel's final dance movements of 'atavistic signature and ritual' (101) ensure that the gates of heaven or, if one prefers, the fences of heaven, open wide for Troy Maxson.

NOTES

1. Lloyd Richards, 'Introduction', in August Wilson, *Fences* (New York: Plume, 1986), p. vii. Further quotations will be cited parenthetically in the text.
2. Sandra G. Shannon and Dana A. Williams, 'A Conversation with August Wilson', in Dana A. Williams and Sandra G. Shannon, eds., *August Wilson and Black Aesthetics* (New York: Palgrave Macmillan, 2004), p. 194.
3. 'August Wilson Interview', *Dialogue* (Summer 1990), p. 9.
4. See Michael Issacaroff and Robin F. Jones's edited collection, *Performing Texts* (Philadelphia: University of Pennsylvania Press, 1988).
5. 'August Wilson,' in Jackson R. Bryer and Mary C. Hartig, eds., *Conversations with August Wilson* (Jackson: University of Mississippi Press, 2006), p. 32. Further quotations from *Conversations* will be cited parenthetically in the text.
6. Julia Kristeva, *Strangers to Ourselves*, trans. Leon S. Roudiez (New York: Columbia University Press, 1991), p. 170.
7. Heather Henderson, 'Building *Fences:* An Interview with Mary Alice and James Earl Jones', *Theater* 16 (1985), p. 70.

11

STEPHEN BOTTOMS

Two Trains Running: blood on the tracks

The 1960s were always going to present August Wilson with a particular challenge in his grand scheme to create a decade-by-decade reflection on African American experience in the twentieth century. As Wilson himself remarks in the prefatory notes for his 1950s play *Fences* (1985), the 'hot winds of change' that began to gather in the postwar era 'would make the sixties a turbulent, racing, dangerous and provocative decade'.[1] The civil rights movement, which began in earnest with the Montgomery, Alabama, bus boycott of 1955 – after Rosa Parks refused to give up her seat to a white man – used peaceful tactics of mass civil disobedience to challenge and shame the often brutally repressive regimes maintained by segregationist cities and states in the American South. By the early 1960s, though, Malcolm X's calls, from the pulpits of the Nation of Islam, for black self-determination 'by any means necessary' had begun to rally support for a more aggressively defiant, anti-assimilationist stance. Although Malcolm X was assassinated in 1965, his spirit remained very much alive in figures such as Stokely Carmichael, who in 1966 challenged Martin Luther King for the moral high ground within his own civil rights movement, invoking the term 'Black Power': 'Power is the only thing respected in this world, and we must get it at any cost.'[2] That same year, the first chapter of the Black Panther Party was formed in California, availing itself of the constitutional right to bear arms in presenting itself as the first fully-fledged black revolutionary organization.

A parallel path of radicalization was apparent among black theatremakers. Lorraine Hansberry's realist family drama, *A Raisin in the Sun* (1959), alerted Broadway audiences to the social injustices and prejudice faced by African Americans in the North as well as the South, and James Baldwin's *Blues for Mr Charlie* upped the ante in 1964 with an uncompromising examination of the rationale behind emerging black radicalism. In the same theatre season, two major new figures emerged Off-Broadway with less commercial, more aesthetically experimental reflections on black experience:

Adrienne Kennedy's *Funnyhouse of a Negro* was an expressionist nightmare of internalized self-hatred; LeRoi Jones's *Dutchman* a subterranean ritual of black-white confrontation, whose central monologue proposed that the major achievements of African American art represent sublimations of the artists' fundamental urge to murder the white oppressor. Thereafter, Jones changed his name to Amiri Baraka and his work became both even more overtly revolutionary in tone, and more experimental in form, as he sought ways to cast off the influence of European theatre forms in search of a more Afrocentric performance style (his 1967 play *Slaveship*, for example, features a mesmeric use of drums, chants and Yoruba dancing). Baraka also, crucially, moved still further from the commercial mainstream of American theatre by targeting much of his work specifically at black audiences in New Jersey. Ed Bullins and others followed suit in Harlem and elsewhere, largely unconcerned with whether or not white audiences or white critics could be bothered to minoritize themselves by journeying into these communities to see their work.

Wilson, who came of age during this fervent period of change, retained something of the revolutionary spirit of the 1960s black arts movement throughout his career. In a speech to the eleventh Theatre Communications Group National Conference in 1996, he famously called for a reenergizing of the notion of a separatist black theatre, in order that young African American artists should not always find themselves defining their art against a dominant white backdrop. Yet Wilson also remained notable for his ability to write plays accessible and digestible enough to intrigue broad, mixed audiences, and thus to succeed repeatedly in an ever more risk-averse Broadway theatre context (an unusual achievement for *any* serious dramatist in recent decades). Considered in relation to the theatrical developments of the 1960s, Wilson's work reads as a return to the more or less conventional realism of a Hansberry, rather than a continuation of the more radical aesthetics of a Baraka or a Kennedy (their legacies are more visibly alive in the work of a playwright such as Suzan-Lori Parks). Indeed, Wilson's work seems sturdily old-fashioned even by comparison with Bullins's neorealist attempts at depicting slices of black American life in plays such as *In the Wine Time* (1968). Bullins, eschewing linear plot development and obvious dramatic symbolism, achieves an in-the-moment theatrical vitality in his writing that *Two Trains Running* (1990) never comes close to. Whereas *Fences* feels, appropriately enough, like a play written in the 1950s – an African American *Death of a Salesman* (1949), perhaps – it is altogether harder to regard *Two Trains Running* as reflecting *aesthetically* on the decade it represents in Wilson's cycle.

There again, 'vitality' is hardly the order of the day in a play dominated by the looming spectre of death. Far from being simply some retrograde assimilationist, Wilson was a writer well aware of his limitations as well as his strengths, and he may well have chosen the year of 1969 as the backdrop for *Two Trains Running* partly in order to avoid attempting to dramatize the hyperkinetic energy of the 'high sixties'. Rather, 1969 was the year when the decade of dreaming came to an increasingly sour end. Following the assassination of Martin Luther King and rioting at the Democratic Convention in 1968, there came the Manson murders, multiple deaths at the Altamont rock festival, and the so-called 'Days of Rage' (in which the white revolutionary group Weatherman incited the casual destruction of public property, ostensibly in protest at the war in Vietnam). For African Americans, 1969 was the year which saw the humiliating spectacle of a black man, Bobby Seale, being bound and gagged in the dock at the so-called 'Chicago 8' conspiracy trial, to prevent him denouncing the court's legitimacy. (His seven white co-defendants, whom Seale claimed not even to know, remained unrestrained.) It was also the year in which Seale's fellow Panther leader, Fred Hampton, was murdered at home in his sleep by a hail of bullets from FBI marksmen. Hampton, a much-loved figure in Chicago thanks to the Panthers' establishment of community self-help schemes such as the 'Breakfast for Children' programme, was publicly mourned by thousands at his funeral.

Death and despair seemed rife in 1969, and it is this mood that Wilson taps into with such unsettling effect in *Two Trains Running*. If, as the back cover of the play's Plume edition suggests, the two trains of the title represent life and death, then there is no question here which one is carrying heavier freight. Fresh deaths frame the beginning and end of the action: 'It don't never stop,' remarks West, the local funeral director, 'Time you bury one nigger you got to go get another.'[3] West's appearance – in black hat, black suit, black shoes, black tie and black gloves (which one character suggests hide a lifeless wooden hand) – casts him as a kind of grim reaper figure haunting the play. Yet the regulars at Memphis Lee's Restaurant, the down-at-heel Pittsburgh diner in which the action is set, fear and resent West (whose funeral parlour is across the street) not only because of his spooky appearance, but because of his relative wealth: death is presently the Hill District's only profit industry. As Memphis – the provider of food to the living – remarks bleakly of the economically blighted area: 'Ain't nothing gonna be left around here. Supermarket gone. Two drug-stores. The five and ten. Doctor done moved out. Shoe store gone. Ain't nothing gonna be left but these niggers killing one other. That don't never go out of style. West gonna get richer and everybody else gonna get poorer' (9).

There is violence in the air, it seems, simply as a result of the helplessness felt by local residents. Sterling Johnson, returning to the district after a spell in jail for bank robbery, is told that his friend Rodney has upped and moved to Cleveland: 'He had to get out of Pittsburgh before he kill somebody' (18). Sterling himself (played in the original production by Laurence Fishburne) subsequently acknowledges that he may yet need to resort again to crime: 'If I can't find no job I might have to find me a gun' (53). The problem is that, try as he might to find honest work, there does not seem to be any. Indeed, he finds himself caught in an absurd Catch-22 situation: the steelworks will not employ him without union membership, but the union will not take him without work. Although Memphis complains that Sterling is simply too lazy to work, noting that he has abandoned a perfectly decent job hauling bricks on a construction site, Holloway (another regular at the restaurant) points out that it paid only ten dollars a day – a starvation wage even in 1969: 'People kill me talking about niggers is lazy. Niggers is the most hard-working people in the world. Worked three hundred years for free. And didn't take no lunch hour. Now all of a sudden niggers is lazy. Don't know how to work. All of a sudden when they got to pay niggers, ain't no work for him to do' (35).

Memphis's conviction that Sterling is merely idle is indicative of the generational faultlines that the 1960s brought sharply into focus. The older man believes that people need to accept their lot and work hard for whatever they can get: this is how he eventually came to own his own restaurant. Holloway and Sterling, conversely, see no reason to accept slavery – or at least indentured servitude – as a precondition for eventual self-determination. Sterling doubts that such law-abiding labour ever really pays off. He tells the story of one 'hard-working man' he knew who worked thirty years in a mill without ever being allowed to join a union (and thus earn a negotiated wage): laid off every five-and-a-half months, before being rehired, he never completed the six months' minimum employment period he needed for union membership. The tale is indicative of a practice Holloway refers to as 'stacking niggers' – an allusion to the piled-up bodies on slaveships, but also to the continuing exploitation of black labour for humiliatingly menial, low-paid tasks. Indeed, Holloway insists, given the structural injustices of the system, even the little money that blacks *are* paid is not really theirs:

> All you got around here is niggers with somebody else's money in their pocket. And they don't do nothing but trade it off on each other. I got it today and you got it tomorrow. Until sooner or later as sure as the sun shine . . . somebody gonna take it and give it to the white man. The money go from me to you and then – bingo, it's gone. You give it to the white man. Pay your rent, pay your

telephone, buy your groceries, see the doctor – bingo, it's gone. Just circulate it around till it find that hole, then – bingo. Like trying to haul sand in a bucket with a hole in it. (33–4)

Perhaps, then, there would be a kind of Robin Hood justice if Sterling were to resort again to armed robbery, except that he would surely end up dead or in jail again, as so many black men do, in this system. 'I'll give you a dollar for every nigger you find that ain't been to jail,' notes Wolf, who tells the story of his own three-month internment without charge, simply for being in the wrong place at the wrong time (54). Later, after a local drugstore is burned to the ground, Wolf reflects that the white owner, Meyer, probably did it for the insurance money, but that somebody else – a black man – will be punished for it: 'Meyer's gonna be down there in Florida playing golf and laying on the beach . . . and the fire inspector's gonna be right there with him. That's the way it works in America' (105).

The play's concerns with structural racial injustice are embodied in the character of Hambone, who has been driven over the edge of his sanity by a deep-rooted sense of having been wronged. A decade ago, we are informed, Hambone painted a fence for the white butcher Lutz (whose premises are across the street from Memphis's restaurant), on the understanding that he would receive a ham in payment if he did a good job. Lutz chose to declare the good job inadequate, though, and offered him only a chicken, which Hambone refused to accept. The play depicts him, ten years on, still demanding his ham on a daily basis from Lutz, and still being rejected: the injustice has gnawed away at his mind to the point where he can only utter the same two sentences over and over again: 'I want my ham . . . He gonna give me my ham' (22). The irony proposed by Holloway is that Hambone may actually have 'more sense' than the supposedly sane – in that he refused to accept the secondary offering of a chicken that many others, confronted with Lutz's intransigence, would probably have taken, to cut their losses. 'Every time we even look at a chicken we gonna have a bad taste in our mouth,' Holloway notes of the likely consequences of such capitulation. Hambone's defiance, conversely, suggests an unwillingness 'to accept whatever the white man throw at him' (30). Picking up on this thread, the critic Harry J. Elam, Jr. argues that the very monotony of Hambone's ever-repeating demands for his ham reflect on the need 'to work specifically and collectively on a local level for change'.[4] Although Sterling tries playfully to educate Hambone in alternative slogans like 'Black is beautiful!' (57) and 'United we stand' (64), these Black Power soundbites remain – Elam notes – 'at the level of rhetoric' by comparison with Hambone's traumatized recitation of a very specific injustice: he calls out Lutz again and again, day after day, challenging him on the wrong he has done.

There again, of course, Hambone's calls fall on deaf ears – and having been driven mad by his futile waiting, he eventually dies unsatisfied (it is the news of his death that draws the play towards its close). Set in the context of the 1960s, his simply *asking* for justice, instead of demanding or even taking what he believes is his, reads in part as an assimilationist acceptance of white authority – an authority which is never going to grant him his due. When Memphis complains that Hambone has 'been around here ten years talking the same thing. I'm tired of hearing it' (44), Wilson is perhaps implying a link to the civil rights movement's insistence on nonviolent protest, which many blacks were indeed 'tired of hearing' by the later 1960s. Having made great headway against segregation laws in the South in its early years, the movement had increasingly run up against nationwide structural and economic inequities that it had no effective means of tackling. Thus the revolutionary radicalism of Malcolm X and his successors began to appeal more and more to a younger generation of activists. Perhaps it is significant that Sterling's cry of 'Malcolm lives!' is the one slogan he cites that Hambone proves unable or unwilling to mimic (64).

Malcolm X is an important figure in *Two Trains Running*, despite having been dead for four years by 1969. The play's events occur around the anniversary of his birthday, which is to be marked locally by a Black Power rally. Memphis dismisses this, too, as a futile gesture – 'Dead men don't have birthdays' (40) – insisting that this continued use of Malcolm's name as a focal point for protest against the white system has a hollow ring to it: 'Niggers killed Malcolm . . . and now they want to celebrate his birthday' (41). Ironically, though, Memphis seems to have very little grasp of what Black Power politics is actually about – perhaps an indicator of just how remote all the activist rhetoric seemed to many ordinary African Americans in this period. Certainly his contemptuous reference to 'these niggers talking about freedom, justice and equality' recalls King more readily than Carmichael. Moreover, despite his derision, Memphis inadvertently endorses the revolutionary agenda when he remarks that 'you can't do nothing without a gun . . . That's the only kind of power the white man understand' (42).

It is left to Holloway to point out the obvious flaw in the militant argument: entering an arms race with the white man is a losing proposition because 'he ain't had nothing but guns for the last five hundred years . . . got the atomic bomb and everything.' 'You can't even use the word "nigger" and "gun" in the same sentence,' Holloway adds, without sparking a repressive panic in the white establishment: 'they'll try and arrest you. Accuse you of sabotage, disturbing the peace, inciting a riot, plotting to overthrow the government and anything else they can think of' (85–6). Given the fates of so many members of the Black Panther leadership, this conclusion is difficult to argue with. But if peaceful protest and violent resistance are equally futile, then what hope is there? This dilemma, palpably felt by the end of the 1960s, is reexamined by Wilson from the historical distance of the 1990s: more than twenty years on, many of the underlying injustices protested against in the 1960s remained fundamentally unaddressed by American authorities – as the 1992 Los Angeles riots made all too clear. Erupting at the end of April, just two weeks after *Two Trains Running* opened on Broadway, these disturbances seemed to many observers like a depressingly predictable rerun of the Watts riots of 1965.

At times, *Two Trains Running* seems so bleak in its perspective – so lacking in faith that America's institutionalized racism can be effectively fought – that the situations faced by its characters acquire the existential overtones of absurdism. Perhaps this is Wilson's version of Eugene O'Neill's *The Iceman Cometh* (1945), with Harry Hope's bar translated as Memphis Lee's restaurant. Certainly the habitués of both establishments are characterized in large part by their resort to comforting 'pipedreams' of a better life which they have no means of realizing. The numbers racket that Wolf acts as an agent for, using the restaurant's menu chalkboard to mark up each day's winning number, is a case in point. Those who play the numbers dream of hitting the jackpot and so escaping the daily grind of their current lives, but it turns out that even this game is rigged by its white owners. When Sterling's number comes up towards the end of the play, he is horrified to discover that, because so many other people have played the same number, the payout to each is only a fraction of the value of the advertised jackpot. 'They been cutting numbers for the past hundred years,' Memphis notes sourly. 'You supposed to understand that when you play your money' (84).

Another pipedream is presented in the shape of organized religion. At the play's outset there is much discussion of Prophet Samuel, a local preacher who has just died, prompting mass shows of mourning in the community. 'God sent him to help the colored people get justice,' believes Risa, the restaurant's waitress, who has 'duly paid all tithing' to be 'a member in good standing of the First African Congregational Kingdom' (87). Holloway speaks of Samuel's colourful past, how he once attempted to preach justice to white people in their own neighbourhoods (25), yet it seems that latterly he has been mostly notable for living very well off his community's 'tithings' (just as West lives very well off their deaths). The play's repeated references to

Samuel's luxurious lifestyle suggest that he has become something of a false prophet: Wolf refers to 'all them jewels and things he had. That big old white Cadillac. Seven or eight women' (8), in terms that perhaps recall the accusations of impropriety that came to surround the Nation of Islam's Prophet Elijah Muhammad. Memphis, though, has no sympathy with the notion that innocent congregants have been fleeced: 'the people ain't thinking about no justice when they lined up there. They thinking about money like Prophet Samuel . . . The people paid Prophet Samuel's way hoping they'd get a financial blessing' (87). Memphis's comments seem harsh in relation to Risa, who certainly does not appear avaricious in this way, but Samuel's death means that he will clearly not now be delivering the justice, or indeed the cash benefits, he had promised.

Although always disparaging of other people's beliefs, Memphis himself turns out to be as dependent on his own pipedream as anyone else: for him, the dream is to return South one day to his hometown of Jackson, Mississippi, to reclaim a piece of land he had bought as a young man, but which had been violently repossessed from him by the former owner, a man named Stovall. The land had been sold because it was believed to be worthlessly dry, but when Memphis found water on the site, a judge upheld a contractual clause invalidating the sale in the event of such a discovery. Memphis thus lost his 'forty acres', and Stovall brutally gutted his mule, too (a kind of displaced lynching?). Yet despite the horror of this experience, which he recounts in graphic detail, Memphis remains stubbornly insistent that he still has his deed (legally invalid though it may be), and that he will one day get his land back. O'Neill's dreamers could not do better.

The particular irony here is that Memphis is now facing a situation in which history is about to repeat itself. For all the pride he takes in his achievement at having worked his way up in the world from nothing, he is about to have his livelihood stripped from him with the imminent forced purchase of his restaurant by the Pittsburgh authorities – apparently as part of one of the flawed 'urban renewal' projects that swept so many cities in the 1960s. Protest as he may, Memphis has no legal recourse because the authorities have 'the right of eminent domain', as West puts it: 'They don't care what you think. They can go anywhere in the city and take any piece of property they want' (39). Bingo! Rather than sell his restaurant to West, though, for what the latter insists will be a better price than the city will ever give him (as a block property owner, West believes he can squeeze more out of them), Memphis stubbornly insists that he will get the price he wants from the city – $25,000 – simply by digging in his heels. Again, he seems wilfully to blind himself to legal realities.

It is to everyone's surprise, then, that at the play's climax Memphis succeeds in securing not $25,000, but $35,000, as part of the purchase order – a sum which he believes will enable him to return to Jackson and repurchase his land. This turnabout, which flies in the face of the play's bleak logic of structural injustice, reads on one level as a fantasy *deus ex machina* conclusion – as Wilson surely knew. Nothing in the play has prepared us to believe that this could occur. So why does it? Is this simply a case of the political need for hope in the future winning out over dramatic coherence? The unexpected optimism is mirrored in news that a crowd six times larger than anticipated has turned out to the Malcolm X rally – including 'niggers that swear up and down on two stacks of Bibles they ain't black . . . they was down there' (104). Is the 'train of life' suddenly picking up speed?

Not entirely, for Wilson is careful to balance these moments of sudden optimism with darker undertones: the news of the burning of Meyer's drug-store, for example, follows directly on from the rally report. There is also more to Memphis's good news than meets the eye: Elam suggests that the city's decision to respect Memphis's financial demands is a result of his having retained a white lawyer, Joseph Bartoromo, to plead his case. Elam reads this with telling ambivalence: 'Wilson does not suggest that Memphis condones white legal superiority, but given the reality of this hegemonic system, he must find a performative strategy that can enable him to prevail.'[5] Given that black lawyers seem to have so little purchase on the system (as Wolf says at the very beginning of the play, 'the NAACP got all kinds of lawyers [that] don't do nobody no good' (2)), and that those who do achieve status have often colluded with power to maintain their positions ('the first black judge' in Pittsburgh, Memphis notes, was 'death on niggers' (58)), then another option is needed. Sometimes, Wilson seems to suggest, Black Power may best be accomplished through a pragmatic manipulation of the existing system, 'by any means necessary', rather than via revolutionary rhetoric. Here, then, the play does offer a tentative, if imperfect way forward, a rejection of despair.

Crucially, though, Memphis himself does not credit Bartoromo with his unexpected payday, but the black conjure woman Aunt Ester. This unseen figure, whom the otherwise sceptical Holloway believes is 322 years old, sounds at first like another Prophet Samuel – another figure whose importance to those who believe in her depends on superstition and pipedreaming rather than any realistic engagement with their problems. Yet she differs significantly from Samuel in that her ministry centres not on the acquisition of money, but on its unimportance. 'Aunt Ester give you more than money,' Holloway explains:

She make you right with yourself . . . Just say you come to see Aunt Ester. You ain't got to tell them what you want to see her about. Just say, 'I come to see Aunt Ester.' You got to pay her, though. She won't take no money herself. She tell you to go down and throw it in the river. Say it'll come to her. She must be telling the truth, 'cause she don't want for nothing. (24)

This is the first of Wilson's cycle plays in which the figure of Aunt Ester is referred to: subsequently she also figures in *King Hedley II* (2000) and *Radio Golf* (2005), and she appears physically as a central character in *Gem of the Ocean* (2003). Indeed, she became for Wilson 'the most significant persona of the cycle. The characters, after all, are her children. The wisdom and tradition she embodies are valuable tools for the reconstruction of their personality', and she represents 'the metaphysical presence of a spirit world that has become increasingly important to my work'.[6] Much of that was still to come, though, when Wilson wrote *Two Trains Running*: in this play she remains a figure whom one might or might not choose to take seriously as a spiritual figure. Rather, her importance in this most materially focused of Wilson's plays lies in the fact that she rejects the materialism dominating the American milieu and encourages other characters to shake off their enslavement to the dollar – to *throw money away* – if they want to receive the blessing of finding themselves.

At the play's climax it becomes clear that both Memphis and Sterling have been to see Aunt Ester, and have followed her instructions. Memphis, para-doxically, has been materially blessed as a result – though his legal winnings should in his case be the means to his ultimate, idealistic end of returning home, to Jackson. In Sterling's case his visit to Aunt Ester has given him the courage to go and confront Old Man Albert, the kingpin behind the num-bers racket, over the injustice of the slashed jackpot. Rather than resorting to self-destructive violence, as the other characters feared he would, Sterling has instead used his wits to win a kind of victory. Demanding and receiving his $2 stake back, by declaring the bet off because Albert has not paid out in full, Sterling nonetheless keeps the $600 he won from the numbers, refusing to return it in exchange. Emboldened by getting away with this challenge to authority, Sterling then carries out the final action of the play – appearing in the final moments carrying a large ham which he has 'liberated' from Lutz's butcher shop in order, belatedly, to right the wrong done to Hambone.

This final image throws the other, unexpectedly upbeat climactic twists of Wilson's otherwise bleak play into fresh perspective. Here is a man who really has found his spirit, and in doing so has committed a criminal act – smashing and grabbing from Lutz's window – which leaves him 'bleeding from his face and hands' (110). The image of the bloodied Sterling holding the ham aloft finally recalls (somewhat ironically?) the revolutionary gestures of Baraka's 1960s dramas, and there is clearly a kind of defiant, cathartic release involved here. Yet the meaning and consequences of the gesture are also complex and conflicted. For one thing, Sterling's destruction of property implicitly challenges Memphis, whose final speech, immediately preceding Sterling's entrance, celebrates the possibility of *acquiring* property – by using his $35,000 to open a bigger, better restaurant with many employees, right there in Pittsburgh. This grand, materialist ambition is apparently at odds with his stated desire to return home to Jackson: will he perhaps 'sell out' his dream, just as Prophet Samuel apparently did? (According to Holloway, Samuel's life, too, changed after going to see Aunt Ester (25); though going to see her may help one to realize oneself more fully, one's inner heart is not always necessarily pure.)

There is also, surely, a question mark over Sterling himself. It is difficult to see his liberation of the ham in straightforwardly joyful terms, because the crime places him in immediate jeopardy of returning to prison. This is precisely where Risa had feared he would end up, which is one of the reasons why she has proved hesitant – throughout the play – in accepting Sterling's touchingly romantic advances. Why open oneself up to someone who cannot be relied on to stand by you? Does Sterling's 'revolutionary' gesture (and a gesture is all it is, in the context of the narrative) jeopardize not only his own future but also hers? Does it render darkly prophetic his earlier gesture of giving her flowers – flowers stolen, for want of money, from the grave of a dead man? Is there a need to distinguish between action that is gestural, and action – such as the formation of a loving partnership of equals – that might really make a difference?

Risa is the most vulnerable character in the play, though also in an odd way the strongest. A beautiful young woman, she has found herself so objectified in terms of her sexuality by the men around her that she has taken the drastic action of scarring her legs to try to repel their lustful stares. She is now treated by most of the men in the play simply as a functionary – a person whose role in life is to be ordered about, to fulfil the menial tasks of serving them. Indeed, Memphis, who as Risa's boss barks humiliating strings of orders at her throughout the play without so much as a thank you, continues to treat her with thoughtless presumption even after his ship has come in at the play's conclusion: 'Risa . . . take this fifty dollars and get some flowers [for Hambone's funeral] . . . Risa, where's my plate, I got to eat something' (110). Is she expected to do two things at once? It is hardly surprising that, as is reported at the beginning of the play, Memphis's wife has just left him: 'She told me she was tired,' he complains derisively, yet 'she ain't got nothing to do but stay home and take care of the house. She got it nice. Talking about she tired. She wasn't too tired to make them four babies' (5). Unfortunately, Memphis's almost laughable blindness to the labours of women in no way makes him unique. Throughout the play, it is clear that the men tend to regard women, and Risa in particular, as second-class citizens – insofar as they regard them at all. Elam notes that Risa's refusal to leave sugar on the restaurant tables, so that the men have to ask her to bring it to them – and in so doing, to acknowledge her existence – is thus a 'subtly subversive act' made all the more telling if the actress takes her own good time about fulfilling these requests.[7]

Wilson has often been accused of being irredeemably male-centric, of being unable to write persuasive parts for women, and certainly complex female characterization is not his strength. In *Two Trains Running*, however – through the quietly influential offstage presence of Aunt Ester, and through the constant but usually silent presence of Risa, toing and froing with the men's orders – it becomes clear just how central, and at the same time just how marginalized, women are in the world Wilson depicts. Even as he compellingly presents the men's justified disquiet about the structural injustices of the economic and legal systems, and about the continuing near-slave status of black men as 'stacked niggers', Wilson presents equally clearly an awareness that the doubled oppression of African American women remained, as late as the 1960s, almost invisible even to their menfolk. This was a time when even Black Power radicals saw no equivalence between the struggles against racial and sexual oppression: Eldridge Cleaver spoke laughingly of women exercising 'Pussy Power', and Carmichael argued that the best position for women in the movement was 'prone'. For the scarred yet subtly defiant Risa, the feminist awakening of the 1970s cannot come too soon.

There is an epilogue, of sorts, to *Two Trains Running*, in the form of Wilson's final play, *Radio Golf*. In the 1990s, at the end of the cycle, a Hill District property is again under threat of enforced purchase for demolition, but this time it is the house in which Aunt Ester lived (and, in the 1980s of *King Hedley II*, died). This architectural embodiment of African American tradition and heritage – whose historic fittings are described lovingly in the dialogue – is to be destroyed not by the white authorities, but by local black property developers, who are actively hoping for the Hill District to be declared 'blighted' in order that their building plans may receive the appropriate financial grants from the federal government. Is this what has become of the black middle class? Are these developers the descendants of Memphis, with his expansionist property plans? Tellingly, the figure who defiantly rallies support against them is the same Sterling Johnson who in 1969 stole a ham from Lutz's window. Sterling, it emerges, has never really found regular work, has never joined a union, has always survived – as he puts it – by 'going through the backdoor'.[8] Yet he has worked, as did Hambone before him, at painting houses (combating time's decay?), and he now commits himself – in the face of the bulldozers – to repainting Aunt Ester's house, so as to restore its faded dignity. Aunt Ester's lessons about what really matters have, for him, been permanent: 'You can't do nothing with money but spend it,' he notes at the beginning of *Radio Golf* (turning around Holloway's complaint about money always going back to the white man):

> After that you back where you started from. Then what you gonna do? I found out I was looking for something that you couldn't spend. That seem like the better of the two. To me. Everybody got their own way of looking at it but if you ask me . . . I'd take something you couldn't spend over money any day.[9]

NOTES

1. August Wilson, *Fences and Ma Rainey's Black Bottom* (London: Penguin, 1988), p. 18.
2. Stokely Carmichael quoted in *The Autobiography of Martin Luther King, Jr.*, ed. Clayborne Carson (London: Little, Brown and Co., 1999), p. 321.
3. August Wilson, *Two Trains Running* (New York: Plume, 1993), p. 91. Futher quotations will be cited parenthetically in the text.
4. Harry J. Elam, Jr., *The Past as Present in the Drama of August Wilson* (Ann Arbor: University of Michigan Press, 2004), p. 70.
5. *Ibid.*, p. 159.
6. August Wilson, 'Aunt Ester's Children: A Century on Stage', *American Theatre* 22:9 (November 2005), p. 30.
7. Elam, *The Past as Present*, p. 100.
8. August Wilson, *Radio Golf*, *American Theatre* (November 2005), pp. 87–108 (p. 99).
9. *Ibid.*, p. 91.

12

DAVID KRASNER

Jitney, folklore and responsibility

> I simply wanted to show how the [jitney] station worked, how these guys
> created jobs for themselves and how it was organized . . . I just wanted to
> show these guys could be responsible.
> August Wilson[1]

Despite being a well-known film star, Danny Glover found himself being
shunned by New York City's taxicab drivers in the autumn of 1999. After
finally being picked up by one cab driver, Glover experienced rude treatment.
'I was so angry,' he said in recounting the event to the *New York Times*. The
Times reported that 'several empty cabs had refused to stop for him, his
college-aged daughter and her roommate. Later, when one finally did, the
driver refused the 6-foot-4 "Lethal Weapon" star access to the front seat
even though he had a bad hip and is entitled under taxi industry rules to
stretch out in front.'[2] Glover filed a formal complaint with New York's Taxi
and Limousine Commission; the incident received attention in the press; a
protest rally was held in Harlem; and even New York's former Mayor David
Dinkins added that he, too, had often been refused cab rides. Despite the
public outrage, refusing cab rides to African Americans is a fact of urban
life and a part of its folklore. In Public Enemy's *Fear of a Black Planet*, for
example, the rap group compared the situation of taxicabs to police and
fire fighters disregarding the black community during 9/11. The lyrics of one
song report, '9/11 is a joke we don't want 'em / I call a cab 'cause a cab will
come quicker.'[3] To compensate, African Americans often use 'gypsy' cabs.

Known as jitneys, gypsy cabs constitute an underground industry in the
African American community. At the beginning of the twentieth century, segregation was institutionalized; by mid-century it had become an embedded
aspect of everyday life. Cut off from the mainstream socially and economically, blacks turned inwards for financial support. As African Americans
moved north in search of jobs, buses, subways and taxis became a necessity. Since 'official' taxicabs were unreliable, blacks instituted their own ser-
vices. Building on the Garvey movement (the concept of nationalism and
separatism fostered by Marcus Garvey and his followers during the 1920s),
African Americans pursued an independent economy. If enforced separation
denied access to the marketplace as suppliers, the reasoning went, why should

African Americans support mainstream business? Jitney cabs were part of a larger internal infrastructure fostering an economy, milieu and even folklore.

Folklore was deemed an essential element in black literature. In his 1937 essay 'Blueprint for Negro Writing', Richard Wright maintains that 'Negro folklore contains . . . the collective sense of Negro life in America.' It is, therefore, the writer's responsibility to flesh out 'aspects of Negro life that illustrate 'the social institutions of Negro people as in folklore'. There is, according to Wright:

> a Negro church, a Negro press, a Negro sporting world, a Negro business world, a Negro school system, Negro professions; in short, a Negro way of life in America. The Negro people did not ask for this, and deep down, though they express themselves through their institutions and adhere to this special way of life, they do not want it now. This special existence was forced upon them from without by lynch rope, bayonet and mob rule. They accepted these negative conditions with the inevitability of a tree which must live or perish in whatever soil it finds itself.[4]

While Danny Glover rejected 'these negative conditions' by asserting his right to a regular cab, jitney cabs continue to serve the African American community.

The literal and folkloric significance of jitneys was not lost on August Wilson. This chapter will examine his 1979 *Jitney* play in the light of Wright's 'Blueprint'. Without being explicit, Wilson follows Wright in his insistence that an African American writer's responsibility is to represent black folklore. *Jitney* premiered at Pittsburgh's Allegheny Repertory Theatre in 1982. The play, originally written with an exclamation mark (*Jitney!*), evolved into a ten-play cycle depicting each decade of African American life in the twentieth century. Until its 2000 New York premiere at the Second Stage Theatre, however, *Jitney* remained a slightly acclaimed and seldom scrutinised drama. It was hardly mentioned in two major Wilson studies of 1994, *May All Your Fences Have Gates: Essays on the Drama of August Wilson*, edited by Alan Nadel, and *August Wilson: A Casebook*, edited by Marilyn Elkins, nor has it ever been the focus of leading Wilson scholars and critics, largely because it remained unpublished until 2000. However, post 2000, the drama of a gypsy cab station managed to move into the spotlight.

The play's main ethical theme is responsibility. Using the cab station as a backdrop, *Jitney* centres on five drivers struggling to lead productive lives. According to Wilson, these drivers 'make jobs out of nothing. The important thing for me was to show these five guys working and creating something out of nothing'.[5] Born of racial segregation, African American ingenuity demonstrates a capacity to meet the challenge by creating 'something out of nothing'. To succeed, African Americans, Wilson's plays suggest, establish specific locations in which they can flourish. These spaces – whether a jitney cab station, a restaurant, a recording studio, a front porch, a back yard, or a boarding house – possess distinctive features identifiable with specific aspects of folklore. Within a segregated society, African Americans have traditionally come together. Each relationship in *Jitney* portrays this tendency. Social cohesiveness and emphasis on responsibility are elevated to folklore status and epitomized by the jitney station owner Becker. The threat of 'eminent domain' (compulsory purchase) looms over the cab station; the city of Pittsburgh, where the play is set, is planning to tear down the block and make way for urban renewal. Becker rallies his fellow drivers, declaring his intention to fight the closure. In the second act he informs them of their responsibilities:

> The people got a right if you hauling them around in your car to expect the brakes to work. Clean out your trunk. Clean out the interior of your car. Keep your car clean. The people want to ride in a clean car. We providing a service. That's why you answer the phone 'car service.' You don't say Becker's Cab's or Joe's Jitney's. Part of that service is providing people with a way to get their groceries home or to get their suitcase down to the bus station or the airport, so they can go home to visit their mama or whoever it is they want to visit.[6]

For Wilson, the cab station makes use of three cultural signifiers – place, time and crisis – establishing its folkloric contours. The locale demonstrates what I will call a 'circumscribed black space', a location using the folklore and traditions of the black community. Time highlights the conditions of African Americans in the late 1970s, which had specific historical connotations. Crises in the play arise in the workplace and the family.

Becker's speech quoted above implies the possibility that passengers might be new arrivals from the South. Going 'home to visit their mama', Becker remarks, would be understood by the black community as a reference to northern migration. A 'bus station or the airport', Becker says, indicates a return visit to family. The Mason-Dixon connection integral to African American history is recognized as such by those in the culture. James N. Gregory has observed that 'Migration is often best understood as a circulation rather than a one-way relocation because, in many instances, migrants at some point circle back toward home'.[7] At the beginning of the twentieth century, roughly 90 per cent of the black population lived in the South; by mid-century, it was evenly divided.[8]

The play's setting, according to the opening stage directions, 'is a gypsy cab station in Pittsburgh, Pennsylvania' (11). Pittsburgh was one of several major northern cities which absorbed large numbers of African Americans.

This movement of people during the twentieth-century diaspora known as the Great Migration occurred primarily during two periods: 1910 to 1930, and post World War II circa 1945 to 1970. Joe T. Darden offers statistical information about the impact on Pittsburgh:

> Continuous migration to a limited number of heavily black populated census tracts and natural increase in these tracts have been the components in the formation and expansion of the 'black ghettos' in Pittsburgh. Lured by the prospect of higher wages and opportunity for social betterment, black migrants from the South crowded into Pittsburgh early in [the twentieth] century to such an extent that, between 1910 and 1930, their numbers increased 93 percent . . . After the Great Depression, another major wave of migration of Afro-Americans began . . . [From 1940 to 1960 migration] and natural increase combined to raise the total black population from 54,983 in 1930 to 100,692 in 1960, the largest three-decade increase in the history of Pittsburgh.[9]

The setting of *Jitney* is therefore much more than a room; the stage space represents the working place of the black people of Pittsburgh and a site for the creation of folklore. Like the memory of Emancipation, the memory of migration Becker alludes to has shaped African American identity as marked by Wilson's prose.

Temporally, *Jitney* takes place during 1977 and relates to a particular juncture of African American history. At the time, the civil rights movement was in decline, having achieved merely a few of its major goals. While certain aspects of society had seen integration, the economy largely had not. As a result, jitneys represent the essence of black economic life. Urban renewal, a persistent motif in Wilson's plays, is a mixed blessing; it brings jobs and housing but undermines tradition and memory. Wilson explains that the setting afforded the playwright 'an opportunity to use this group of men to expose the culture, to get at some of the ways that this particular community of people solved its problems, abused itself, and all those kinds of things'.[10] Fusing family and business crises illuminates the characters' predicaments. Pamela Jean Monaco observes that Wilson 'favors drama of the interior setting that focuses on an individual and his or her family construct'. By situating the protagonists in a specific time, place and crisis, the playwright 'demonstrates the impact of political and social changes on the individual and the community'.[11] These changes impact on characters caught in the ebb and flow of social upheaval.

The play's crises incorporate three main relationships. First, there is the father-son conflict common to Wilson's dramas. Becker worked for nearly three decades at the local Pittsburgh mill. Upon retiring with a pension, he used his savings to build his own business. The station, although in disrepair, proudly displays a sign on the wall reading: *'Becker's Rules: 1. No overcharging; 2. Keep car clean; 3. No drinking; 4. Be courteous; 5. Replace and clean tool'* (11). Yet despite his best efforts to establish himself as a pillar of the community, he experiences a major catastrophe. His only son, Clarence (nicknamed Booster), is sentenced to twenty years in the penitentiary. Booster had shown great promise in high school and was accepted by the University of Pittsburgh at a time when few, if any, African Americans were allowed to enroll. At college he became involved with a white woman whose father was vice-president of Gulf Oil. Coincidentally, on a night when Booster and his girlfriend drove for a tryst in a dead-end street the girl's father rendezvoused at the same spot with a black prostitute. Seeing his daughter in the arms of a black man enraged the father. He attacked Booster. Booster, not knowing who the man was, retaliated.

At the preliminary court proceedings, the girl, intimidated by her family, lies: she claims that she was forcibly abducted and raped. Becker is able to get his son freed on bail, but instead of letting justice take its course, Booster takes matters into his own hands. He goes to her home, where he murders both daughter and father. The killings anger Becker, who feels that his son has senselessly thrown his life away. He stops attending the trial, leaving his then wife (he subsequently remarries) to attend the proceedings alone. Booster is found guilty and sentenced to death, the shock of which causes his mother to stop eating; she eventually dies. Booster's capital punishment is suspended, but for twenty years father and son blame each other for the death of Booster's mother (Booster claims that his father failed to help her through her suffering). The climactic final scene of Act 1 occurs when Booster returns to the jitney station to confront his father.

The second relationship focuses on Darnell Williams (nicknamed Youngblood) and his girlfriend, Rena. Youngblood, one of Becker's drivers, is a Vietnam veteran who moonlights as a skilled car mechanic. He also works as a UPS driver, attempting to earn enough money to support his family by holding down three jobs. He has fathered Rena's child and is trying to do the right thing by investing what little he has in a down payment on a house. Because he wants to surprise Rena, he withholds the details. For her part, Rena suspects him of philandering. In a central scene of Act 2, Youngblood and Rena become reconciled and learn the importance of responsibility.

The third relationship is that between the remaining characters. They joke, banter, argue, fight, reconcile and unite. Turnbo is a driver and a mordant busybody, well meaning but intrusive (often 'studying' someone). Fielding, the fourth driver, has squandered his talent as a tailor. He is an alcoholic and is threatened with dismissal by Becker, but the two men reconcile. The threats and reconciliations are in all probability a cycle that Becker and Fielding have experienced numerous times. Doub, the fifth driver, is the voice of reason. He cools overheated arguments and pursues solidarity. Rounding out the cast are Shealy, a numbers runner, and Philmore, who makes a brief appearance as a passenger. The men bond despite mutual agitation. As Sandra Shannon explains, 'Becker's jitney station is more than just headquarters for dispatching taxis. It also doubles as home for several men who have lost their way in the world'.[12]

The station is a place where tall tales are frequently exchanged. Keith Clark remarks that 'Wilson's multiple dramatic discourses – simultaneously realist and naturalist, fabulist and mystic, ritual and spiritual – are rooted in black men's retrieval and voicing of personal histories, which inform the plays' thematic and formal configuration. Hence, personal stories take precedence over the erection of a seamlessly crafted dramatic story'.[13] The play emphasizes language, social interaction and symbolism and highlights characters possessing a sense of responsibility. The opening exposition reveals that Booster is being released from prison. The atmosphere is leisurely. Men are playing checkers and answering the payphone. People call for appointments and rides. Although hostility arises between Youngblood and Turnbo, Shealy takes his payments for the numbers (an underground lottery game connected to the daily horse races) and Doub and Turnbo swap neighbourhood stories.

In the next scene Rena suspects Youngblood of infidelity involving her sister, Peaches. Her suspicions are encouraged by a gossiping Turnbo, who informs her that Youngblood's 'business is on the street' (i.e., the news of his philandering is everywhere). Despite Turnbo's meddling, an important point about responsibility is made in criticizing young men for their lack of commitment not only to spouses but also to the community. As Turnbo says, 'These young boys don't know nothing about that . . . and it's gonna take a lifetime to find out. They disrespect everybody and don't think nothing about it. They steal their own grandmother's television' (31). The emphasis on shared values is a significant component to the drama as a whole.

The cab station is scheduled for demolition. This is conveyed rather cavalierly by Becker:

> DOUB I was just talking to Clifford next door. He says the man is gonna board his place up next month.
> BECKER Yeah, I know. The man from the city was by here two weeks ago, too. They gonna tear it all down, this whole block.
> DOUB The man was by here and you ain't told nobody! What he say?
> BECKER They're gonna board the place up first of next month.
> DOUB Why in hell didn't you tell somebody!
> BECKER I'm telling you now. (36)

Becker avoids informing his employees because he initially believes that the station will relocate and the demolition will prove to be little more than an inconvenience. However, he is soon overcome by despondency. In explaining his feelings to Doub, Becker invokes the spirit of Christianity, a recurring theme in Wilson's plays.

> I used to question God about everything. Why he hardened Pharaoh's heart? Why he let Jacob steal his brother's birthright? After Coreen [his wife, named Ruth in other versions of the play] died I told myself I wasn't gonna ask no more questions. Cause the answers didn't matter. They didn't matter right then. I thought that would change but it never did. It still don't matter after all these years. It don't look like it's never gonna matter. I'm tired of waiting for God to decide whether he want to hold my hand. I been running cars out of here for eighteen years and I think I'm just tried of driving. (36)

His despondency stems from the fact that his son is to be released the next day. The tension of potentially losing their jobs results in a fight between Youngblood and Turnbo.

In the final scene of Act 1, Booster arrives, '*dressed in his prison-issued suit, and a white shirt without a tie*' (51). When Becker enters, the stage is set for the climactic confrontation. Wilson, a playwright prone to melodrama and the moral high ground, constructs an emotionally powerful scene as Becker announces:

> I am the boss of a jitney station. I'm a deacon down at the church. Got me a little house. It ain't much but it's mine. I worked twenty-seven years at the mill . . . got me a pension. I got a wife. I got respect. I can walk anywhere and hold my head up high. What I ain't got is a son that did me honor . . . The Bible say 'Honor they father and they mother.' I ain't got that. I ain't got a son I can be proud of. (55)

Booster counters by describing how his childhood emulation of his father inspired his revenge:

> I don't know if you knew it Pop, but you were a big man. Everywhere you went people treated you like a big man. You used to take me to the barbershop with you. You'd walk in there and fill up the whole place. Everybody would stop cussing because Jim Becker had walked in. I would just look at you and wonder how you could be that big. I wanted to go to school and try to make myself feel big. But I never could. (56)

He explains that his father once had to cower in the face of a landlord's ranting because the rent was overdue. At that moment Booster had seen his father as a coward, and he now informs him that 'you had got smaller. The longer he shouted the smaller you got. When we went back to the barbershop you didn't seem so big no more. You was the same size as everybody else' (57). Booster's 'big and small' symbolism is tangentially related to Wilson's own relationships with his biological father, a white German who abandoned the family, and his stepfather, a black ex-football player and felon. There is, in Wilson's plays, an inner conflict, a felt need to stand tall in the face of adversity, while simultaneously hubris proves costly. This conflict of courage and foolhardiness is often played out in Wilson's father-son relationships. Harry J. Elam, Jr. contends that even as the plays demonstrate the 'faults and frailties of the father, the underlying objective is to reconcile and restore the position of the patriarch within the fabric of the family, precisely because the black father seems so apparently lost'. Given the history of slavery and displacement, the black family unit had 'existed as property, absented by legislation, even from their humanity'. Wilson, therefore, 'considers how we can recuperate the black father as a presence in images of masculinity'.[14] Booster, as the play's narrative suggests, must learn that 'big' has less to do with confrontation and more to do with channelling rage productively.

The second act begins with another 'symbolic' father-son relationship, this time between Doub and Youngblood. Doub, the play's *raisonneur*, supplies a lesson: take the initiative and suppress anger towards whites. He says to Youngblood, 'You want to make something of your life, then the opportunity is there. You just have to shake off that "white folks is against me" attitude. Hell, they don't even know you alive' (65). He reminds him that he is not the only African American to have served in the military; Doub served in the Korean War collecting bodybags. This proved a sobering experience. He urges Youngblood to take responsibility, acquire an education, and should the station close and jitney driving fall through, obtain a job in the mill. Youngblood recoils: 'The mill sucks the life out of you. That's not for me. I don't want that. I'll do anything but I don't want that' (66). But Doub remains sanguine: 'It ain't all the time what you want. Sometimes it's what you need. Black folks always get the two confused' (67).

When Rena enters, Youngblood confesses that he has been with her sister Peaches looking for a house and asking her to assist him in choosing the right place. This desire to own a home prompts comparison with Lornaine Hansberry's *A Raisin in the Sun* (1959). In that play it is the mother, Lena Younger, who wants a home, and only in the end will Walter Lee, her son, understand its significance. Hansberry and Wilson join in conveying the sense of responsibility which success at marriage and family entails. The home for Youngblood and Rena, as it is for the Younger family, is at the root of their loving relationship and the core of their identity as a couple.

Becker assembles the drivers to explain the extent of the city's demolition plans. The jitney station is not alone in being marked for demolition. As he

insists, 'If we don't do something they'll put Clifford out of business. Put
Hester out of business [their neighbours]. Put us out of business' (85). The
other drivers come round to Becker's way of thinking. 'If everybody stick
together they can't do nothing,' Fielding says (86). As in another taxicab
drama, Clifford Odets's *Waiting for Lefty* (1935), Wilson paints a powerful
portrait of workers' solidary. For Odets, unions are the solution; for Wilson,
too, solidarity and teamwork can overcome adversity.

Despite the hopeful conclusion of the scene, the final two scenes take an
abrupt turn. Becker dies. The drivers mill around praising him until Booster
arrives. They convey the news, bringing Booster to an anguished state. In the
final scene, Booster comes by to show his appreciation of the support for his
father shown by Becker's colleagues. He closes the play with the following
testimonial that is worth quoting at length:

> I never knew him too much, you know. I never got to know him like you all
> did. I can't say nothing wrong by him. He took care of me when I was young.
> He ain't run the streets and fuss and fight with my mama. The only thing I ever
> knew him to do was work hard. It didn't matter to me too much at the time
> cause I couldn't see it like I see it now. He had his ways. I guess everybody do.
> The only thing I feel sorry about . . . is he ain't got out of life what he put in.
> He deserved better than what life gave him. I can't help thinking that. But you
> right . . . I'm proud of my old man. I'm proud of him. (*The phone rings*.) And
> I'm proud to be Becker's boy.
> (*He stops and catches himself*.)
> I didn't come here to preach no sermon.
> (*He starts toward the door. He stops and turns around. The phone continues
> to ring. He crosses to it and picks up the receiver*.) (*Into phone*) Car service.
> (*The lights go down to black*.) (6)

This final moment lays bare the play's meaning. When Booster answers
the telephone, he picks up more than a receiver; he picks up where his father
left off. He does so in full view of the others, thereby reassuring them of
his continued support of the jitney station and his willingness to fight for
their rights. The family business connects father and son, with Booster now
embracing his role in life. The ending attests to Wilson's romanticism. The
literary historian René Wellek contends that the three criteria of Romanticism are 'imagination for the view of poetry, nature for the view of the world,
and symbol and myth for poetic style'.[15] *Jitney* follows these principles in its
use of poetic language, the father-son relationship as a form of 'nature' (or
nurturing), and the ambience of myth and symbolism common to African
American life. Wilson once said that the 'foundation of my playwriting is
poetry. Not so much in terms of the language but in the concept . . . [T]he

mental process is poetic: you use metaphor and condense. I try to find a metaphor to carry the work'.[16]

Despite the play's emotional resonance, it is not without its weaknesses. Wilson readily admits that at the time he wrote *Jitney*, 'You could fit in a thimble what I knew of theater'.[17] The play's fault lies in its melodramatic contrivances. Youngblood's desire to surprise Rena with the house is manipulated, enabling Rena to suspect infidelity, thereby creating a conflict where one could easily be avoided. This conflict allows Wilson to orchestrate a potboiler break-up-then-make-up ending. Becker's sudden death also conveniently draws the curtain (in much the same way as Troy Maxson's death ends *Fences* (1985)). It allows Booster his better-late-than-never reconciliation. Similarly, the fight between Youngblood and Turnbo seems engineered. *Jitney* tells the story of salvation and redemption. Wilson's later plays are far less optimistic, more realistic and less naïve. Still, the roots of superb dramas to come are evident in *Jitney*, both in its dialogue and in its social portrayal. As Wilson's work matured, the plays became increasingly complex.

Wilson's concept of social bonding serves him as a playwright in much the same way it served Arthur Miller. Miller's play *All My Sons* (1947), like *Jitney*, is meant to teach us that community and social responsibility must take precedence over selfishness. The closing testimonial at Willy Loman's funeral in Miller's *Death of a Salesman* (1949) can be viewed as anticipating the message Wilson sends regarding Booster's homage to his father. When Linda Loman utters the play's famous moral dictum, 'attention must be paid', over Willy's grave, she is referring not merely to her husband, but to something conceptual – the common man – a family breadwinner who works hard, plays by the rules, and deserves better than the raw deal he endures. Similarly, Booster says of his father that 'he ain't got out of life what he put in. He deserved better than what life gave him.' For Miller and Wilson, hard working, morally upright characters like Loman and Becker deserve recognition. Wilson represents a tradition of African American dramatists whose work and conduct spotlight those who live by the rules and have earned the respect they too rarely receive.

NOTES

1. August Wilson, quoted in Sandra G. Shannon, *The Dramatic Vision of August Wilson* (Washington, DC: Howard University Press, 1995), p. 95.
2. 'New York's Cabbies Show How Multi-Colored Racism Can Be', *New York Times*, 7 November 1999, Section 4, p. 4. The cab driver in question was from southern Asia.
3. Public Enemy, '9/11 Is a Joke', http://www.publicenemy.com/index.php?page=page5&item=3&=58num

4. Richard Wright, 'Blueprint for Negro Writing', *New Challenge: A Literary Quarterly* 2:11 (Fall 1937), p. 57.
5. Shannon, *Dramatic Vision*, p. 56.
6. August Wilson, *Jitney* (Woodstock, NY: Overlook Press, 2003), p. 86. Further quotations will be cited parenthetically in the text.
7. James N. Gregory, *The Southern Diaspora: How the Great Migrations of Black and White Southerners Transformed America* (Chapel Hill: University of North Carolina Press, 2005), p. xii.
8. For studies of migration, see Neil Fligstein, *Going North: Migration of Blacks and Whites from the South, 1900–1950* (New York: Academic Press, 1981); Alferdteen Harrison, ed., *Black Exodus: The Great Migration from the American South* (Jackson: University of Mississippi Press, 1991); Daniel M. Johnson and Rex R. Campbell, *Black Migration in America: A Social Demographic History* (Durham: Duke University Press, 1981); and Joe William Trotter, ed., *The Great Migration in Historical Perspective* (Bloomington: University of Indiana Press, 1991).
9. Joe T. Darden, *Afro-Americans in Pittsburgh: The Residential Segregation of a People* (Lexington, MA: Lexington Books, 1973), pp. 6–7.
10. August Wilson, 'August Wilson on Playwriting', in Jackson R. Bryer and Mary C. Hartig, eds., *Conversations with August Wilson* (Jackson: University of Mississippi Press, 2006), p. 225.
11. Pamela Jean Monaco, 'Father, Son, and Holy Ghost: From the Local to the Mythical in August Wilson', in Marilyn Elkins, ed., *August Wilson: A Casebook* (New York: Garland, 1994), p. 90.
12. Shannon, *Dramatic Vision*, p. 60.
13. Keith Clark, *Black Manhood in James Baldwin, Ernest J. Gaines, and August Wilson* (Urbana: University of Illinois Press, 2002), p. 97.
14. Harry J. Elam, Jr., *The Past as Present in the Drama of August Wilson* (Ann Arbor: University of Michigan Press, 2004), p. 131.
15. René Wellek, *Concepts of Criticism* (New Haven: Yale University Press, 1963), p. 161.
16. August Wilson, quoted in David Savran, ed., *In Their Own Words: Contemporary American Playwrights* (New York: Theatre Communications Group, 1988), p. 292. New York:
17. Shannon, *Dramatic Vision*, p. 63.

13

JOAN HERRINGTON

King Hedley II: in the midst of all this death

In African societies, life is closely associated with blood. When blood is shed in making a sacrifice, it means that human or animal life is being given back to God who is in fact the ultimate source of life. Therefore the purpose of such sacrifice must be a very serious one. Such sacrifices may be made when the lives of many people are in danger. The life of one person or animal, or of a few of either, is destroyed in the belief that this will save the life of many people. Thus the destruction of one becomes the protection of many.[1]

Set in the 1980s, August Wilson's *King Hedley II* (1999) reveals a world in which the lives of many people are in danger. Twenty years after the passage of the Voting Right Act and its accompanying promise of social change, conditions for African Americans in the inner cities are, perhaps, worse than ever. Reaganomics has failed to trickle down, black-on-black crime is at its height, the youth of the community suffer the oppression of crack culture, and, by 1990, the unemployment rate for black men is twice as high as for white.[2] US Department of Justice statistics for the late 1980s reveal that African Americans represented 12 per cent of the population but were responsible for 50 per cent of all homicides and 66 per cent of all robberies; 50 per cent of all urban blacks were arrested for a serious crime at least once in their lifetime.[3] Most of the crimes occurred within dominantly or completely African American communities. The victims were rivals, neighbours, enemies, relatives. The availability of drugs and guns and the distinct lack of opportunities determined the fate of many young men and women whose isolation from community and history made them easy prey. They had lost their cultural connection; Aunt Ester was dead.

This is the world of *King Hedley II*. As Wilson himself notes, 'Look at the sets . . . we've got a torn-down building where the guy plants some seeds and then puts barbed wire around the seeds, and everyone's walking around with 9mms under their belts. It looks like a war zone – like someone dropped a bomb there.'[4] The play is filled with darkness and despair and, at its outset, marked by the death of a recurring Wilson character whose spiritual presence has guided the characters in several of his other plays. The unnaturally old Aunt Ester has survived from the trials of slavery to the turmoil of the civil rights movement. She has offered strength, guidance and renewal throughout most of the century chronicled by Wilson; but in *King Hedley II*, she dies.

The disconnection of the community from its cultural heritage is represented in Aunt Ester's demise – a stunning response to the rampant apathy. In Stool Pigeon's Prologue to *King Hedley II*, the character foreshadows the death as he bemoans the state of his world:

> Everything done got broke up. Pieces flying everywhere. Look like it's gonna be broke up some more before it gets whole again. If it ever do. Ain't no telling . . .The people wandering all over the place. They got lost. They don't even know the story of how they got from tit to tat. Aunt Ester know but the path to her house is all grown over with weeds, can't hardly find the door no more.[5]

The monologue sets the stage for the play's central dilemma but also for its association with African culture. The language here is reminiscent of the chant of a Yoruba priest, bemoaning the chaos that has resulted from the failure of the community to make sacrifice.

> The world is broken into pieces;
> The world is split wide open,
> The world is broken without anybody to mend it;
> The world is split open without anybody to sew it.[6]

In his call for a vital reconnection, Wilson himself reengages with African culture. In contrast to the play's Judaeo-Christian imagery, he includes the traditional Yoruba demand for ritual and sacrifice as a means of achieving harmony. Here the sacrifice is not intended to 'reunite alienated sinners with God', but rather to find solutions for the problems of daily life. This sacrifice is not designated by God but rather self-determined through divination, embodying an effort to reconnect with ancestral spirits, here represented by Aunt Ester.[7] But the characters in *King Hedley II* have failed to make any sacrifice. Separated from their ancestors, their gods and their history, their tragedy, like that of Yoruban traditional drama, 'is the anguish of this severance, the fragmentation of essence from self'.[8] Within this framework Wilson makes an impassioned plea for African Americans to reconnect with the cultural roots almost completely abandoned in the deadly 1980s.

The action of the play, set in the decaying, violent Hill District of Pittsburgh in 1985, continues the lives of characters that first appeared in Wilson's *Seven Guitars* (1995). The story revolves around the title character's striving to start a new life after a seven-year jail term for manslaughter. He lives with his wife Tonya, a 35-year-old grandmother who has just learnt of her new pregnancy, and his mother Ruby, a singer who has been on the road most of King's life, leaving his upbringing to her now-deceased sister. While King and his friend Mister scam and steal in an effort to open their own business, King's future is influenced by the arrival of Elmore, his mother's old lover, and King's neighbour Stool Pigeon, who collects newspapers obsessively so that those who come after him will know what 'went on' (27). The play is set in the rundown back yard of the family home where the characters spin their wheels in the dirt, repeating their mistakes, making desperate and violent choices, and further isolating themselves from family and community.

The play concludes with the shooting of the title character by his mother. It is a heartstopping moment, seemingly epitomizing the agonizing cycle of violence that defines this generation. But Wilson has framed it differently. Immediately following King's shooting, the stage directions read, '*Stool Pigeon suddenly recognizes that the sacrifice has been made*' (102). King's blood has fallen on the grave of a black cat belonging to Aunt Ester. It is the sacrifice that Stool Pigeon has been awaiting, one that will enable the resurrection of Aunt Ester and the reconnection of the community to a lost past. It is a moment of transition – of hope.

King's journey begins with Wilson's stark presentation of the reality of a life in which separation and inequality plague the characters. King's inability to have even his most modest expectations met is evidenced in his failure to collect photographs from a Sears store. Despite the fact that, as instructed, he brings his receipt, he is unable to fulfil even this simple quest: 'The problem is they tell me my receipt don't count. That's what the problem is . . . You see what I'm saying. That's like telling me I don't count' (53).

Indeed, at every turn King is told he does not count and he quickly comes to recognize the basic injustice of his world. 'They got everything stacked up against you as it is. Every time I try to do something they get in the way. It's been that way my whole life. Every time I try to do something they get in the way' (54). Raised at the height of the civil rights movement, King and his wife Tonya expected better but now realize that there 'Wasn't nothing for me and now ain't nothing for [my children] . . . Seem like something should have changed' (42).

Not only have things not improved, it is clear in *King Hedley II* that they have deteriorated, with the death of Aunt Ester standing as the greatest evidence of the present danger for the community. Aunt Ester made her first entrance into Wilson's drama in *Two Trains Running* (1990), set in the 1960s. In that play Holloway notes, 'Aunt Ester give you more than money. She make you right with yourself.'[9] Unseen but present in this play and the three that follow, she is defined by her actions and words related by those onstage. For Wilson's characters, she holds the potential for spiritual renewal through connection to the past. She preaches self-knowledge and personal responsibility. As Holloway tells Sterling, 'You don't want to do nothing for yourself. You want somebody else to do it for you. Aunt Ester don't work that way. She say you got to pull your part of the load.'[10]

For Aunt Ester, and Wilson, pulling the load means acknowledging where you have come from. In *Two Trains Running*, Memphis comments, 'Aunt Ester clued me on this one. I went up there and told her my whole life story. She says, "If you drop the ball, you got to go back and pick it up. Ain't no need in keeping running, 'cause if you get to the end zone it ain't gonna be a touchdown."'[11] Aunt Ester stands as Wilson's ever-present reminder of the need for connection to the past. For his characters, she is the conduit to the source. She finally makes her stage appearance in *Gem of the Ocean* (2003), chronologically the first play in the ten-play cycle, set in 1904 but written after *King Hedley II*. In this play she attends Citizen Barlow who is troubled by having committed a robbery for which an innocent man has chosen to give his life rather than be branded a thief. In order to make Barlow 'whole', Aunt Ester takes him on a journey to the City of Bones, recreating the experience of the Middle Passage and enabling him to find peace through acknowledgement of that history. It is the first time the audience is allowed to witness her work. Her ability to bridge the years is an impressive sight.

Born in 1619 and, at the opening of *King Hedley II*, 366 years old, Aunt Ester has spanned the presence of the African people on Western soil.[12] Wilson notes, 'Aunt Ester carries the memory of all Africans, the memory of the ancestors. She embodies the wisdom and traditions of all those Africans, starting with the first one. It is a tremendous responsibility to carry all this – to remember for everyone as well as to remember for yourself – and she's accepted the responsibilities of it.'[13]

Despite the fact that she makes an appearance in only one play, *Gem of the Ocean*, Wilson notes, 'Aunt Ester has emerged for me as the most significant persona of the cycle. The characters, after all, are her children. The wisdom and tradition she embodies are valuable tools for the reconstruction of their personalities and for dealing with a society in which the contradictions, over the decades, have grown more fierce, and for exposing all the places it is lacking in virtue.'[14]

In the plays preceding *King Hedley II*, Wilson did not envision the death of Aunt Ester, despite his characters' disbelief that anyone could live that long. In 'How to Write a Play Like August Wilson', the playwright says of *Two Trains Running*, 'there are so many references to death . . . In the midst of all that, though, in the midst of all this death, you have that which doesn't die – the character of Aunt Ester which is the tradition.'[15] His sentiment is embodied in the character of Holloway, who remarks, 'She get sick sometime.

As you can imagine, somebody 322 years old is bound to get sick once in a while. But she ain't gonna die, I guarantee that!'[16] Read in the context of *King Hedley II*, written ten years later, *Two Trains Running*, set in 1969 but written in 1989, seems oddly optimistic. Twenty dramatic years later, Aunt Ester is dead, King Hedley is dead, and the community, represented in its families, is disintegrating

The 'death' of Aunt Ester, and the demands this event makes on Wilson's characters, stand as the metaphysical core of *King Hedley II*. Ester's nearly impossible old age brings to the fore the question of her existence in a world defined by twentieth-century Western culture, deeply dependent on linear chronological progression and clear lines between life and death. Throughout Wilson's century-long saga, his characters consistently note that Aunt Ester is unnaturally old, unnaturally wise and, indeed, otherworldly. But viewed from the African, particularly the Yoruban perspective, her presence is less unusual. Called forth and made present by their descendants, ancestors exist within the same world as those who succeed them. They exist in the here and now and one encounters them at the crossroads of life or invokes them in moments of crisis. Wole Soyinka describes this expanded perspective as 'contemporaneous existence within . . . daily experience', wherein 'life, present life, contains within it manifestations of the ancestral, the living, and the unborn'.[17] In *King Hedley II*, Stool Pigeon buries Aunt Ester's black cat in the back yard. Given societal restrictions, it is the closest he can come to burying Aunt Ester herself at the site of the house, in keeping with a tradition wherein ancestors were kept close to home. Despite objections, Stool Pigeon creates the grave in preparation for his anticipated spilling of blood on to the site so that the cat (representative of Aunt Ester) can come back in seven days. The ritual sacrifice is not needed so much to resurrect Aunt Ester as to regenerate the community through a reconnection to its spiritual and cultural past.

For eighty-one years, Wilson allows Aunt Ester to serve the community, to be its glue, to heal its soul.[18] But in *King Hedley II*, she dies. Perhaps, the characters conjecture, she died of grief, certainly a possibility as she surveyed a landscape in which she had no place. 'Part of the picture in *Hedley*', Wilson explained, 'is that the path to Aunt Ester's house is all grown over with weeds and leaves. You can hardly find the door anymore.'[19] Whether she lives on the earth in a mortal state or whether her 'death' is merely the symbolic identification of the severing of the ties to her 'children', whose acknowledgement of her existences is necessary for her sustenance, her death is the core of the tragedy. As Molefi Kete Asante notes in 'The Future of African Gods: The Class of Civilizations', 'the abandonment of our history, indeed the abandonment of our gods, the gods of our ancestors, have brought us deep into the quagmire of misdirection, mis-orientation and self-pity – a quagmire demanding a sacrifice.'[20]

In the extremely complicated final scene of *King Hedley II*, Wilson clearly provides such a quagmire. The title character learns that he is not, as he has been told, the son of crusading, prophetic King Hedley I, introduced in *Seven Guitars*, but rather the son of his mother's earlier lover. The revelation is doubly devastating, first in the denial of the lineage on which he has built his identity, and second in his recognition of the need to avenge the death of his true father. The last moments of the play are wild, violent and irrational. In the final scene King's mother accidentally shoots him in an attempt to save his life. '*The bullet strikes King in the throat. Tonya screams. King falls on the ground near where the cat is buried*', providing the blood Stool Pigeon awaited for his sacrifice (102). Although the killing is 'accidental', a mother, a wife, an unborn child and the community have offered sacrifice.

According to Professor George Brandon, the African-Cuban Santeria religion provides a useful context for the study of Africanisms in American culture. Santeria, which literally means worship of saints, is an 'African based religion with a clear dual heritage. Imported into the United States from Cuba, its component traditions include European Christianity . . . traditional African religion (in the form of orisha worship practices by the Yoruba of Nigeria) and Kardecan spiritualism'.[22] The word for sacrifice in Santeria is *ebo*, translated as 'to do' or 'the thing done'.[21] As John Pemberton explains:

> Ebo is Santeria's answer to the problem of suffering, a means to achieve harmony in a universe composed of teeming forces, both good and ill, whose relationships continually change and whose configurations are manipulable through sacrifice. Through the medium of ebo and communication with ancestors, deities, and malevolent spirits, the disordered universe is replaced by freshness, clarity and peace.[23]

Perhaps it is Aunt Ester herself, along with Wilson, who has demanded the sacrifice that concludes the play, although, in her usual oblique fashion, Aunt Ester has not designated its details. In explaining the Yoruba idea of 'ori', a 'personal, prenatal, destiny', Pemberton has stressed its emphasis on the need for an individual to determine the proper path, the intended road, 'to know security and hope in the midst of struggle'.[24] Throughout Wilson's work, it has been Aunt Ester who has helped others to find the path that necessarily demands a reconnection to the past in an attempt to move forward. In their own pursuit of security and hope, Wilson's characters continually sought her guidance to determine the proper road to follow, to address their desire, and, like their ancestors, to determine the correct sacrifice necessary to restore harmony.

In the Yoruba tradition such answers come from the diviner priests who recite the verses of the Odu ('the 256 figures or patterns which appear on the dust of the divining tray and which refer to a vast collection of verses'). 'The objective of Ifa divination ("the most universal and oft-performed ritual of the Yoruba") is to determine the correct sacrifice necessary to secure a favorable resolution of the problem confronting the client'.[25] In Wilson's plays Aunt Ester is the diviner, offering advice to be deciphered. As in ancient African tradition, the supplicant listens to the verses and selects the one that best answers his question, a question that may or may not have been asked of the diviners. Thus a sacrifice and its method of enactment are determined. As with the diviners whose prescriptions are deeply metaphoric, Aunt Ester's answers must be extracted from her wise words, the true question sometimes being known only to the seeker. Aunt Ester knows that 'without sacrifice, obligation would not be met, all would be in disorder, and the world would fall apart'.[26] Indeed, the stories of the diviners make clear that sacrifice is necessary – the gods do not support those who do not make ebo; 'For persons plagued by illness, bad luck, poverty, or stress, ebo is the only way they can alter their fate.'[27]

But in *King Hedley II*, the diviners have been abandoned; the self-serving community prefers not to give up anything, neglecting an ancient under-standing that

> Nothing in the universe is obtained by doing nothing. You must always give something to get something. It's extremely basic; you can't fill up a cup without giving its contents first. You can't move to a new place in a room without giving up the space you now occupy. In other words, sacrifice is a basic concept of our universe.'[28]

The death of Aunt Ester facilitates a sacrifice that might otherwise have been neglected as the danger of the schism between the children of the 1980s and their forefathers is denied. The absurdity of the situation is clearly evident to Stool Pigeon, whose collection of newspapers is largely burned by street punks during a mugging. He did not fight for the $63 they took; he fought for the history:

> This is my papers. What's left of them. What them kids gonna do now? They burned up their history. They ain't gonna know what happened. They ain't gonna know how they got from tit to tat. You got to know that. They ain't gonna know nothing. I ask myself, 'Why they do that?' I have to tell myself the truth. I don't know. If somebody know and they tell me then I'll know. But the truth is I don't know. I can't figure it out. (69)

The neglect of the next generation is made all the more profound in the physical nature of the assault on Stool Pigeon and, symbolically, those who came before.

Wole Soyinka notes that the gulf between one area of existence and another – man and ancestors, man and deities – 'is what must be constantly diminished by the sacrifices, the rituals, the ceremonies of appeasement to those cosmic powers which lie guardian to the gulf. Spiritually, the primordial disquiet of the Yoruba psyche may be expressed as the existence in collective memory of a primal severance.' Soyinka speaks of the mythological separation of man and gods and further explains, 'I would render this more cogently today in terms of race origination, uprooting, wandering and settling.'[29] Stool Pigeon, like Soyinka, recognizes a disruption of the community so intense that it demands a sacrifice to repair it. 'The people wandering all over the place. They got lost' (8) as, in play after play, Wilson explores migration, wandering, cultural separation, uprooting. 'Characters sever ties to their families and their histories, and once those ties are broken, communities crumble.'[30]

Wilson recognizes that 'disturbances in the social or natural order can only be corrected by ritual means', in this case, sacrifice.[31] King's blood falls on the grave of Aunt Ester's black cat, whose death closely followed that of her mistress. According to Stool Pigeon, blood on the grave of this animal will ensure its return in seven days – and the blood he demands is clearly that of a traditional sacrifice: 'If I knew where to get a goat I'd kill him and spill his blood on there. That might work. Either that or a fatted calf' (60.)

Stool Pigeon is humorously stymied in his efforts to access these animals, perhaps because Wilson recognizes the need for a grander gesture on behalf of the community – the sacrifice of a king. Thus Wilson must build King's character so that his nobility is clearly apparent despite his failings. Although King, lacking other opportunities, dreams of opening a video store – in fact one video store in each state – he finances his entrepreneurial dreams by selling refrigerators of questionable origin and by robbing the local jewellery store. He is not unlike previous Wilson characters who feed their families – and their sense of justice – through illegal activity. Wilson does not judge these men negatively but rather sees them as warriors, respecting those 'who look around to see what the society has cut out for them, who see the limits of their participation, and are willing to say, "No I refuse to accept this limitation that you are imposing on me"'[32]

Throughout Wilson's plays, there are men who take what they are owed or offer what is due. Solly, in *Gem of the Ocean* a past conductor of the underground railroad, burns down the mill whose owners abuse their workers.

Sterling, *Two Trains Running*'s growing black nationalist, steals the ham that was owed to Hambone who was never adequately paid for work done.

While Wilson's respect for the valiance of these undertakings is clear, they are not separable from their other, less valiant actions. Wilson's concern is expressed by the women of his plays, who recognize the inherent challenge to the structure of the community and its families posed by these choices. In *Two Trains Running* Risa tells the proposing Sterling, 'You ain't got no job. You going back to the penitentiary. I don't want to be tied up with nobody I got to be worrying is they gonna rob another bank or something.'[33] In *King Hedley II* King's wife Tonya tells his mother, Ruby, 'Every time he go out somewhere I hold my breath. I'm tired of it. I'm suffocating myself. I done told him if he go back to jail I'm through with it. I gonna pack up my little stuff and leave. I ain't goin' through that again. I ain't visiting any more jailhouses' (78). Society has taught these men to 'prize masculinity over community in the forms of family, home, neighborhood'.[34] And while Wilson respects the necessity of the choice these men make, he recognizes, nonetheless, the need to change the culture that breeds these choices through radical action – the sacrifice of a king.

King Hedley II is a rebel, an unwilling leader, but he is also a man touched by a mystical presence in his heritage. He is named for the man he believes, through most of the play, to be his father. King Hedley I comes from the coterie of Wilson characters whose unpredictable but prophetic natures separate them from the other characters. Gabe in *Fences* (1985), Hambone in *Two Trains*, Hedley in *Seven Guitars* and Stool Pigeon in *King Hedley II* are all regarded by the other characters in their plays as being off balance. But Harry J. Elam, Jr. notes that 'In Wilson's work it is the characters that appear mentally or physically impaired, besieged by madness, unable to grasp the reality of the world around them, who represent a connection to a powerful, transgressive spirituality, to a lost African consciousness and to a legacy of black social activism.'[35]

A product of his generation, King has lost touch with this element of his nature, but his choice to closely align himself with King Hedley I rarefies his awareness of a thread connecting him to an empowering past.

Stool Pigeon, himself prophetic, recognizes King's potential. As a child, King cut Aunt Ester's grass and she gave him a gold key ring. Stool Pigeon identifies this with the biblical story of 'the key given to the righteous that they might enter the kingdom', and he challenges King: 'Aunt Ester gave you the key ring, that mean you got to find the key' (21). Stool Pigeon believes in King's potential to climb the mountain – to fulfil his ori/destiny. But in his confused and overwhelming world, King's path, like Aunt Ester's walk, is hard to find. As Stool Pigeon notes, 'King get a Key to the mountain and he'll be all right. Only he don't know he looking for it. He liable to walk right by it' (60). King senses his potential. He has dreamed of himself with a halo around his head, a dream that has such presence for him that he asks the other characters if they can see it. Unable to find a spirituality in themselves, King's family and friends do not see it and they do nothing to reinforce his visions, telling him the seeds he plants will never grow.

But King's final actions of the play establish him among those deserving of a place on the mountain. Stool Pigeon presents him with the machete that King Hedley I had used to kill a man. It is the machete of the 'Conquering Lion of Judea', as Stool Pigeon defines Hedley I (61). He tells King, as he presents it, 'You can do with it what you want. If you find a way to wash that blood off you can go sit on top of the mountain. You be on top of the world.' Giving away the machete that was used to kill Stool Pigeon's friend is an act of forgiveness and a challenge to King, whose first instinct is to get it sharpened and take it down to Sears 'to see them talk about their system then' (63).

King is conflicted. He has already served time for murder but late in the play he notes, 'Anybody kill somebody is living without God. You ain't even got no right to pray' (73). Still, following the scene in which King learns of his true parentage, knowledge that reveals that his mother's current lover, Elmore, is the killer of King's biological father, King's friend Mister remarks on King's visit to the nearby cemetery where his first wife is buried:

> He always do that when something happen. Then when he come back he be a new man. Somebody kill you daddy, that seem like blood for blood to me. I know King. That's just what he thinking. He just wants to think about it a while. Elmore need to go on to Cleveland if he wanna get there. Otherwise somebody gonna have to busy him. I know King. Your blood is your blood and ain't nothing thicker than that. King be looking for ways to prove it . . . His daddy dead and he looking at the man who killed him. He ain't supposed to be looking long. (98)

The cycle of violence, so prevalent in the decade in which the play is set, is embodied in King at this moment and in the moments that follow, as his duelling angels appear in the men at his side. As he plays a vicious game of dice with Elmore, Mister urges, 'Blood for blood, King. Be the man!' while Stool Pigeon reminds him, 'You got the Key to the Mountain. You can go sit on Top of the World' (100). In the final moments King puts the machete to Elmore's throat, epitomizing the black-on-black, often friend-on-friend violence that defined this decade. But King proves himself a worthy sacrifice as the stage directions read, '*Unable to harm Elmore, King turns and sticks the machete into the ground*' (101). As Wilson explains, 'His forgiveness of Elmore is the key to the mountain through forgiveness – so it gives birth to a new tradition that's based on forgiveness and reconnecting to that new tradition.'[36]

For the renewal and rebirth to truly begin, the community must rebuild from the start and in ancient African cultures the kings 'were often sacrificed as part of a ritual of reenactment and reinforcement of this cycle of death and resurrection'.[37] The focus was always on the new life. Sometimes ritual regicide was practised so that the spirit of the king could enter his successor. Sometimes the ritual anticipated the resurrection of the king. According to Yoruban culture, since King is childless at the time of his death, his spirit is destined to return to earth as opposed to joining the ancestral world.

Ultimately, what may make King most worthy of sacrifice is that he represents hope. Despite King's less admirable qualities, we care for him, root for him and find him heroic even in his effort to grow a flower. In the opening scene of the play, King arrives in his yard and plants seeds from a packet. Throughout the play, despite discouragement from others, he draws energy from his modestly growing plant. He even ironically protects his seedling with barbed wire. It is an admirable effort in a dead zone of humanity. As Ladrica Menson-Furr writes, 'Wilson's dramas re-define and represent the image of the black man on the farm, transforming him into a hero and his farm work into a noble profession through which he is given the power of creation, and the "green thumb" of life, to save his race and himself.'[38] It is a gesture of independence following in the footsteps of his namesake King Hedley who, in *Seven Guitars*, has dreams of owning a plantation and facing the day when 'the white man not going to tell me what to do no more'.[39] King Hedley I wanted to be 'big man and landowner', and he longed to have a son.

It is King Hedley I's commitment to being a parent that results in King Hedley II's confused lineage. In *Seven Guitars*, Ruby, who will later bear King Hedley II, says of her pregnancy and King I, 'I'm gonna tell [King] it's his. He's the only man who ever wanted to give me something. And I want to have that. He wants to be the father of my child and that's what this child needs. I don't know about this messiah stuff but if it's a boy – I hope to God it is – I'm gonna name it after him. I'm gonna name him King.'[40] Like the man he believes to be his father, King II wants to establish his legacy. His act of planting is 'a physical metaphor for King's desire to see the harvesting of his own biological seed so that others will know that he has lived.'[41]

In one of the play's darkest twists, King's wife Tonya decides to abort their child. At thirty-five, she does not want to 'have a baby that younger than my grandchild. Who turned the world around like that? What sense that make?' (39). Her choice is also determined by the likely fate she sees for her child, and the intense violence that will define his world; 'I ain't raising no kid to have somebody shoot him. To have his friends shoot him. To have the police shoot him. Why I want to bring another life into this world that don't respect life? I don't want to raise no more babies when you got to fight to keep them alive' (39).

In a stunning defence of her design, Tonya relates the story of a tragically disturbing malaise that haunts her and epitomizes the times:

> You take little Buddy Will's mother up on Bryn Mawr Road. What she got? . . . One minute her house is full of life. The next minute it's full of death. She was waiting for him to come home and they bring her a corpse. Say, 'Come down and make the identification. Is this your son?' Got a tag on his toe say 'John Doe.' They got to put a number on it. John Doe number four . . . Somebody come up and tell her, 'Miss So-and-So, your boy got shot.' She know before they say it. Her knees start to get weak. She shaking her head. She don't want to hear it. Somebody call the police. They come and pick him up off the sidewalk. Dead nigger on Bryn Mawr Road. They got to quit playing cards and come and pick him up. They used to take pictures. They don't even take pictures no more . . . The only thing to do is call the undertaker. The line is busy. She got to call back five times. The undertaker got so much business he don't know what to do . . . I ain't going through that. I ain't having this baby . . . and I ain't got to explain it to nobody. (39–40)

In an ironic parallel, King himself was almost aborted – chronologically just following the close of *Seven Guitars*, the play in which his character was conceived. In *King Hedley II* King's mother Ruby tells of being sent to see Aunt Ester, who Ruby assumed performed abortions. But it is not this child who is to be sacrificed, and in the divination of Aunt Ester, a different path is carved. Ruby remembers:

> She put her hands on my head. I got real peaceful. Seem like all my problems went away. She told me man can plant the seed but only God can make it grow. Told me God was a good judge. I told her that's what scared me. She just laughed and told me, 'God has three hands. Two for that baby and one for the rest of us.' (41–2)

Thirty-five years later, Tonya stands at this crossroad. Ruby tells Tonya, 'You never know what God have planned', but the world Tonya faces is even more challenging than that faced by Ruby; Aunt Ester's restful hands are gone, and the disintegration of the community has created even more confusion. King argues for the life of his baby: 'I need this baby not 'cause I took something out the world but because I wanna put something in it . . . Even if you have to call the undertaker. Even if somebody come along and pull it out by the root. It still deserves to live' (84). But Tonya demands change – a new society, a new definition of family, and the ability of a child to know its father. This requires sacrifice. 'Sacrifice is essentially the conversion of a situating of death, or potential death in any of its manifestations, into a situation of life . . . so the sacrificial victim dies to give life, to reverse the death-bound temporal process.'[42] As with Ruby, the sacrifice of the unborn child will not suffice. In an ultimate expression of the danger of the dissolution of heritage and disconnection from family and community, the magnitude of the sacrifice is determined and King is killed by his mother.

King's death is necessary for the birth of the child. New life cannot begin until the old life has been destroyed. The old king must die – in this case, be sacrificed – before the new king can rise. As Wilson notes, 'There's always new life somewhere, here with Tonya being pregnant King dies but then he lives.'[43] With the enactment of the sacrifice, the potential for reconnection is considerable. In Stool Pigeon's final monologue, he praises the forces beyond his world, welcoming both the God of Abraham and his African ancestors, here embodied in the conquering Lion of Judea. Soyinka notes that 'tragedy in the Yoruba, traditional drama, is the anguish of this severance' between man and ancestors, between man and gods.[44] Stool Pigeon welcomes an end to the severance and tragedy; according to Wilson, 'It's really a joyful play. We start a new tradition, we can reconnect.'[45]

NOTES

1. John S. Mbiti, *Introduction to African Religion* (Oxford: Heinemann Educational Publishers, 1991), p. 63.
2. Peter Wolfe, *August Wilson* (New York: Twayne, 1999), p. 23.
3. Edward S. Shihadeh and Nicole Flynn, 'Segregation and Crime: The Effect of Black Social Isolation on the Rates of Black Urban Violence', *Social Forces*, 74: 4 (June 1996), p. 1325.
4. Rob Kendt, 'August Wilson', *Backstage West*, 10 February, 2000, p. 8.
5. August Wilson, *King Hedley II* (New York: Theatre Communications Group, 2005), pp. 7–8. Further quotations will be cited parenthetically in the text.
6. John Pemberton, 'Eshu-Elegba: The Yoruba Trickster God', *African Arts* 9:1 (October 1975), p. 67.
7. Gailyn Van Rheenan, 'Communicating Christ among Folk Religionists', at www.missiology.org/folkreligion.
8. Wole Soyinka, *Myth, Literature and the African World View* (London: Cambridge University Press, 1976), p. 145.
9. August Wilson, *Two Trains Running* (New York: Penguin, 1999), p. 22.
10. *Ibid.*, p. 76.
11. *Ibid.*, p. 109.
12. The calculation of Aunt Ester's age from play to play is inconsistent but the characters agree she predates American Slavery.

13. Randy Gener, 'Salvation in the City of Bones', *American Theatre* (May/June) 2003, p. 21.
14. Wilson, *Preface King Hedley II*, p. x.
15. August Wilson, 'How to Write a Play Like August Wilson', *New York Times*, 10 March 1991, Section 2.5, p. 17.
16. August Wilson, *Two Trains Running*, p. 40.
17. Soyinka, *Myth, Literature*, p. 144.
18. Although the character was not created in Wilson's first four plays, her presence can certainly be read into them all and she is similarly manifest in the characters of Herald Loomis in *Joe Turner's Come and Gone* (1986) and Boy Willie in *The Piano Lesson* (1987).
19. August Wilson quoted in Gener, 'Salvation in the City of Bones', p. 21.
20. Molefi Kete Asante, 'The Future of African Gods: The Clash of Civilizations', published by the author at www.asante.net/news/ptare-accra-speech.html.
21. George Brandon, 'Sacrificial Practice in Santeria, an Africa-Cuban Religion in the United States', *Africanisms in American Culture* (1990), p. 120.
22. *Ibid.*
23. Pemberton, 'Eshm-Elegba', p. 127.
24. *Ibid.*, p. 67.
25. *Ibid.*, pp. 27, 67.
26. *Ibid.*, p. 67.
27. Brandon, 'Sacrificial Practice', p. 126.
28. *Ibid.*
29. Soyinka, *Myth, Literature*, p. 144.
30. A. Bryant, 'The Storyteller', *New Crisis* 108:3 (May/June 2001), p. 46.
31. B. E. Kipkorir. *The Marakwet of Kenya* (Nairobi: Esater African Literature Bureau, 1973), p. 42.
32. Bill Moyers, 'August Wilson', in Betty Sue Flowers, ed., *A World of Ideas: Conversations with Thoughtful Men and Women about American Life Today and Ideas Shaping our Future* (New York: Doubleday, 1989), p. 179.
33. Wilson, *Two Trains Running*, p. 100.
34. Carla McDonough quoted in Wolfe, *August Wilson*, p. 38.
35. Harry J. Elam, Jr., *The Past as Present in the Drama of August Wilson* (Ann Arbor: University of Michigan Press, 2004), p. 58.
36. Wilson quoted in *ibid.*, p. 86.
37. Clyde W. Ford, *The Hero With an African Face* (New York: Bantam Books, 1999) p. 49.
38. Ladrica Menson-Furr, 'Booker T. Washington, August Wilson, and the Shadows of the Garden', *Mosaic: A Journal for the Interdisciplinary Study of Literature* 38:4 (December 2005), p. 176.
39. August Wilson, *Seven Guitars* (New York: Penguin, 1996), p. 24.
40. *Ibid.*, pp. 95–6.
41. Menson-Furr, 'Booker T. Washington', p. 178.
42. Pemberton, 'Eshu-Elegba', pp. 68, 70.
43. Bondo Wyszpolski, 'Guns of August', at www.easyreader.info/archive/news2000/0921/coverstory.php.
44. Soyinka, *Myth, Literature*, p. 145.
45. Bryant, 'The Storyteller', p. 43.

14

MARGARET BOOKER

Radio Golf: the courage of his convictions – survival, success and spirituality

Hey, you have to go forward into the 21st century. I figure we could go forward united . . . I'm talking about the black Americans who share that 400-year history of being here in America. One of the things with *Radio Golf* is that I realized I had to in some way deal with the black middle class, which for the most part is not in the other nine plays. My idea was that the black middle class seems to be divorcing themselves from that community, making their fortune on their own without recognizing or acknowledging their connection to the larger community. And I thought: We have gained a lot of sophistication and expertise and resources, and we should be helping that community, which is completely devastated by drugs and crime and the social practices of the past hundred years of the country . . .

If you don't recognize that you have a duty and a responsibility, then obviously you won't do that. Some people don't feel that responsibility, but I do, so I thought I would express that in the work. In the 21st century we can go forward together. That was my idea behind the play.[1]

Radio Golf (2005) is both August Wilson's Old Testament to the past and his New Testament to the future. Never one to mince words, even in the last few months of his life, he sounds his challenge to the black middle class to engage in the battle for the black man's soul.

Wilson selects a specific era out of the homogeneous course of history to illustrate a 'state of emergency' which Walter Benjamin in *Illuminations* (1969) calls the rule rather than the exception for those who subscribe to the tradition of the oppressed.[2] *Radio Golf* depicts Pittsburgh's Hill District in 1997, a year which marks the critical moment of its possible extinction in the name of progress. As the city proceeds to rid itself of blight, it also creates a 'moment of danger' which affects both the historical content of the African American tradition and its receivers. The Hill's current desolation and impending demolition could lead to a redevelopment of black culture and community or to the erasure of African American memory and history when faced with the appeal of material success, wealth and status promised by the

American Dream. Wilson presents the dilemma but leaves us to contemplate the solutions.

In his entire ten-play chronicle, Wilson teaches his own community and the diverse American audience to recognize and respect the role African Americans have played in both an ethnic and a national historical context. Simultaneously proud of his cultural roots and his American citizenship, he wants to support and celebrate both. To do so, he has wisely chosen his old neighbourhood, the Hill District of Pittsburgh, as the location for all but one of his plays. Containing many landmarks, with Aunt Ester's house as its red-doored heart, it was once a lively hub made up of houses with yards, numerous businesses (Miss Harriet's fried chicken place, Hop's Construction, Sam Green's grocery, Mr Redwood's Orphanage, Wilks Realty), schools (St Richard's, Connolly Trade), hospitals, churches, entertainment and sports centres (the Crawford Grill or Kennard Field). Poverty, crime and unemployment now walk its once busy streets. Poor blacks and street gangs, pawnshops, the mission, Hill House, and busy undertakers populate the district. Even TV trucks, as Mame Wilks points out, will not drive up to the Hill unless there is a shooting. Socially mobile blacks have moved out of the inner city to Shadyside and other suburban neighbourhoods. The Hill District is the cycle's overriding "*lieu de mémoire*" to use Pierre Nora's term, the setting

> where memory crystallizes and secretes itself at a particular historical moment, a turning point where consciousness of a break with the past is bound up with the sense that memory has been torn – but torn in such a way as to pose the problem of the embodiment of memory in certain sites where a sense of historical continuity persists.[3]

What happens when the local handyman paints the front door of an old house slated for demolition and decides to invite the neighbourhood to a party? All hell breaks loose. 1839 Wylie Avenue is sacred ground, the home of the now-deceased Mother of the Race, the 'most significant persona'[4] of Wilson's ten-play chronicle of the African American experience. She is none other than the ultimate ancestor, Aunt Ester. Aptly named after the woman who saved her people in the Old Testament and as old as slavery itself, she signifies the presence of the black man in America and bears witness to his history and worth. The impending destruction of her home serves as the catalyst for the play's dramatic action.

Significantly, the stage setting for *Radio Golf* is the Bedford Hills Redevelopment Company construction office and *not* Aunt Ester's home. One is visible and the other invisible; one concrete, the other spiritual. One points to the future, the other connects to the past. Decorated with posters of contemporary international golf champion Tiger Woods and the 1960s icon of the civil rights movement Martin Luther King, Jr., it is a site of memory that exists within the larger one of the Hill District. The old building, a former Centre Avenue storefront, complete with antique embossed tin ceiling, belongs to Wilks Realty, the black business with a history which reaches back to Caesar Wilks, the first black constable on the Hill and the man who invaded Aunt Ester's sanctuary in 1918 (*Gem of the Ocean* (2003)). This location becomes the arena in which the drama's spiritual conflict takes place.

The play's protagonist, Harmond Wilks, is representative of the black middle class, which moved out of the Hill District years earlier to a more affluent part of the city (Shadyside) and lost touch with those left behind. He is a real estate developer, wealthy owner of Wilks Realty, local leader and potential mayoral candidate. His Cornell roommate, and the drama's antagonist, Roosevelt Hicks, is an avid golfer, soon-to-be Mellon Bank Vice-President and part owner of and golf talkshow host on WBTZ radio. The two friends have long played golf together and have just become partners in a new, black enterprise – the Bedford Hills Redevelopment, Inc. Funded by a combination of their own and government (Model Cities) money, the pair plan to revive the Hill District and make a tidy profit on their $200,000 investment in the process. The author uses their shared interest in the game of golf to contrast their personal histories, ethics and relationship to African American history and values.

Titles are always keys to an understanding of Wilson's dramas, and *Radio Golf* is no exception. The title metaphorically alludes to the aspirations of the black middle class towards the accumulation of wealth and social status, including celebrity, within the larger American context. Golf is, after all, an upper-class individual sport played on manicured greens as opposed to team baseball played on backlots in urban neighbourhoods (*Fences*) (1985). Wilson chooses golf – a professional sport once inaccessible to blacks – to examine the erosion of African American cultural values in the pursuit of success as defined by the dominant white society. Ever since '22 noblemen and gentlemen' at St Andrews, Fife, Scotland set up the Society of St Andrews Golfers in 1754 and adopted its present name of the Royal and Ancient Golf Club of St Andrews by permission of William IV in 1834, the game of golf has been associated with upper-class society both in Great Britain and later in America. Historically, African Americans were the caddies, not the players, on American courses. The Professional Golf Association did not admit blacks until Charlie Sifford, first black in the World Golf Hall of Fame and author of *Just Let Me Play* (1992), pioneered the way in 1961. Wilson issues a warning: 'We're all trying to imitate the British to become lords and aristocrats, have a bunch of servants and a gardener . . . We were founded as a British colony.'[5] Wilson is a typical Pittsburgh sports fan who admires the athletic excellence of Tiger Woods, Muhammad Ali, Joe Louis and others who pioneered the way for blacks in professional sports. Simultaneously, he criticizes the conversion of their talent and heritage into mass-marketable products, such as the Nike endorsement or, much earlier, Ma Rainey's recorded songs. This commodification[6] is tantamount to stealing their heritage, like Aunt Ester's house, in the name of progress.

The play's language and music capture this commodification and shattering of history. Harmond and Mame speak with near-perfect grammar about marketing and business deals and their relationship. Harmond, like a true politician, can adjust his speech pattern to his constituency. Roosevelt retains the poor grammar and colourful swearing of his youth in addition to the vocabularies he learnt in college. Ben Brantley, in his *New York Times* review of *Radio Golf*, describes what Wilson is doing as an artist:

> The inspiring antiseptic slang of much of the dialogue in 'Radio Golf' is deliberate . . . Mr Wilson intends that at least three of his characters sound as out of place as they do. They may be transacting business in that section of Pittsburgh known as the Hill, . . . but they have forgotten its language, an organic poetry shaped by decades of hard living. They are people who've lost their natural voices. In Mr Wilson's world, that's the same thing as losing their souls.[7]

Old Joe and Sterling possess the 'Shakespearean richness that Mr Wilson has devised for residents of the hill . . . the wayward anecdotal vigor that is Mr Wilson's blissful specialty'.[8]

Wilson signifies a break in the African American tradition with the noticeable absence of the blues, a 'way of remembering, a congenital instinctive force that reaches back through the centuries to the first slave ships'.[9] Old Joe Barlow pawned his guitar in 1970. The two developers sing white man's music: 'Hail, Hail the Gang's All Here' and 'Blue Skies'. Harmond, who has lost the way to 'leave his mark on life'[10] in a unique song of his own, will eventually transform the notion of 'gang' into a new alliance with Sterling, the war-painted Cochise of the play's close, in a last-ditch effort to celebrate the history contained in Aunt Ester's house.

Wilson utilizes contrasting attitudes towards the game of golf in the drama's five characters to explore the dilemma of entrepreneurial self-interest versus community welfare. The five characters are living embodiments of chronological history ranging from 1918 through 1997, and reference back to the founding of America as a nation. Wilson includes allusions to the Indian Wars, African ancestry in Ethiopia, the Middle Passage, slavery, the underground railroad, abolition and reconstruction, black northward migrations, the industrial revolution, the Depression, World War II, middle-class black flight from the inner cities and the residue of poverty and crime left behind, the demise of the steel mills and small businesses, the civil rights and Black Power movements, and the consequent advancement of blacks into positions of prominence in entertainment, sports, business and politics.

Both Harmond Wilks and Roosevelt Hicks are beneficiaries of the expanding opportunities for blacks made available through the civil rights movement and affirmative action policies of the 1960s, 1970s, 1980s and 1990s. Both are graduates of one of the nation's finest private universities, Cornell. While Harmond inherited wealth, Roosevelt is still scrambling to amass it. Harmond's monogrammed golf set, bought 'before taxes' twelve years earlier, is now a part of him. He is comfortable with government officials (both city and federal) and experienced in urban politics. His hero and champion of the community is Martin Luther King, Jr. At the play's beginning, Roosevelt is hungry for financial success and recognition and is comparatively naïve, as is evident by his elation over an invitation to play golf with a set of white Pittsburgh businessmen for the first time. His hero is Tiger Woods. Aided by the notion that golf has taught them how to succeed in life, both men believe that a world of opportunity lies before them. They are excited by the possibility of erecting a driving range at Kennard Field and a golf camp for kids which could give young, poor blacks a head start.

Wilson delineates three other nongolfing *dramatis personae* to fill out the spectrum of characters inside his geographical Hill District/*lieux de mémoire*. He brings us Harmond's wife Mame, a public relations professional and future spokesperson for the governor's office as well as loyal, loving spouse. She prefers the posh neighbourhood of Shadyside to the downtrodden Hill and views Harmond's golf clubs as 'stuff', easily replaceable if you have insurance and file a police report. The two Hill denizens – Elder 'Old Joe' Barlow (World War II veteran, divorced father of eight children, vagrant with a criminal record, the son of Caesar Wilks's sister Black Mary and Citizen Barlow of *Gem of the Ocean* and the current owner of Aunt Ester's house) and Sterling Johnson (local handyman, Aunt Ester protégé, ex-con and warrior spirit who first appeared in *Two Trains Running* (1990)) – can view golf clubs only as useless weapons or stolen goods for sale, especially in a neighbourhood which cannot boast the necessary grass to play on. They carry the history of the neighbourhood through personal memories in vigorous anecdotal voices, speaking a language lost to the three strangers – Harmond, Mame and Roosevelt. History, however, conflicts with the process of gentrification.

Wilson focuses on the two black business partners to build the conflict which powers the drama. The real estate developers are, by definition, erasers of history and memory. And there is not much of the old Hill District left to preserve, as Sterling points out: 'How you gonna bring it back? It's dead. It take Jesus Christ to bring it back. What you mean is you gonna put something else in its place. Say that. But don't talk about bringing the Hill back. The Hill District's dead.'[11] Harmond tells him about the plan to rebuild the whole neighbourhood with shops, houses and stores (later revealed to be a 180-unit apartment building and chain businesses like Starbuck's, Barnes and Noble, and Whole Foods (one exists in Shadyside today)). He tempts Sterling with potential construction work. Wilson, however, has other plans for his central character. As he begins a journey to acknowledge the importance of African American history, Harmond will discover the real meaning of that 1960s anthem 'We shall overcome', and what inclusive civic leadership really demands.

As the grandson of Caesar Wilks, the Hill's first black policeman, Harmond inherits his ancestor's belief in the structure provided by the rule of law. He sees golf as a game of honour, concentrated individual effort and skill governed by an international, uniform set of rules. He declares, 'You teach the kids how to play golf and they have all the rules they need to win at life.' (93). A man of integrity, Harmond has played by the rules. He follows his father into the business, remains loyal to his wife, and believes some things are not replaceable or for sale, like the embossed tin roof, the decorations in Aunt Ester's house, or a family bloodline. Citizens' rights and responsibilities are very important to this man. He views the law as a means to set standards for everyone (black and white), curb violence, protect individual rights and ensure social order and wellbeing. He protests about police brutality in his candidacy speech in the face of his wife's resistance and promises to attract future employers, such as Wilson Sporting Goods, to provide jobs and a means to combat poverty. He wants to be the mayor for all Americans. He holds to the notion that 'The law protects you when you own your house and pay the taxes. But the law also protects the city when a property's left abandoned' (96).

The currently controversial concept of 'eminent domain', which permits the state to seize private property for the 'public good' or a city to remove someone's home and turn it over to a private developer, goes one step further. Ironically, Harmond's one illegal act, buying derelict houses from the city before public auction, hoists him on his own petard in a way he could not have predicted at the outset. He discovers his own complicity in buying stolen property, whether it be the club set from Sterling or the house belonging to his cousin, Old Joe Barlow. Wilson puts Harmond to the test; he must make a choice between hiding his fraudulent activity, thereby ensuring huge financial success and social prominence if the development moves forward, or eliminating the corruption by rescuing Aunt Ester's house from demolition and risking the ruin of his career. Ultimately, he confronts Mame and Roosevelt with his moral dilemma:

HARMOND: Bedford Hills acquired 1839 illegally. It bought it from me but I didn't own it. I bought the house before it went to auction. That's against the law. That's corruption. I'm going down to the courthouse and file an injunction to stop the demolition.
MAME: Harmond, if you do that you're throwing everything away. All your hard work. Your career. Your reputation.
HARMOND: All I'm trying to do is save Bedford Hills Redevelopment. You got to have rule of law. Otherwise it would be chaos. Nobody wants to live in chaos. (105)

While Harmond believes 'I've got the law on my side', it is Sterling who knows from experience that rules change, especially if you are not the one making them. Even Old Joe recognizes the uselessness of protest if you are 'invisible'. Sterling, who went to Black Power leader Malcolm X's rally in *Two Trains Running*, spells out the nature of the game:

You got too big too fast. They don't like that. If you hadn't did it to yourself they was laying for you. They don't mind you playing their game but you can't outplay them. If you score too many points they change the rules. That's what the problem was . . . you scored too many points. If things had kept on going like that you was gonna have to buy you a gun. Time this is over you ain't gonna be able to walk down the street without somebody pointing at you. If they point and whisper you in trouble. You'd have to move out the state. Start over again somewhere fresh. That is if you still wanna play the game. If you still wanna play the game you gonna have to relearn the rules. See . . . they done changed. If you relearn the rules they'll let you back on the playing field. But now you crippled. You ain't got but one leg. You be driving around looking for handicapped parking. Get back on the field and every time you walk by somebody they check their pockets. That enough to kill anybody right there. If you had to take a little hit like that all day every day how long you think you can last? I give you six months. (107)

Roosevelt, on the other hand, has to be 'in the game', no matter what the cost. He tells his partner:

I hit my first golf ball, I asked myself where have I been? How'd I miss this? I couldn't believe it. I felt free. Truly free. For the first time. I watched the ball soar down the driving range. I didn't think it could go so high. It just kept going higher and higher. I felt something lift off of me. Some weight I was carrying around and didn't know it. I felt like the world was open to me. Everything and everybody . . . I must have hit a hundred golf balls trying to get that feeling.

But that first time was worth everything. I felt like I had my dick in my hand and was waving it around like a club: 'I'm a man! Anybody want some of this come and get it!' That was the best feeling of my life . . . That's why I keep my golf clubs in the trunk of my car just in case I drive by a golf course. I keep looking for that feeling. That's what I want these kids to have. That'll give them a chance at life. I wish somebody had come along and taught me how to play golf when I was ten. That'll set you on a path to life where everything is open to you. You don't have to hide and crawl under a rock just 'cause you black. Feel like you don't belong in the world. (90–1)

Sounding like Boy Willie in *The Piano Lesson* (1987), Roosevelt associates golf with freedom and self-respect, making money (Tiger Woods's Nike endorsement), achieving celebrity status, and playing the game with white heavy hitters. Because his need to belong is so strong, he believes that success in America comes through playing by the white man's rules, just as in golf. To transact business on the green, he prints his new business cards as Vice-President of Mellon Bank and partner in the Bedford Hills Redevelopment Company because 'Without them cards they'll think I'm the caddie' (92).

Roosevelt naïvely believes that the white businessmen included him at their table because of his great golf game:

I was the center of the table and the conversation was going as good as my game. There I was holding my own, breaking out ahead of the pack at a table of millionaires. Then I look up and it was just me and Bernie sitting there. Man to man. I thought to myself, This is where I've been trying to get to my whole life. And then it happened. Bernie Smith wants to partner with me to buy WBTZ radio . . . I'd be in charge. Bernie wants to be a silent partner . . .(97)

The more practised Harmond recognizes their manipulation of his partner's love for golf and need to belong. Bernie's payment of green fees, drinks, etc. is not much of an outlay when compared with the profit margin possible via media or urban redevelopment.

Roosevelt, however, is more than happy to trade on his 'black face' to garner government subsidy to buy the local radio station at a reduced price. Particularly when he can both make money and be the host of a programme about his favourite sport. As he says:

This is how you do it! This is how everybody does it. You don't think Mellon has ever been used? We're talking about an eight million dollar radio station! This is the game! I'm at the table! There was a time they didn't let any blacks at the table. You opened the door. You shined the shoes. You served the drinks. And they went in the room and made the deal. I'm in the room! Them mother-fuckers who bought and traded them railroads . . . how do you think they did it? This is business. This is the way it's done in America . . . I get to walk away with a piece of an asset worth eight million dollars. I don't care if somebody else makes some money 'cause of a tax break. I get mine and they get theirs . . . Harmond, I have to take this. This is not going to come along again. The window of opportunity is already starting to close. If I don't do this Bernie will get somebody else. (97–8)

As an old friend, Harmond supports him with advice about lawyers, deal percentages and a promise to watch his back. Roosevelt wants to celebrate with another round of golf, but, in a funny, ironic and prophetic twist, Harmond cannot play. His golf clubs have been stolen by members of his own African American community. At the play's close, Roosevelt will sacrifice his best friend to the lure of wealth and status promised by a new partnership with the same Bernie Smith in the Bedford Hills Redevelopment project. Roosevelt follows his own radio broadcast advice. He knows he is 'one hole from disaster' (101) if he sticks with Harmond and decides to eliminate the handicap (1839 Wylie) which threatens the entire redevelopment scheme. Ultimately, he does not care whose rules he plays by, if he wins the game and gets his cut. He is, as Sterling declares, a 'Negro':

> Sterling: [*to Roosevelt*] . . . You a Negro. White people will get confused and call you a nigger but they don't know like I know. I know the truth of it. I'm a nigger. Negroes are the worst thing in God's creation. Niggers got style. Negroes got blind-eyetist. A dog knows it's a dog. A cat knows it's a cat. But a Negro don't know he's a Negro. He thinks he's a white man. It's Negroes like you who hold us back. (107)

Unlike Roosevelt, Harmond discovers the value of history and memory contained within the community whereas Roosevelt threatens its very existence.

Harmond takes action testifying to his newly evolved community loyalty. He attempts to pay Old Joe for his house, recognizes the Wilks family role in supporting Aunt Ester, and tries to include 1839 Wylie in the new redevelopment plan. He learns that rules change when the court denies his temporary injunction against the demolition of Aunt Ester's house. When all else fails, he significantly gives Roosevelt his Tiger Woods poster in a painful goodbye and destroys his participation in a partnership that would later include Bernie Smith. At the end of the play, Harmond, paintbrush in hand, joins Sterling, war-painted like Cochise, the Apache chief who resisted white colonization of the tribe's homeland in the Southwest. Theirs is a grassroots uprising in the style of Malcolm X. Harmond's actions cost him his political career and Roosevelt's friendship, but redeem his soul. He is one of the gang, one of Aunt Ester's children, and the proud possessor of '[t]he wisdom and tradition she embodies which are valuable tools for the reconstruction of their personality and for dealing with a society in which the contradictions, over the decades, have grown more fierce, and for exposing all the places it is lacking in virtue'.[12]

Wilson's characters

> still place their faith in America's willingness to live up to the meaning of her creed so as not to make a mockery of her ideals. It is this belief in America's honor that allows them to pursue the American Dream even as it remains elusive. The conflicts with the larger society are cultural conflicts . . . in what has been a difficult and sometimes bitter relationship with a system of laws and practices that deny us access to the tools necessary for productive and industrious life.[13]

In the final analysis, the Harmond/Roosevelt conflict embodies and crystallizes in time (the turn of the century) the moment of danger in which the unique African American history and cultural values could disappear, if those in leadership positions do not assume responsibility for their continuance. It is time for the next generation of Aunt Ester's children to step up.

NOTES

1. Suzan-Lori Parks, 'The Light in August', *American Theatre* (November 2005), pp. 22, 24.
2. Walter Benjamin, *Illuminations*, ed. Hannah Arendt, trans. Harry Zohn, (New York: Schocken Books, 1969), p. 263.
3. Pierre Nora, *Les Lieux de Mémoire* (*Realms of Memory: Rethinking the French Past*), ed. Lawrence D. Kritzman, trans. Arthur Goldhammer (New York: Columbia University Press, 1996), vol. 1, p. 284.
4. August Wilson, 'Aunt Ester's Children: A Century On Stage', *American Theatre* 22:9. (November 2005), p. 26.
5. Parks, 'The Light in August', p. 24.
6. Paul Gilroy, *The Black Atlantic: Modernity and Double Consciousness* (Cambridge, MA: Harvard University Press, 1993).
7. Ben Brantley, 'Voices Warped by the Business Blues', *New York Times*, 30 April 2005, p. B11.
8. *Ibid.*, p. B15.
9. *Ibid.*, p. B11.
10. August Wilson, *Joe Turner's Come and Gone* (New York: Penguin, 1988), p. 10.
11. August Wilson, *Radio Golf*, in *American Theatre* (November 2005), p. 91. Further quotations will be cited parenthetically in the text.
12. Wilson, 'Aunt Ester's Children', p. 30.
13. *Ibid.*, p. 28.

15

DAVID K. SAUER AND JANICE A. SAUER

Critics on August Wilson

> The only research I do is to listen to the music. There's a lot of
> history of our people in the music. When I was writing *Ma Rainey's*
> *Black Bottom*, I didn't want to know anything about Ma Rainey.
> I figured what I needed to know I'd get out of her music. Listening
> to her singing gave me a good sense of who she was. . . . When
> I did *Joe Turner's Come and Gone*, I certainly did not think about
> anything that happened in 1911, but I had a sense that they didn't
> have cars but had horses. And I envisioned people coming into the
> cities, and there were boarding houses and people setting down
> roots. I believe if you do research, you're limited by it . . . It's like
> putting on a straitjacket. August Wilson[1]

It is not for nothing that Harry J. Elam, Jr.'s 2004 book is entitled *The Past as*
Present in the Drama of August Wilson, in that it acknowledges the extent to
which Wilson's plays, set in the past, nonetheless address current concerns.
Wilson may not have been interested in conducting historical research but he
was concerned to trace the history of individual lives and the unfolding story
of the African American community in such a way that present attitudes and
values are seen in the context of past experiences.

Some critics have chosen to treat the plays as if they were written in the
era in which they are set. So, for example, a number of articles approach
Ma Rainey's Black Bottom (1984) in terms of the history of the blues (Adell,
Crawford, Gener, Mills, Plum, Smith, Snodgrass, Taylor),[2] or jazz (Hay,
Werner, Wolfe); the Great Migration (Anderson, Bogumil, Gates, Pereira,
Shannon 'Transplant'); the conflicting views of African spirituality ver-
sus African American Christianity (Richards, Shannon 'Good Christian');
patriarchal roles (Brewer, Clark, Hampton, Sterling); women's roles (Elam
'Women', Kubitschek, Marra); 'Southernness' (Gantt) or 'folk traditions'
(Harris).

Elam, however, has warned of the dangers of ignoring the complexity of
works which resist too programmatic a response, observing, for example,
that 'The ending of *Ma Rainey*, in which one of the band members murders
another, is a complex and confounding blues moment' ('August Wilson' 324),

adding that 'Forged in and from the economics of slavery as a method of mediating the pains and dehumanization of that experience, the blues are purposefully duplicitous, containing a matrix of meanings' (321). He draws a distinction, however, between this play and later ones:

> It [*Ma Rainey*] stands in stark contrast to endings of Wilson's later dramas such as *Fences, Joe Turner*, and [The]*Piano Lesson*, in which characters reach moments of spiritual fulfillment, acknowledge their relationships to the African American past, and perform actions of self-actualization, self-determination, and collective communion. Present in the final moment of *Ma Rainey*, in contrast, is the ironic anguish of the blues wail. (324)

Arguably, though, the 'blues wail' is to be heard throughout Wilson's work and the endings of several of his plays are unresolved and ambiguous. Mary Bogumil, in her book *Understanding August Wilson*, captures some of that complexity when she concludes, with particular relevance to *The Piano Lesson* (1987), that 'Wilson lets the audience know that those ancestral voices must be heard; otherwise they can paralyze, as they do in Berniece's case, or confound as they do when Boy Willie attempts to overcome them with sheer brute force, and contribute to, throughout most of the play, the Charles family's disintegration instead of spiritual reconciliation' (93).

Choosing sides: African or American?

Margaret Booker, in her study of August Wilson and Lillian Hellman, sees the former's work in the context of American notions of national identity. Joanne Gordon, however, insists on the centrality of the African dimension of an African American writer, contrasting him with the South African playwright Athol Fugard who 'dreams of a world without distinctions based on race. Wilson, in contrast,' she suggests, 'wants to assert the African in his characters' (29). Similarly, for Patricia Gantt, Wilson's position is that 'The Message of America is "Leave your Africanness outside the door." My message is, "claim what is yours"' (85). It is this dimension that is stressed, too, by Pamela Jean Monaco: 'Holding up to his audience the struggles and triumphs of the ordinary men and women who have come before, he demonstrates how tradition can sustain one through any hardship and challenge' (103).

For other critics, the key to Wilson's work lies in his characters' attitudes to the white world. Thus Cigdem Usekes, in *American Drama*, argues that 'August Wilson appears to be contending in his plays that unless blacks can discover a means to assert their own physical power, they will continue to be terrorized and victimized by their white compatriots' (62), while in "We's the Leftovers" he suggests that Wilson's 'black characters find themselves in an ongoing struggle with a hostile social and economic structure and its white representatives' (124).

John Hanlon, in contrast, sees the principal issue in *Ma Rainey's Black Bottom*, for example, as capitalism, pointing out that those who control the music business may be white but they are also rich, or at least control the means of production. For Kim Marra, meanwhile, it is gender that is central, as she argues that Wilson favours the 'male protagonist and constructs female characters as the Other' (123). As a consequence, 'The tyranny and eventual overthrow of black matriarchy charted through Wilson's history cycle reinforce dominant gender ideology and contribute to the author's canonization and commercial success' (155).

For most critics, however, race lies at the centre of Wilson's work and, still more, Africa, though this could cause problems for audiences. Indeed, Sandra G. Shannon, in *African American Performance and Theatre History*, argues that white audiences cannot fully appreciate the most African elements. The reason for this is that 'without knowledge of African rituals, superstition, religion, or music, which continue to inform Africans in America, audiences are forced to assess Wilson's work using awkward yardsticks that contain little, if any, relevance to Wilson's intentions' (155). For Elam (based on his performance of the role of Sylvester in *Ma Rainey's Black Bottom*), the various handicapped characters in Wilson, 'besieged by madness, unable to grasp the reality of the world around them, represent a connection to a powerful, transgressive spirituality, to a lost African consciousness, and to a legacy of black social activism' (611). He attributes the madness to the loss of African roots.

Still other critics have chosen to stress Wilson's universality. Joan Fishman, for example, traces the development of *Fences* (1985) through its drafts, arguing that 'It is Wilson's approach to responsibility which ultimately makes the play universal and allows him to examine issues which cross cultural lines' (164). Terms such as 'universal' and 'cultural lines' seem to indicate an appeal to white audiences as well as others.

Alan Nadel's anthology tends to find more of a synthesis between racial polarities. For him, Wilson's project is 'an attempt to make history, that is, an attempt both to construct an event and to construct the story in which it figures'(103). In that anthology Michael Morales argues that 'For Wilson ... retention of a cosmological perspective is equally important as historical experience in accounting for cultural difference' (113). Morales tries to balance (American) history and (African) mysticism, the historical and the cosmological. Mark William Rocha, meanwhile, starts with performance theory but grounds it in a form of Henry Louis Gates, Jr.'s 'signifying', suggesting that 'The loud-talking of Wilson's play "tricks" members of the audience into demonstrating their ignorance of the African sensibility that produced the play and shaped the basic assumptions of black culture, especially that of signifyin(g)' (117–18). Thus the white audience must confront the ignorance which Shannon claims blinds it.

The Piano Lesson: seeking a balance

The play in which critics most clearly try to balance binaries is *The Piano Lesson*. They recognize the claims of both Berniece and Boy Willie, and try to combine them in generalizations. Wilson's endings, however, are extremely tricky and do not offer a complete victory of one side over the other. And Wilson does not play fair. Although his plays construct such binaries, he twists them in ways that create ambiguity and complexity. Thus, all critics agree that *The Piano Lesson* opposes Berniece and Boy Willie. All understand the terms of the opposition – she wants to keep the piano which she sees as family history, and he wants to sell it to buy the land of the former slave master of their family. She stands for allegiance to family and past, and he stands for the future. But, as the play unfolds, the simple opposition is dramatically twisted. Berniece, it turns out, stands for repression of the past, not telling her daughter about the family history and how it is embodied in the piano. She, after all, had left the family home, moving north in the migration to Pittsburgh. Boy Willie, by contrast, is not exactly a forward-moving capitalist who will sell the family heritage, as he initially seems to be. He does not want to move to Pittsburgh. He wants to stay in the South and work the family farm, but under his own control. Their roles are ostensibly reversed from the values they espouse.[3] The ending of the play exorcises the ghost, leaves the piano with Berniece, and exhumes the family history for her daughter Maretha. Boy Willie leaves the piano in returning to the South, but there is no precise resolution.

Amadou Bissiri attempts a synthesis: 'The link between womanhood and cultural continuity', he asserts, 'is a universal truth that Wilson particularly emphasizes here' (103). However, since the piano stays in the North with Berniece, Wilson sees that continuity as sustained in industrial rather than rural America. 'So ultimately Wilson's point is an assertion of black culture and identity within the industrializing culture' (103). For Devon Boan, though, the essential point is that 'Wilson has redefined the frustration of carrying the burden of the past, which is at the center of his other plays, into a question of how best to utilize the past' (263). Thus 'the family's slave narrative yields to the piano's pragmatic use, where its focus becomes the present and future, not the past' (270).

For Booker, 'the battle is an interior one in the house, rather than out in the yard. Berniece supports her brother's ascent up the stairs with all the ancestral force at her disposal' (123). The tension between the two of them, however, is not, from Susan Abbotson's point of view, to be easily resolved. As she explains, 'Wilson does not want us to take sides; in fact, he feels it is important that we do not. What we need to do is carefully balance the pros and cons of each character's behavior, to ascertain what is the best combination of responses to the dilemmas these people face' (84). Much the same, she suggests, applies to *Ma Rainey's Black Bottom*: 'Whom should we support – Ma or Levee?' (100). Nor, Eric Bergesen and William Demastes argue, is the crucial tension in the play between the races, insofar as Wilson is interested in both 'interracial tensions and tensions within the African-American community itself' (219).

Exploring other perspectives

Viewed from the perspective of performance, the plays offer a significant challenge. The actor Charles S. Dutton, who played not only Boy Willie but also the leads in the initial productions of *Ma Rainey's Black Bottom* (Levee) and *Joe Turner's Come and Gone* (1986) (Loomis), remarked that 'Herald Loomis is probably one of the most difficult characters to play in literature, period' (180), a view supported by Delroy Lindo, who played Loomis in subsequent productions. He was not, he insisted, 'the kind of man you just walk on stage and pick up' (Nemy 'On Stage').

Joyce Moss and George Wilson choose to foreground the significance of the plays' social and economic context. In their analysis of *Fences*, they note the 'tough economic times' that have affected 'several generations of black Americans' (145), times which lead Wilson's characters into crime. Troy becomes a hold-up man, shot and jailed in *Fences*, while West has been convicted of theft in *Two Trains Running* (1990). Floyd Barton holds up a jewellery store in *Seven Guitars* (1995) while Boy Willie's stories in *The Piano Lesson* all involve and imply minor theft. For Wilson, all his characters are rebelling against their constrained circumstances and discrimination, the most revolutionary of them being Solly Two Shoes in *Gem of the Ocean* (2003), who burns down a mill rather than allow the workers to be exploited by the company.

The conflict between capitalist and worker is to be found, at least by inference, in practically all the plays in the cycle, but once again the issue is far from simple. As Shannon observes in her book on *Fences*, the play 'raises a series of stark contrasts between a time when having sufficient amounts of food on the table was a child's biggest concern to a time when having access to a television set was in vogue' (67). All the homes in Wilson's plays are owned by those who live in them, from Aunt Ester's through Seth's in *Joe Turner's Come and Gone*, Doaker's in *The Piano Lesson*, Troy's in *Fences*, Memphis's diner in *Two Trains Running*, the jitney station in *Jitney* (1982), Ruby's house in *Seven Guitars* (1995) and *King Hedley II* (1999), to the vast real estate development planned in *Radio Golf* (2005). Capitalism itself is not rejected. What is at stake is something more than ownership, something more profound than a conflict between money and labour.

At base, the ground on which Wilson stands is clearly race, and although his characters struggle, survive and, sometimes triumph in American society, what holds them together, beyond immediate circumstances, is their awareness of a common past, a shared language, a mythology which braids together with history, a history, however, that lives because they personally and collectively bear its marks and inherit its truths.

As Christopher Bigsby has argued:

> August Wilson chooses deliberately to situate his characters historically, but his are not historical dramas in the sense that the past is treated as icon, faithfully reconstructed in its detailed realism. For him the past constitutes something more than a series of way-stations on a journey to the present, though it is that, too. The past is the present. It provides the images, the language, the myths which we inhabit, with which we debate and against which we define ourselves. (292)

In this way, Wilson's plays have contemporary resonance even as they seek to recreate the past. In the dialogue between the two, there is a collision of perspectives that affects our understanding of both.

NOTES

1. August Wilson quoted in Herb Boyd, 'Interview with August Wilson', august wilson-net, 26 April, 2000. Rpt. in Jackson R. Bryer and Mary C. Hartig, eds., *Conversations with August Wilson* (Jackson: University of Mississippi Press, 2006), p. 238.
2. See the Bibliography for works cited by author surname, in this chapter.
3. Wilson's major characters who are not so contorted are Aunt Ester from the beginning of the century and Sterling Johnson at the end.

SELECTIVE BIBLIOGRAPHY

Abbotson, Susan C. W. 'What Does August Wilson Teach in *The Piano Lesson*?: The Place of the Past and Why Boy Willie Knows More than Berniece.' *Journal of American Drama and Theatre* 12 (2000), pp. 83–101.

Adell, Sandra. 'Speaking of Ma Rainey/Talking About the Blues.' *May All Your Fences Have Gates: Essays on the Drama of August Wilson*. Ed. Alan Nadel. Iowa City: University of Iowa Press, 1994, pp. 51–66.

Anderson, Douglas. 'Saying Goodbye to the Past: Self-Empowerment and History in *Joe Turner's Come and Gone*.' *CLA Journal* 40 (1997), pp. 432–57.

Bergesen, Eric, and William Demastes. 'The Limits of African-American Political Realism: Baraka's *Dutchman* and Wilson's *Ma Rainey's Black Bottom*.' *Realism and the American Dramatic Tradition*. Ed. William W. Demastes. Tuscaloosa: University of Alabama Press, 1996, pp. 218–34.

Bigsby, C. W. E. *Modern American Drama: 1945–2000*. Cambridge: Cambridge University Press, 2000.

Bissiri, Amadou. 'Aspects of Africanness in August Wilson's Drama: Reading *The Piano Lesson* through Wole Soyinka's Drama.' *African American Review* 30 (1996), pp. 99–113.

Boan, Devon. 'Call-and-Response: Parallel "Slave Narrative" in August Wilson's *The Piano Lesson*.' *African American Review* 32 (Summer 1998), pp. 263–71.

Bogumil, Mary L. *Understanding August Wilson*. Columbia: University of South Carolina Press, 1999.

Booker, Margaret. *Lillian Hellman and August Wilson: Dramatizing a New American Identity*. New York: Peter Lang, 2003.

Boyd, Herb. 'Interview with August Wilson.' *AugustWilson.net*. 26 April 2000. <http://www.augustwilson.net/An%20Interview%20with%20August%20Wilson.htm>. Rpt. in *Conversations with August Wilson*. Eds. Jackson R. Bryer and Mary C. Hartig. Jackson: University of Mississippi Press, 2006, pp. 235–40.

Brewer, Gaylord. 'Holy and Unholy Ghosts: The Legacy of the Father in the Plays of August Wilson.' *Naming the Father: Legacies, Genealogies, and Explorations of Fatherhood in Modern and Contemporary Literature*. Eds. Eva Paulino Bueno, Terry Caesar and William Hummel. Lanham, MD: Lexington, 2000, pp. 120–39.

Clark, Keith. 'Healing the Scars of Masculinity: Reflections on Baseball, Gunshots, and War Wounds in August Wilson's *Fences*.' *Contemporary Black Men's Fiction and Drama*. Ed. Keith Clark. Urbana: University of Illinois Press, 2001, pp. 200–21.

Crawford, Eileen. 'The B^b Burden: The Invisibility of Ma Rainey's Black Bottom."
August Wilson: A Casebook. Ed. Marilyn Elkins. New York: Garland, 1994, pp. 31–48.

Elam, Jr., Harry J. 'August Wilson's Women.' *May All Your Fences Have Gates: Essays on the Drama of August Wilson*. Ed. Alan Nadel. Iowa City: University of Iowa Press, 1994, pp. 165–82.

'August Wilson, Doubling, Madness, and Modern African-American Drama.' *Modern Drama* 43 (2000), pp. 611–32. Rpt. in *Modern Drama: Defining the Field*. Eds. Ric Knowles, Joanne Tompkins and W. B Worthen. Toronto: University of Toronto Press, 2003, pp. 173–92.

The Past as Present in the Drama of August Wilson. Ann Arbor: University of Michigan Press, 2004.

'August Wilson.' *A Companion to Twentieth-Century American Drama*. Ed. David Krasner. Malden, MA: Blackwell, 2005, pp. 318–33.

Fishman, Joan. 'Developing His Song: August Wilson's *Fences*.' *August Wilson: A Casebook*. Ed. Marilyn Elkins. New York: Garland, 1994, pp. 161–81.

Gantt, Patricia. 'Ghosts from "Down There": The Southernness of August Wilson.' *August Wilson: A Casebook*. Ed. Marilyn Elkins. New York: Garland, 1994, pp. 69–88.

Gates, Jr., Henry Louis 'The Chitlin Circuit.' *New Yorker*, 3 February 1997, pp. 44–50; 52–5.

Gener, Randy. 'Salvation in the City of Bones: Ma Rainey and Aunt Ester Sing Their Own Songs in August Wilson's Grand Cycle of Blues Dramas.' *American Theatre* 20:5 (2003), pp. 20–4, 64–7.

Gordon, Joanne. 'Wilson and Fugard: Politics and Art.' *August Wilson: A Casebook*. Ed. Marilyn Elkins. New York: Garland, 1994. 17–29.

Hampton, Gregory J. 'Black Men Fenced in and a Plausible Black Masculinity.' *CLA Journal* 46 (2002), pp. 194–206.

Hanlon, John J. '"Niggers Got a Right to Be Dissatisfied": Postmodernism, Race and Class in *Ma Rainey's Black Bottom*.' *Modern Drama* 45 (2002), pp. 95–124.

Harris, Trudier. 'August Wilson's Folk Tradition.' *August Wilson: A Casebook*. Ed. Marilyn Elkins. New York: Garland, 1994, pp. 49–67. Rpt. in *Modern Dramatists: A Casebook of Major British, Irish, and American Playwrights*. Ed. Kimball King. New York: Routledge, 2001, pp. 369–82.

Hay, Samuel A. *African American Theatre: An Historical and Critical Analysis*. Cambridge and New York: Cambridge University Press, 1994.

Kubitschek, Missy Dehn. 'August Wilson's Gender Lesson.' *May All Your Fences Have Gates: Essays on the Drama of August Wilson*. Ed. Alan Nadel. Iowa City: University of Iowa Press, 1994, pp. 183–99.

Marra, Kim. 'Ma Rainey and the Boyz: Gender Ideology in August Wilson's Broadway Canon.' *August Wilson: A Casebook*. Ed. Marilyn Elkins. New York: Garland, 1994, pp. 123–60.

Mills, Alice. 'The Walking Blues: An Anthropological Approach to the Theater of August Wilson.' *Black Scholar* 25:2 (1995), pp. 30–5.

Monaco, Pamela Jean. 'Father, Son, and Holy Ghost: From the Local to the Mythical in August Wilson.' *August Wilson: A Casebook*. Ed. Marilyn Elkins. New York: Garland, 1994, pp. 89–104.

Morales, Michael. 'Ghosts on the Piano: August Wilson and the Representation of Black American History.' *May All Your Fences Have Gates: Essays on the Drama of August Wilson*. Ed. Alan Nadel. Iowa City: University of Iowa Press, 1994, pp. 105–15.

Moss, Joyce, and George Wilson, eds. 'August Wilson: *Fences*.' *World War II to the Affluent Fifties (1940–1950). Literature in Its Time: Profiles of 300 Notable Literary Works and the Historical Events that Influenced Them*. Detroit: Gale Group, 1997, pp. 145–50.

Nadel, Alan. 'Boundaries, Logistics, and Identity: The Property of Metaphor in *Fences* and *Joe Turner's Come and Gone*.' *May All Your Fences Have Gates: Essays on the Drama of August Wilson*. Ed. Alan Nadel. Iowa City: University of Iowa Press, 1994, pp. 86–104.

Nemy, Enid. 'On Stage.' *New York Times*, 15 April 1988, p. C2.

Page, Yolanda Williams. 'The Ground on Which He Stands: Charles S. Dutton on August Wilson.' *August Wilson and Black Aesthetics*. Eds. Dana A. Williams and Sandra G. Shannon. New York: Palgrave Macmillan, 2004, pp. 177–87.

Pereira, Kim. *August Wilson and the African-American Odyssey.* Urbana: University of Illinois Press, 1995.

Plum, Jay. 'Blues, History, and the Dramaturgy of August Wilson.' *African American Review* 27 (1993), pp. 561–67.

Richards, Sandra L. 'Yoruba Gods on the American Stage: August Wilson's *Joe Turner's Come and Gone.*' *Research in African Literatures* 30:4 (1999), pp. 92–105. Rpt. in *African Drama and Performance.* Eds. John Conteh-Morgan and Tejumola Olaniyan. Bloomington: Indiana University Press, 2004, pp. 94–106.

Rocha, Mark William. 'American History as "Loud Talking" in *Two Trains Running.*' *May All Your Fences Have Gates: Essays on the Drama of August Wilson.* Ed. Alan Nadel. Iowa City: University of Iowa Press, 1994, pp. 116–33.

Shannon, Sandra G. 'A Transplant That Did Not Take: August Wilson's Views on the Great Migration.' *African American Review* 31 (1997), pp. 659–66.

'The Good Christian's Come and Gone: The Shifting Role of Christianity in August Wilson's Plays.' *Melus* 16 (1989–90), pp. 127–42.

'Audience and Africanisms in August Wilson's Dramaturgy: A Case Study.' *African American Performance and Theater History: A Critical Reader.* Eds. Harry J. Elam, Jr. and David Krasner. Oxford: Oxford University Press, 2001, pp. 149–67.

August Wilson's 'Fences': A Reference Guide. Westport, CT: Greenwood, 2003.

Smith II, Philip E. '*Ma Rainey's Black Bottom*: Playing the Blues as Equipment for Living.' *Within the Dramatic Spectrum.* Ed. Karelisa Hartigan. Lanham, MD: University Press of America, 1986, pp. 177–86.

Snodgrass, Mary Ellen. *August Wilson: A Literary Companion.* Jefferson, NC: McFarland, 2004, pp.

Sterling, Eric. 'Protecting Home: Patriarchal Authority in August Wilson's *Fences.*' *Essays in Theatre/Etudes Théâtrales* 17 (1998), pp. 53–62.

Taylor, Regina. 'That's Why They Call It the Blues.' *American Theatre* 13:4 (1996), pp. 18–23.

Usekes, Cigdem. '"You Always Under Attack": Whiteness as Law and Terror in August Wilson's Twentieth-Century Cycle of Plays.' *American Drama* 10:2 (2001), pp. 48–69.

'"We's the Leftovers": Whiteness as Economic Power and Exploitation in August Wilson's Twentieth-Century Cycle of Plays.' *African American Review* 37 (2003), pp. 115–25.

Werner, Craig. 'August Wilson's Burden: The Function of Neoclassical Jazz.' *May All Your Fences Have Gates: Essays on the Drama of August Wilson.* Ed. Alan Nadel. Iowa City: University of Iowa Press, 1994, pp. 21–50.

Wolfe, Peter. *August Wilson.* New York: Twayne, 1999, pp.

16

CHRISTOPHER BIGSBY

An interview with August Wilson

This interview was conducted in London, in November 1991, on the occasion of the National Theatre's production of *Ma Rainey's Black Bottom*.

BIGSBY You were born in Pittsburgh in 1945. What sort of world were you brought up in?

WILSON Actually I lived in a mixed neighbourhood. There were, as I recall, quite a few Syrians, Jews, Italians and blacks, all mixed together. It was very interesting.

BIGSBY Does that mean that you were insulated from segregation?

WILSON It doesn't mean that at all because one encounters that early on. I suspect that from the time one is about seven or eight one begins to notice that all the people who are in positions of authority, whether it is the owner of the grocery store, the landlord, the teachers at the school, the bus drivers, or the people downtown in the shops and stores, all these people are white. So one begins to notice that early on, even though one may not quite understand it. So you are isolated.

BIGSBY Looking back, can you recall what it was like as a child, slowly becoming aware of this process?

WILSON I suspect my first raw encounter with racism was when I was four-teen. Every day when I went to school there was a note on my desk saying, 'Go home, nigger'. That was my first encounter with both individual and institutional racism.

BIGSBY What happened when you read that note?

WILSON I would take it, ball it up, put it in my pocket and proceed with my studies, which was difficult to do because I was the only black in the school and this was a school of about fifteen hundred or so. I had my own lunch table. The guys would stand up and eat lunch elsewhere rather than sit down beside me. When I went from that school I went to trade school. My mother always wanted me to be a lawyer, you see, and she said, 'Well, if you're not going to be a lawyer, go learn to fix cars.' I went to the auto-mechanic shop and ended up in a sheet-metal class. When I was in the sheet-metal class I was assaulted by my teacher, physically assaulted, for hammering a thumbtack in with a T-square. I promptly left that school. All the while that I was going out of my neighbourhood to these two schools there was a public school across the street but my mother did not have great faith in public schools. So she told me, 'OK, go to Gladstone High School.' I enrolled in Gladstone High School. I was in the ninth grade, officially. They put me in all tenth grade subjects, but I was in the ninth grade. The work was boring because it was not a very good school.

I had a history teacher who assigned us a paper to write. I had been in his class for probably about two months and I didn't do any work because it was boring, so I decided here was something I could do, write. So I wrote a twenty-page paper on Napoleon. It was fascinating. It was about what Victor Hugo called Napoleon's will to power. My sister rented a typewriter and typed up this paper for me and I submitted it to him. He called me in after class and said he had an A-plus, which was the highest grade, and he had an E, which was the lowest, and he said, 'I am going to give you one of these two grades.' It struck me as a rather odd thing. He wanted me to prove that I wrote the paper and I felt the fact that I had put my name on it, that I had said I wrote it, should have been enough. My mother told me to be honest and I had all my footnotes and my bibliography and all the things that we were supposed to have. I didn't feel that I had to prove to him that I wrote the paper, so I told him, 'I don't want to talk with you about this. I just said I wrote it.' And so he took the paper and he drew a circle around the E and he handed me back the paper. I tore it up and I threw it in his wastebasket and walked out of the school. I never went back and I was fifteen years old.

BIGSBY As a result, you didn't go on to college in the way that some American dramatists did: Tennessee Williams, Arthur Miller, David Mamet. Do you think that you lost something by not going on, or possibly gained something?

WILSON I think I gained. It was actually the best thing that ever happened to me. I didn't want my mother to know that I had dropped out of school so I would get up every morning, as though I was going to school, and I would go to the library and spend the time that I should have been in school at the library. I would come home at three o'clock and pretend that I had been to school. This is what I did for about three or four months. However, as I began to sleep later and later, I didn't really go to the library. Eventually, I told her. But I think it freed me. I found it very liberating because I was confronted with these stacks of books, and I felt fortunate in that all the knowledge that man had accumulated was in the books. I thought about the time when this stuff wasn't written down and you had to go see whoever it was when you wanted to learn something. But here it all was and I could learn anything that I wanted to learn. So I explored the library and all those subjects that interested me, things like anthropology and theology. I read books that I never would have read had I not been free. I was fulfilling the responsibility to educate myself.

BIGSBY You have mentioned your mother, but not your father.

WILSON My father was not around. He was a very sporadic presence in the household. My mother is really the one who raised me.

BIGSBY Your father was white and your mother was black.

WILSON My mother was black, from North Carolina. Yes.

BIGSBY Did that leave you then, or subsequently, with any ambiguity about your own identity?

WILSON No, because the cultural environment of my life and the cultural environment of my mother's household was always black.

BIGSBY When was the writer in you born?

WILSON I have always had a fascination with words. My mother taught me how to read when I was four. It was something about the idea that there were these symbols and that you could actually tell someone what you were thinking by using them that appealed. I can remember learning the word 'breakfast' and the fact that it was two words 'break fast'. I didn't know the other meaning of the word 'fast', but I recognised those two words in there. I was in kindergarten at the time and I thought, this is wonderful, you can take two words and put them together and make a third word. I think from that moment I was gone. Then in the seventh grade there was this girl called Nancy.

BIGSBY How old were you in seventh grade?

WILSON Twelve years. Nancy was a girl that even the third graders were in love with. I would write these poems for Nancy and I would leave them on her desk. I didn't sign them. And shortly after I began writing poems, Nancy and Anthony took up with each other and I always thought that she thought Anthony was writing the poems. So from that time I suspect that in many ways I have written poems for Nancy, although her name has changed many times. But now I've learnt to write my name to them. The first thing I can remember writing, though, was the poems for her.

BIGSBY Where is Nancy today?

WILSON I have no idea. I lost contact with her from ninth grade on. So many years ago.

BIGSBY So you started with poetry and then moved on to short stories. How was the dramatist born out of the short story writer?

WILSON I first got involved in theatre in 1968, in the middle of the Black Power movement in the United States. I felt a duty and honour to participate as we black Americans were debating the character of our culture and seeking ways to alter our relationship to American society. I thought one of the best ways I could participate, since I was an artist, was in the theatre, using that as a means to raise the consciousness of the people, a way of politicizing the community. So, with a friend, I started a theatre called the Black Horizons Theatre and I decided I would go home immediately and try to write a play. I couldn't do it because I couldn't write dialogue. But it was alright because I didn't have to write a play. I could direct and I had my poetry and short fiction and so it didn't really disturb me. Plays were simply not my thing.

That was my first encounter with theatre. I didn't see my first professional production until 1976.

BIGSBY This was the decade of Black Power, black nationalism and the civil rights movement. Where, on that spectrum, would you have placed yourself – with the black cultural nationalists?

WILSON Yes, absolutely. I notice that you got all three of them in there. There were these various factions, but, yes, I called myself a cultural nationalist and I still do.

BIGSBY James Baldwin once said that he felt a conflict between two parts of himself. As a writer he felt the need to step back from the situation in order to see it more clearly, while as a black American he felt the need to be in there, on the firing line, tearing down the slums. In other words, there was a curious kind of guilt about writing because writing implied detachment. Were you ever aware of that kind of conflict?

WILSON No. I was just the opposite. I thought writing was a tool, a weapon that enabled one to fulfil oneself and to participate even more fully. There was never any question in my mind of a writer being removed, or stepping back from the situation. I always felt that because of the writing I was involved. I always thought it was a cultural war. Writing and art are part of culture and I was there in that regard.

BIGSBY So the theatre was concerned to bring about change in society, to raise consciousness, to influence the way people thought of their situation?

WILSON Yes. Change the way people thought about their situation.

BIGSBY Is that still your function?

WILSON Yes, to an extent it is still the same.

BIGSBY What is the proviso?

WILSON Well, there are other things that I try to do with my art besides simply raising people's consciousness. I am trying to show that there is a culture among black Americans that is uniquely theirs and which is capable of offering sustenance. There is a whole and complete culture and I am trying to illuminate its values and show it exists.

BIGSBY A significant moment in your career, and your life seems to have been when you left Pittsburgh and went to St Paul, Minnesota, in the late 1970s. Why did that prove such a crucial move?

WILSON Yes. It was a significant moment. I went there on 5 March 1978. I went from a neighbourhood of fifty-five thousand blacks to a state in which there were only thirty-five thousand. This was a tremendous change. In Pittsburgh it was a question of not being able to see the forest for the trees. The reason I couldn't write dialogue was because I didn't respect the way blacks talked. I didn't see a value in it. I was always trying to alter the language into something else. So I asked a friend how to make characters talk and he said, 'You don't. You listen to them.' I thought he was being funny at the time but it actually turned out to be one of the most profound things he has ever said to me. So I moved to St Paul, a city of about ten thousand blacks. For the first time I was removed from a black community and, perhaps as a result, for the first time I began to hear the voices that I had grown up with all my life. And I began to discover, to recognize, the value of those voices and the fact that I did not have to change the way they talked in order to create art. That was one of the really important moments in my life.

BIGSBY How far are you one of the beneficiaries of the changes that have taken place in the American theatre in the 1970s and 1980s, the growth, in particular, of regional theatre? Plays now begin in cities like St Paul and move to Broadway, whereas in earlier decades they would move in the other direction. Has that been important to you?

WILSON It has been very important to me in the sense that my plays generally started in St Paul and from there I was fortunate to get productions in other theatres in Boston, Chicago, San Diego and elsewhere. What this does is enable us to go back into rehearsal. So I have a second crack at it, if you will. I have an opportunity to go back and apply the things that I learnt from the first production and change the script, continue to work on the play.

BIGSBY That means that you learn from your audiences?

WILSON Oh, yes, I do, sure. I learn from the community ultimately.

BIGSBY: And who is that audience?

WILSON The audience is whoever comes to the theatre. Blacks do not, as a rule, go to the theatre, partly because they can't afford the tickets. The audience is generally a mixed one. We get good black audiences in Chicago, but theatre in America is mostly white. It is an elite form of culture, of entertainment, and the number of people who consistently go to the theatre is very small.

BIGSBY Isn't there any irony in that? If one of your concerns is to raise black consciousness, how can you do that working in theatre which, as you say, is not a place black Americans tend to go?

WILSON Since I have started writing plays, since my first production in 1984, more and more blacks go to the theatre and more and more blacks go to the theatre simply because, in many of the regional theatres, my play was the first black play they have ever mounted. Blacks don't go to the theatre primarily because the theatre is not responsive to them. So if I have a production there, they will go. I am able to reach blacks, although I do not write exclusively for them. I don't write for anyone. I write for the audience of one which is the self. The play is the thing and whatever its requirements are, that is what I work for.

BIGSBY How did you arrive at this idea of reexploring black history in America, decade by decade? Was that a decision you made before you wrote any of them, or did it emerge in the process of writing?

WILSON I wrote a play which was set in 1971, and then I wrote a play called *Fullerton Street*, which was set in 1941. Then I wrote *Ma Rainey's Black Bottom*, which was set in 1927. It was then that I discovered I had written a play in three different decades and that was when I decided to continue to do that. But I did not start off with any grand ideal of trying to write a play for every decade. It is simply that having written the first three, it seemed a natural thing to do.

BIGSBY What interests me is that this is not a public history you are telling. *Fences*, for example, takes place between 1957 and 1965, which brackets a major part of the civil rights movement, from Little Rock, Arkansas, in 1957, through to the Voter Registration Act of 1965. None of that appears in the play. It is a private history that you are more concerned with articulating, isn't it?

WILSON Yes. I am concerned with the situation, the condition, of blacks in a particular decade. There is a 1930s play, but it doesn't deal with the Depression, because I am not interested. I have a 1960s play [*Two Trains Running*], but I don't believe the words Black Power are ever mentioned [in fact, he was wrong – they are], and it doesn't deal with Martin Luther King. So what? It deals with the people, people who live their lives in a certain social condition that could not have existed other than in those particular decades. There are things happening that are peculiar, say, to 1968, but the 1960s did not just spring up out of nowhere. They were a direct result of the 1940s. So you try to look at those kinds of things. I am not particularly interested in history as such. You can get that in the history books.

BIGSBY You seem to be taking people who have been pushed to the very margins of society, economically, socially, in almost every way, and putting them literally in the centre of the stage. It is almost as though you are recovering people.

WILSON That's interesting. Romare Bearden, the artist, was once asked to comment on his art. He said, 'I try and explore in terms of the life I know best those things which are common to all culture.' When I read that I thought, this is something that art should do. So the life I know best, I suspect, is that life so that is what I write about: those characters, those dispossessed people, if you will. That's what I know and that's what I write best about.

BIGSBY What led you to *Ma Rainey's Black Bottom*?

WILSON: I actually started *Ma Rainey* in 1976. I wrote a one-act play called *The Homecoming*, which dealt with economic exploitation. It took place in an abandoned train station. These two black guys encounter two recruiting scouts from the record companies. Then I started working on *Ma Rainey's Black Bottom*, which is about the economic exploitation of early black performers. I planned a third play about Otis Redding and so *Ma Rainey* fitted naturally into this trilogy that I was calling *Dangerous Music*. I wrote the first when I wrote *Ma Rainey* and the second one hasn't been written. But I listened to female blues singers. I bought this double album because I was very poor and had to save money. There was a song on there called *Ma Rainey's Black Bottom*. I began to think about writing a play that took place in a recording studio and there was something about the fact that Ma

Rainey's name was in the title of the song that intrigued me. So I began to write a piece about the day that they recorded this particular song.

BIGSBY But it is not just a play about white exploitation of black culture, is it, though that is a part of it? It is about the tensions within the black community or, in this case, among the black musicians.

WILSON Yes. It started out, in 1976, as a study of economic exploitation, but I abandoned the play after about twelve pages. Those pages were about things that happened in the studio. They made constant reference to a band offstage rehearsing and by 1980 I decided that I would bring the band on stage. So I said, let me go see this band that they keep talking about. So I opened the door and there were these four guys sitting there talking and I went in and wrote down what they said. Once I discovered the four musicians, these characters in the play, then I realized that I would have to write something larger than a study of economic exploitation. I thought then that what I wanted to do was show the content of the lives of the people in order to show where this music came from, where the blues came from. I was fuelled by the ideas and attitudes I absorbed from reading, between 1976 and 1980, and from listening to the male blues singers. So I felt confident and capable of characterizing the four musicians. Then it was a matter of blending the two together.

BIGSBY But music isn't only important in your plays as subject, is it? It keeps coming back as an image. You talk of characters looking for their song and their song means their life, their identity.

WILSON Identity, yes. No, music is very important. I think the blues has been a music that is terribly misread. It is actually the carrier of philosophical ideas for black Americans. It is their cultural response to the world. In an oral tradition one obviously passes along information orally. The best way to do that, though, is to make it memorable. If I tell you a story, something that you want to pass on to someone else, music and song is a way of doing that. And it offers a bonus because the music grants you an emotional reference to the information that is being passed on. It is either sanctioned by the community or it dies. Those ideas sanctioned by the community survive in that people continue to sing them. Culture is an organic thing. It is constantly growing and changing. So when I discovered that and began to look at this particular music and how it related to this group of people, then the whole world just opened up for me.

BIGSBY I am interested in the fact that you use the word 'story', because another common thread in your plays is that your characters are instinctive storytellers.

WILSON Yes, well, that is part of the African tradition. In various parts of Africa, the mark of a good personality is how long you can keep the story going. There are various techniques and ways of telling stories, and I became fascinated with that because I have been around people who have told the same story in three or four different ways depending on who they were talking to. A person will tell me a story differently from the way he would tell you the story. So I just began to mark the structure of these stories, feeling the drama in them. I have stood around in Pat's Cigar Store in Pittsburgh and watched these guys using Aristotle's Poetics much better than some university students because theirs is an intuitive sense. Some of the stories were absolutely incredible – incredible, too, in the way in which they were told. The story is basically simple but it is the telling and the structure of the story that is fascinating.

BIGSBY But if there is a risk of the appropriation of black culture by whites, as has proved true in music, is there not a risk with your own work that the same process may be at work?

WILSON That's a very, very interesting question. I think not, because I think that just as blacks can claim the blues, so they can claim my work as part of their tradition, as part of their culture, and that exists separately from any use that whites may put it to.

BIGSBY LeRoi Jones/Amiri Baraka, warned, in the 1960s, against becoming, what he called, fluent in the jargon of power. As you begin to pick up prizes from the New York critics and the Pulitzer Prize committee, are you at all worried that you may be becoming too fluent in this sense?

WILSON Quite the contrary. I think as my work goes on it gets stronger and deeper, more mature. When my work changes, then we can talk about that. All the prizes and awards and whatnot are all very fine, and I take them and hang them up on my wall, but I understand and recognize them for what they are and I continue with my work. My work has not changed because of that. It has gotten sharper.

BIGSBY *Ma Rainey* was followed by *Fences*, which I gather was originally about four and a half hours long. What is the process of the refining of a play from the moment you create the first text to the moment of production?

WILSON I have been fortunate in having an opportunity to work at the Eugene O'Neill Playwrights Conference. I actually submitted five scripts there before they accepted *Ma Rainey's Black Bottom*. The way they work is to have the playwright read his play, each and every word of it, to the other playwrights and the staff of the Playwrights Conference. In reading your play, it is amazing how much you discover about it. You always get to a part of a play and you turn a page and you don't want to read that page because in your subconscious you have identified one of the problems of the play. So I found the process of simply reading it aloud to be very helpful. They then do two staged readings of the play and I try to use that opportunity to present different endings, try different things, because you have actors to work with. The first performance of *Ma Rainey* was four and a half hours long. In the second performance I cut forty-five minutes off the script. Then people tell you all these things that they want to tell you about your play. I get a lot of input and I take it all and I use what I can. I go home and do another rewrite of the play, which is the second or third rewrite, and that usually is the one we go into rehearsal with. But as a result of the process of rehearsal, I come out with a fourth rewrite, because you discover things in rehearsal. So by the time we have done the first production, the script has gone through four revisions and sometimes these are pretty substantial in the sense that I have changed characters. It is a matter of finding what works and what doesn't and how best you can clarify those ideas that you think the audience is not getting. Then from there it is a matter of finetuning.

BIGSBY You didn't mention the director in this. You have a very close working relationship with Lloyd Richards.

WILSON Yes. Lloyd is not only the artistic director of the National Playwrights Conference, but is also the dean of the Yale Drama School and artistic director of the Yale Repertory Theatre. From the time I first met him, Lloyd has taken me under his wing. He has directed all my plays and it has proven to be a good relationship. We work together very well.

BIGSBY *Fences* has a central character, a one-time baseball player who couldn't get into the leagues because they were then all white, and who now works on a garbage truck. It seems like the story of a life that falls apart, of dreams that come to nothing. *Ma Rainey* ends with the death of one of the musicians. Yet in both those plays there is a countercurrent, a current moving towards some kind of reconciliation and harmony.

WILSON Yes. I think it is interesting to note that the two avenues that have long been open to blacks for participation in America are music and sport. I think it is interesting, therefore, and unconscious on my part, that *Fences* deals with sport and *Ma Rainey* with music. That both of those avenues have failed these particular characters, as opposed to leading to success, is ironic. I don't know why I chose them, but I find that interesting.

BIGSBY But they are not stories of failure?

WILSON They are not stories of failure, no. I think Troy, in *Fences*, is a magnificent spirit because, no matter what the circumstances of his life, he reveals a willingness to engage life and to live life with zest and purpose, to live it with as much vividness and force and vibrancy as he can. I think it is a testament to his spirit. This is what I discovered, too, in the blues, despite the seeming sorrowfulness of the music. There is a great vitality and life affirmation despite the circumstances.

BIGSBY Beyond that, the musicians in *Ma Rainey* have come together as musicians to create something through cooperation. There is a kind of unity which they discover while they are playing, whatever the differences are between them outside of their music. Similarly, in *Fences* there is an act of reconciliation, though admittedly after the central character is dead. The son is reconciled to his father and that reconciliation seems to be central to the play.

WILSON Oh, without question. I think each of the characters in *Fences* has to make his or her own reconciliation with Troy: the brother, the two sons, the wife. In the middle of all that, you have this illegitimate child representing the future, the hope of the future, though I would never use the word illegitimate. Everyone in the play is institutionalized. They are the victims of some institution or other: the army, the jail, the hospital and the church. The only one free from any constraint is the seven-year-old daughter with her garden. That is the new life. The future is her and all the hope is represented in her.

BIGSBY That sense of reconciliation is even stronger in the next play in the cycle, *Joe Turner's Come and Gone*. There is one character whose self-imposed job it is to go around and bring people back together again, to reunite those who have been broken apart. There is another character called Bynum, who likes to think that his function is to bind people together. I wonder if that isn't also part of your function?

WILSON Well, I certainly identify with that and with the attempt to heal. I suspect I say heal thyself, however. It is this attempt to heal, to bind together, to recognise the one simple fact that they are African people which is central. Troy, for example, played baseball in the Negro baseball leagues. I think we should still have a Negro baseball league. I think that if we had that now it would be a good thing for black America. I think it would provide us with a focus. I think it might even be economically viable.

BIGSBY You mean you want to reinvent segregation?

WILSON It's not a reinvention of segregation. Troy could not make the major leagues because the assumption was that white is better. I am saying it is not necessarily better. He was a baseball player but in this particular play he is better because he did not have an opportunity to play in the white leagues.

BIGSBY You mentioned Africanness, and *Joe Turner's Come and Gone*, set in 1911, has a powerful component of African elements. How real could that be today for a black community in America?

WILSON I think that this is just as real as in 1911. I think it is something that is part of the blood's memory. There is a sensibility that is still distinctive, despite the fact that we have been in America and the North American continent for 370-some years. We walk down the street differently. There is a certain style. We decorate our houses differently. Our ideas about the world are very much different and our world views are different. These are things that have survived for hundreds of years. What I am saying is that culture is very much alive and as strong today as it was in 1911. It might be a bit easier to trace the African connections in 1911, because I think they were stronger, more identifiable, in 1911 than they are in 1989, but this is a small bit of time in the course of history. We are talking about seventy or eighty years. They are still there. They are very much a part of the people.

BIGSBY The latest play in the cycle, *The Piano Lesson*, set in the 1930s, is about a brother and sister who inherit a piano, a piano that dates back to the days of slavery. They have a discussion about what to do with the piano which becomes almost a discussion of what to do with history, the need to face history, the need to use it positively. Is that really what this whole cycle of historical plays is about?

WILSON I think ultimately, yes. I think this is the theme that I keep coming back to over and over again: the need to reconnect yourself. Having been uprooted from Africa, an agrarian land-based society, and taken into the South, the blacks created a culture which was a very separate culture from that which had existed in Africa. They were then uprooted again and attempted to transplant that culture to the pavements of industrialized cities in which there was no housing. The cities were not welcoming. I think it was a terrible mistake. I think that we would have been better had we stayed in the South. I think our culture would have been stronger if we had stayed in the South. It would have continued to grow and develop along the lines that it was going. When we left, we left people behind there. We left old people who were unable, or unwilling, to make the trip north to the new life. They died.

BIGSBY So you left history behind?

WILSON Yes. No one bothered to tell them. These kids today in 1991 don't even know about those people. They know nothing about that part of their lives and their connection to it. I think this is a flaw in African American culture. That connection is broken. I am standing in my grandfather's shoes, you see, but people don't realize that. This is what I am trying to do with my plays: make that connection. Unless we acknowledge a common past, we can't have a common present or a common future, and you have to make an intelligent decision about where, as a people, we are going, how we are going to participate in this society. Are we going to accept the idea of cultural assimilation, or insist on the idea of cultural separatism? This is what we have been debating for hundreds of years. My plays are part of that debate.

BIGSBY And what are the parameters of this sequence of plays to be? How far back are you going to go and how far forward?

WILSON I want to deal with the twentieth Century. I don't want to go past that. I have done all of the 1940s and 1980s and since I rely on an historical perspective I think that the 1980s will be the last period I will cover. I have just finished a play, called *Two Trains Running*, which is set in 1968. That's the period I know best, I think. That's when I came into manhood and I always felt that that would be the most difficult one, so I decided that I would do that one next and get it out of the way so I could then do the 1940s and the 1980s. So I have finished it and I feel good about that.

BIGSBY Do each of these plays stand on their own or do they gain resonances from one another?

WILSON Both. They stand on their own, certainly. Each one is crafted as an individual work of art. They could exist, and definitely do exist, separately. However, I think if you take them all together, and place them side by side, they lend weight to one another. I'd love to see them all done together. It would have a cumulative effect. But they are certainly individual. I don't repeat any of the characters in any of the plays [plainly a decision he later revised]. The circumstances, the situations, are different and I explore different dramatic ideas in the plays.

BIGSBY Richard Wright once used a very startling image for the black American. He went into a facility where they were carrying out experiments on animals. There were rows of dogs with their vocal cords out, baying, as he said, silently at the moon. For him that was an image of what had happened to the black American: suffering pain, but silenced. Is there a sense in which what you are doing is giving those voices back?

WILSON I don't think they ever lost them. It is there in the blues. In *Joe Turner's Come and Gone* Loomis has not lost his song, he has simply forgotten how to sing a song because of the circumstances of his life. But he still has it. All he has to do is to learn how to sing it. So, for me, it is a matter of reconnecting with the past, with your culture at its strongest. It is a matter of identity, the idea of accepting responsibility for your own presence in the world.

INDEX

Smith, Bessie 18
Smith, Anna Deveare 58
Smith, Bernie (*RG*) 190, 191
Smith, Bessie (blues musician) 40
Smith, Carl (Dingbat) 53, 62, 63
social bonding 167
social contexts 197
social injustice, reflection in King Hedley II's lack of self-worth 171
social system, black manipulation of 153
Solly Two Shoes (*Gem*) 75, 84, 85, 197
  naming and identity 82, 83
  symbolic of black self-determination 86
  as warrior 176
son-father conflicts
  Fences 139–40, 141
  Jitney 161, 164, 166
Sotiropoulos, Karin, on racial humour 123
soul, loss, reflected in language usage in *RG* 186
Southern states (America), AW characterizes as ancestral land 12
Soyinka, Wole
  on ancestors 173
  on Armah's *Two Thousand Seasons* 90
  Kongi's Harvest 9
  relationship between cultural traditions and sacrifice 176
  on tragedy in Yoruban traditional drama 181
spiritualism 63
spirituality 194
  in *Gem* 75
  in *MR* 193
  in *PL* 120
  Yoruba people 77
sport
  black participation 186, 210
  desegregation 3
'stacking niggers' 148
Sterling (*RG*) 186
  attitudes to law 189
  Harmond's alliance with 191
  on Negroes 191
Sterling (*TTR*) 148
Stool Pigeon (*KHII*) 171, 177
  on King Hedley II's spirituality 177, 178
  Prologue 170
  resurrection of the community through Aunt Ester 173
  sacrifice of King Hedley II 174
  sense of cultural traditions through sacrifice 175, 176

on spirituality 181
stories, in *PL* 120
storytelling 32, 208
  AW's use of 70
  in *Fences* 135
Stovall (landowner, *TTR*) 152
Sullivan, Arthur 72
Sullivan, Dan, AW objects to his directing his plays 23
supernatural, AW's use of 32
Sutter, ghost (*PL*), symbolism 117–8, 119, 121
Sutter, James (*PL*) 114, 115
Sutter, Robert (*PL*) 115
symbolism, Levee's sense of the world 110

taxicabs, African Americans denied access 158
Theatre Communications Group, 11th biennial conference, AW delivers 'The Ground on Which I Stand' 12, 56, 146
theatre
  audiences 11
  AW's involvement with 204, 205
  black theatre 8
  blacks' role 3, 5–6
  development in 1970s and 1980s and their importance for AW 206
  inclusivity within American theatre envisaged by AW 59
Thompson, Robert Farris 85
Tillery, Miss Poochie (*SG*) 132
Tillery, Wilford Ray (*SG*) 127, 131
time, control, within *MR* 107–8
titles, AW's use 185
Toledo (*MR*) 105, 106, 108, 109, 128
Tony Award, won by *Fences* (1987) 135
Tonya (*KHII*) 177, 179
tragedy
  in *MR* 128
  in *SG* 127
  Yoruba traditional drama 181
Troy (*Fences*) 197, 210
Tulane Drama Review 8, 9
Turnbo (*Jitney*) 162, 163
Turner, Joe (*JT*) 92, 94
Turner, Pete (*JT*) 92
Two Trains Running 2, 4, 30, 212
  absurdism 151–5
  artistic evolution 48
  Aunt Ester's role 76, 77, 171, 172
  Black Power in 150

Cambridge Companions to...

AUTHORS

Edward Albee edited by Stephen J. Bottoms

Margaret Atwood edited by Coral Ann Howells

W. H. Auden edited by Stan Smith

Jane Austen edited by Edward Copeland and Juliet McMaster

Beckett edited by John Pilling

Aphra Behn edited by Derek Hughes and Janet Todd

Walter Benjamin edited by David S. Ferris

William Blake edited by Morris Eaves

Brecht edited by Peter Thomson and Glendyr Sacks (second edition)

The Brontës edited by Heather Glen

Frances Burney edited by Peter Sabor

Byron edited by Drummond Bone

Albert Camus edited by Edward J. Hughes

Willa Cather edited by Marilee Lindemann

Cervantes edited by Anthony J. Cascardi

Chaucer, second edition edited by Piero Boitani and Jill Mann

Chekhov edited by Vera Gottlieb and Paul Allain

Coleridge edited by Lucy Newlyn

Wilkie Collins edited by Jenny Bourne Taylor

Joseph Conrad edited by J. H. Stape

Dante edited by Rachel Jacoff (second edition)

Charles Dickens edited by John O. Jordan

Emily Dickinson edited by Wendy Martin

John Donne edited by Achsah Guibbory

Dostoevskii edited by W. J. Leatherbarrow

Theodore Dreiser edited by Leonard Cassuto and Claire Virginia Eby

John Dryden edited by Steven N. Zwicker

George Eliot edited by George Levine

T. S. Eliot edited by A. David Moody

Ralph Ellison edited by Ross Posnock

Ralph Waldo Emerson edited by Joel Porte and Saundra Morris

William Faulkner edited by Philip M. Weinstein

Henry Fielding edited by Claude Rawson

F. Scott Fitzgerald edited by Ruth Prigozy

Flaubert edited by Timothy Unwin

E. M. Forster edited by David Bradshaw

Brian Friel edited by Anthony Roche

Robert Frost edited by Robert Faggen

Elizabeth Gaskell edited by Jill L. Matus

Goethe edited by Lesley Sharpe

Thomas Hardy edited by Dale Kramer

Nathaniel Hawthorne edited by Richard Millington

Ernest Hemingway edited by Scott Donaldson

Homer edited by Robert Fowler

Ibsen edited by James McFarlane

Henry James edited by Jonathan Freedman

Samuel Johnson edited by Greg Clingham

Ben Jonson edited by Richard Harp and Stanley Stewart

James Joyce edited by Derek Attridge (second edition)

Kafka edited by Julian Preece

Keats edited by Susan J. Wolfson

Lacan edited by Jean-Michel Rabaté

D. H. Lawrence edited by Anne Fernihough

Primo Levi edited by Robert Gordon

David Mamet edited by Christopher Bigsby

Thomas Mann edited by Ritchie Robertson

Christopher Marlowe edited by Patrick Cheney

Herman Melville edited by Robert S. Levine

Arthur Miller edited by Christopher Bigsby

Milton edited by Dennis Danielson (second edition)

Molière edited by David Bradby and Andrew Calder

Toni Morrison edited by Justine Tally

Nabokov edited by Julian W. Connolly

Eugene O'Neill edited by Michael Manheim

George Orwell edited by John Rodden

Ovid edited by Philip Hardie

Harold Pinter edited by Peter Raby

Sylvia Plath edited by Jo Gill

Edgar Allan Poe edited by Kevin J. Hayes

Alexander Pope edited by Pat Rogers

Ezra Pound edited by Ira B. Nadel

Proust edited by Richard Bales

Pushkin edited by Andrew Kahn

Philip Roth edited by Timothy Parrish

Salman Rushdie edited by Abdulrazak Gurnah